THE MAKING OF A TELEVISIO

DAD'S ARI

BILL PERTWEE

THE MAKING OF A TELEVISION LEGEND
DAD'S ARMY
BILL PERTWEE

CONWAY

ACKNOWLEDGEMENTS

This work could not have been compiled without Jimmy Perry and David Croft; after all, *Dad's Army* was their first co-operation as writers. Their care in researching the period, their eye for casting and character building for their first 'baby' – and their other co-productions since then – have given them a special place in television history. I'd like to thank David and Jimmy and many others for their help: Joan Lowe had the foresight, thank goodness, to put diary notes into print, which gave me a great insight into Arthur's career; Joan Le Mesurier, Althea Ridley, Kay Beck and Gladys Sinclair gave me their unstinting help. Clive Dunn is always able to put me right on certain facts during various phone calls from his home in Portugal. Frank Williams laughs a lot when we meet to talk about the show, but then Frank always does laugh a lot! Harold Snoad has a great memory and was able to recall many details of the television and radio productions in the early years.

For permission to use the pictures, thank you to Brian Fisher, *Woman* Magazine, Doug McKenzie, Lynn News, Jon Kimble and the *Daily Mirror*, Michael Fresco, Columbia Tristar Pictures, National Screen Services, *The Blackpool Gazette*, The Imperial War Museum, the Dad's Army Appreciation Society and the Barmy Army. Several of these carried no identification and therefore I have not been able to credit them; for this I apologise. Thanks also to *Punch* for permission to reproduce their cartoons.

As with other books I was jolly grateful for the help I had with the 1997 edition from my late wife Marion, and good friend Geraldine, who always gave me lots of encouragement. My thanks to Paul Carpenter and Tony Pritchard and others of the DAAS, and it's always good to have Charles Garland around; and he's been around a long time!

I don't think I would have taken on this new project unless I was sure that Maggie Bourgein would be part of it with me. She has been fantastic in so many ways, spending hours in front of her computer, checking facts on the internet and corresponding with people by email. There has been the odd, 'Bill are you listening to me? Now concentrate!' when I've been looking for the cricket scores in the paper – but nobody's perfect.

The man at the helm in all this is Tony Mulliken of Midas. He fixes my book deals and if there's a problem, no matter how busy he is, I hear the familiar 'Don't worry mate, I'll sort it out.' I can then relax and have a glass of wine – and a quick glance at the cricket.

I've dealt with several publishers since my first effort in the late 70s, with *Promenades and Pierrots*, and I feel sure that my association with Anova Books is going to be a long and happy one.

I hope you enjoy the book, folks, and if you come to a book signing anywhere, do come and say hello.

First published in Great Britain in 1997 by
Pavilion Books Limited.

This edition first published in 2009 by
Conway
An imprint of Anova Books Ltd
10 Southcombe Street
London W14 0RA
www.anovabooks com
www.conwaypublishing.com

Original edition © 1997 PRC Publishing Ltd., part of Anova Books.
Updates © 2009 Anova Books Group Ltd

A CIP catalogue record for this book is available from the British Library.

ISBN 978 18448 6105 7

10 9 8 7 6 5

Printed and bound by 1010 Printing International Limited, China.

CONTENTS

INTRODUCTION

I can hardly believe that we have recently celebrated the 40th anniversary of *Dad's Army*. Who would have thought, so long after those first rehearsals in a back room in a pub in Chiswick, that there would still be regular screenings of the show at weekends and Christmas, radio episodes could be heard every week on Radio 7, that one would be able to buy a small box containing the entire nine years' worth of episodes on DVD, and that the programme would have its own large appreciation society which attracts members from all over the world? Of course, when we were working on the series, Radio 7 and the DVD hadn't even been heard of. There have been so many changes in every area of life in the last forty years, and it's testament to the strength of the show and its writing that it truly has withstood the test of time. This book tells the story of the making of *Dad's Army* and what has happened to it, and its actors, since.

Over 40 years ago Jimmy Perry was walking past Buckingham Palace when he remembered that he had seen a Home Guard detachment standing guard in the quadrangle there during World War II. Jimmy's thoughts then went back to his own Home Guard experience as a 16-year-old on Barnes Common in South West London. Those thoughts gave him the inspiration to write a script of a 30-minute situation comedy about the Home Guard. When it was finished, he took it to television producer David Croft, with whom Jimmy had worked previously, to assess its possibilities. It was the beginning of an extraordinary collaboration that has become part of entertainment history.

Right: The 'Magnificent Seven'. L-R: Clive Dunn, Jimmy Beck, John Le Mesurier, Arthur Lowe, John Laurie, Ian Lavender and (behind) Arnold Ridley.

'They don't like it up 'em!'

The day in the summer of 1968 that I received a phone call from BBC producer David Croft offering me two lines as an air raid warden in a new television series called *Dad's Army* turned out to be the key moment in my career. Until then I had been involved mainly in radio, summer shows and cabaret, but suddenly I found myself in the company of a delightfully warm group of film, television and stage actors, all of us being in at the start of what was to become one of the great television programmes this country has produced. *Dad's Army* became beloved by the viewing public, including the Royal Family, and was eventually adapted into a long-running radio series, a stage musical – including an appearance in a Royal Command Performance in the presence of Her Majesty the Queen at the London Palladium – and a full-length feature film made by Columbia Pictures. This book is not just the story of a successful television series of 80 episodes that were made over nine years, but also a story about the families and friends of those actors who became legends because of it.

Today, thanks to *Dad's Army*, everyone knows about the Home Guard but when the series started, several generations after the last war, for many younger people, the idea of one's country being guarded by a lot of men who were mostly too old or frail to fight, seemed just ridiculous. Who then would be interested in a television programme about these (with one or two exceptions) senior citizens trying to look like soldiers, guarding their country with pitchforks, broomsticks and any other items of domestic hardware they could lay their hands on? But wasn't it the exceptional optimism of those loyal countrymen that might prove to be the catalyst for the television public to latch on to? The original concept of the Home Guard, or Local Defence Volunteers as they were first called, had been deadly serious even though their weapons were primitive. Reminiscing in this way Jimmy

BEN ELTON

Dad's Army is quite simply the finest sitcom this country has ever produced. Like P.G. Wodehouse before them, Croft and Perry created a Britain that will never fade. A timeless place which we can visit in order to refresh our souls. The men of the Walmington platoon remind us that though life may be a ludicrous farce, it can be lived with decency, dignity and enthusiasm.

The casting was perfect, every player in perfect harmony with the script. All in all a classic of the popular arts, utterly hilarious and also very moving.

Perry realised that here was a ready-made comedy situation, one that could be written about without in any way belittling the efforts of the guard.

When Anthony Eden made his historic speech in June 1940, calling for men under and over the age of active service in the armed forces to form a local defence corps, there was an immediate response from every eligible male in the country. It was a dark hour, and Britons everywhere realised they must stand firm in the face of heavy odds. In the Low Countries and France the Germans had carried all before them. The rescue of the British Army – minus most of its heavy armaments and vehicles – from Dunkirk had been but a small victory; the Battle of Britain was about to begin and it seemed only a matter of time before the Nazis invaded the British Isles

Opposite: Volunteer: 'Tell Hitler not to come over tonight because the wife's cooking her carrot pudding'.

ERIC MERRIMAN

I have to be honest. When I first heard about a projected comedy series featuring the Home Guard I thought it would never work. The war was too long ago; a younger generation would not appreciate it; and nostalgia wasn't what it used to be. As it became a phenomenal success, I felt rather like the Hollywood Director who film-tested Fred Astaire and reported, 'can't act, can't sing, can dance a little ...' So I was wrong too. And as a comedy writer myself I should have known better – in as much as the best comedy is usually that nearest to the truth. The absurdity of our unpreparedness at that time was, indeed, almost laughable. Let's face it, any country that has to collect its saucepans to be made into fighter planes is in trouble. Or forms a Home Defence Fighting force and then is unable to give them weapons – well!

We schoolboys used to call them the 'Pitchfork Brigade', and were it not such a laughing matter then it would have been deadly serious. Come the invasion and I doubt if we would ever have survived. But I know one thing for sure; every single one of those civil soldiers would have fought to the death to protect every inch of British soil. **Dad's Army** was a brilliantly funny portrayal of life in those times. The writing was immaculate, the casting impeccable, and the production faultless. I would have been proud to have written any one of the many hilarious episodes, and the fact that I doubted its potential is shameful. All I can say to myself is ... 'you stupid boy!'

(The lad in the picture is Eric's grandson, Daniel.)

from their positions on the Channel coast. Winston Churchill, who had taken over from Chamberlain and been made Prime Minister in charge of a coalition government, told the British people that they would have to fight on the beaches, and never surrender; but his government's master stroke was to ask all those men not fit for active service to form themselves into a Home Guard, as his request boosted the flagging morale of the country. Many families had already been touched by war. Husbands, sons and sweethearts had left the comfort of their homes for the rigours of battle. Some had already perished or been taken prisoner in the fighting in France, and the Navy had endured horrific losses at sea. but in Britain itself, every home was to be involved in the war with the formation of the Local Defence Volunteers. Houses, pubs, village halls and the like became the headquarters of Britain's new 'fighting force'. It says a great deal for the sincerity of the men and their involvement in the war effort that the British people felt that they could sleep easy in their beds at night with the 'boys', albeit most of them 'old boys', watching over them, even though some people must have had doubts as to the Home Guard's ability to cope with the expected German invasion from land, sea and air when they had only pitchforks, broomsticks and, if they were lucky, a shotgun and a few cartridges between them.

It was with these thoughts that Jimmy Perry returned home one day in the late 1960s and contacted producer David Croft, for whom he had worked on a few television programmes, and asked if it would be possible to create a series about the Home Guard. Perhaps Jimmy had remembered a very funny radio comedian called Robb Wilton – very much a Captain Mainwaring – who in the 1940s had caricatured the Home Guard;

'The day I joined the Home Guard my missus said to me, "What are you?"

'I said, "I'm one of the Home Guard." She said, "What do you do?"

'I said, "I've got to stop Hitler's army from landing."

'She said, "What, just you?"

'I said, "Oh no, there's me and Charlie

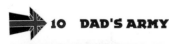

"I've laid your uniform out, my Lord."

Left: Bill Cotton, then Head of Variety at the BBC.
Above: This Leslie Baker cartoon pokes fun at the shortage of uniforms suffered by the Home Guard when it was first formed.

Evans and Harry Bates, and ... well, there's seven or eight of us altogether."

'She said, "Do you know this feller Hitler?"

'I said, "Of course not."

'She said, "Well, how will you know if it's him if he lands?"

'I said, "Well, I've got a tongue in me head haven't I?"'

Remembering the very good reaction that Robb Wilton had in making gentle fun of the Home Guard might have prompted Jimmy and David to take the thought of creating a series about *Dad's Army* seriously and to hurry to the typewriter.

Although the BBC programme makers had commissioned Jimmy and David to write an initial short series of scripts about the Home Guard, there was some doubt in their minds that a comedy programme based on this subject would prove successful. The then Head of Variety, Bill Cotton, son of one of Britain's best loved band leaders Billy Cotton, said of *Dad's Army*: 'As with all great comedies *Dad's Army* had the first qualifications of

a smash hit. It was very well written and cleverly cast. Huw Weldon always used to tell the story of being confused whilst watching the show being rehearsed – he thought Arthur Lowe would be the Sergeant and John Le Mesurier would be the officer. He considered reversing it to be a stroke of genius. *Dad's Army* to me was a wonderful surprise. When David Croft told me he wanted to do a comedy about the Home Guard I told him he was out of his head. I am very grateful I was not heeded. In fact, in later years I had the enormous joy of travelling to Thetford, where they were filming, to tell the cast they had topped the ratings with an audience of 21 million. *Dad's Army*, in my opinion, is a wonderful document of social history – it captures so much of the atmosphere of the Second World War. I am positive that in a hundred years' time people will be watching it to get a feel of the period. Meanwhile, I am sure we will be kept in touch with Walmington-on-Sea with seasons of repeats. If we don't, I'll write and complain!'

THE CREATORS

JIMMY PERRY, OBE

If a small boy's sole ambition is to own a full suit of white tie and tails, a pair of riding breeches and a trilby hat and to adorn the whole outfit with a pipe, you can be sure that sooner or later the young man in question will make the entertainment industry sit up and take notice. Although few people at the age of five or six know exactly what they want to do when they grown up, Jimmy Perry certainly did. Looking back he says: 'I had no family inheritance of show business. My father was in antiques and I got bored hearing them discussed from morning to night.' Some of that talk of antiquity must have rubbed off on young Jimmy because he is now very knowledgeable on the subject.

'I was taken to the theatre by my mother as a very small boy and was smitten by this wonderful world of bright lights, extrovert people and exciting atmosphere. We went to see plays and the great variety comedians of the day in music halls in and around London. I was taken to a pantomime when I was seven and when we got home I sulked for two hours because I hadn't wanted it to end. I lived in a complete world of fantasy. I hated school and particularly one of the masters who was a nasty piece of work. I pretended I was a member of the Secret Service and I went to the Headmaster and told him that the nasty piece of work was a German spy and must be sacked! I knew even as a young teenager that I wanted to act, I wanted to wear smart clothes and go out with beautiful women. I tried to grow a moustache but this was a failure; so

Top: Jimmy Perry, who hit on the idea of writing a comedy about the Home Guard.

Above: 'What are the silly asses up to now?': Jimmy Perry and David Croft.

Opposite: Jimmy Perry during his season as a Butlin's redcoat (standing third from right).

was the pipe I tried to smoke! When the war started I wanted to get into uniform, but I had to wait until the summer of 1940, when I joined the Home Guard in Barnes where we lived. I loved going out on the common and doing night duty and I had no fear of being killed by the bombing, although it had already flattened the school I had attended. My mother was always fearful of me being out at night and catching cold, (shades of Private Pike), but I enjoyed it.'

After being bombed out, Jimmy and his family moved to Watford and that town was eventually to play an important part in his life. In 1943 Jimmy became Gunner Perry of the Royal Artillery and was posted to Oswestry. He immediately asked who ran the Base Concert Party and said that if they didn't have one, perhaps he should start one? A concert party was not uppermost in the commanding officer's mind at that time as there were more serious and pressing problems to

VINCE POWELL

Dad's Army was, and still is today, one of the funniest sitcoms ever to be shown on television. The series, created by Jimmy Perry, and written by David Croft and Jimmy, was the perfect example of a combination of a brilliant script performed by a team of talented performers. And what a team! Who will ever forget the bumbling pomposity of Captain Mainwaring, the self-effacing hesitance of Sergeant Wilson, the outrageousness of Lance Corporal 'they don't like it up 'em, Sir' Jones, the canny pessimism of Private Frazer, the spivish villainy of Private Walker, the innocence of Private Pike or the frailty of geriatric Private Godfrey? Add to those the slightly effeminate vicar and the irascible Air Raid Warden Bert Hodges and one has an unforgettable group of comic characters, which the public took to their hearts. Is it any wonder that the repeats gain higher audience figures than most of the present-day new sitcoms? Long may it be repeated!

be dealt with, such as Hitler and preparation for the second front. However, Gunner Perry had to be listened to and the concert party of Oswestry was duly organised with Perry to the fore.

He now had an outlet for his need to perform, and was able to do his impressions of various radio entertainers such as Ned Sparks, Gordon Harker and Robb Wilton and public figures, including President Roosevelt and Winston Churchill, all of whom were well-known to the young soldiers in the audiences.

One day there was upheaval in the camp when practically all of the personnel were sent south in preparation for D-Day – the invasion of Europe. Only a handful, including Gunner Perry, remained behind. Did the Second Front in France not need a Concert Party? What would Eisenhower and Montgomery do without impressions of Ned Sparks and Gordon Harker? As it happened most of the battalion were cut to pieces on the beaches of Normandy, so Jimmy was lucky to escape that bloody conflict.

One night, a captain at the camp who had by then taken over compering the shows, was very drunk and Jimmy complained bitterly about his unprofessional conduct on stage. The captain immediately took revenge on Jimmy and had him posted to the Far East, and so another chapter in the life of Gunner Perry began. At some point Jimmy climbed to the rank of Sergeant but for the sake of this narrative we'll stick to 'Gunner'. The unit left Liverpool in a convoy of 50 ships and travelled via America, and not the Mediterranean, because of the threat of attack by German U-boats. This was very worrying for everyone involved in that convoy – everyone, that is, except Gunner Perry who was far more concerned that the ship did not have a concert party.

After a short stay at Cape Town, the ship arrived at Bombay, five weeks after leaving Liverpool. From Bombay Jimmy was posted to an anti-aircraft unit at Deolali, then to Assam in the jungle. This was Jimmy's opportunity to form an entertainment unit and to give the Far East a taste of his impressions. Many years later, the memory of that period of entertainment in the jungle and all it meant to those troops became the basis for the television series, *It Ain't Half Hot Mum!*

In 1945 the atom bomb was dropped on Japan and the war in the Far East was over, but there were plenty of Japanese who were still carrying on their own private war in that area. Jimmy became ill and was sent back to Deolali. In 1946 he went to Delhi where he joined one of the renowned Gang shows, which were in the process of being amalgamated with the Combined Services Entertainment Unit (CSE as it was known for many years after). Indian independence was now on the horizon and Indians themselves were being killed and wounded in the turmoil. The week before independence Jimmy left India on the SS *Franconia*, together with hundreds of other troops. They docked at Southampton and shortly afterwards he was demobbed during the freezing winter of 1947.

At that time Jimmy weighed a meagre 8½ stone and spent three months sitting in front of the open fire at his parents' home. He now had to decide about his future and felt that his chosen course was a career in the theatre. He went to see an old friend who was appearing at Collins Music Hall in Islington and before long Jimmy was back smelling the greasepaint. He was coached in drama by an old army mate, Joe O'Connor, and then applied for and won a scholarship to the Royal Academy of Dramatic Art in London. During his training at RADA he met and worked with other aspiring actors and actresses, including Robert Shaw, Joan Collins, Laurence Harvey, Lionel Jeffries, Warren Mitchell and Dorothy Tutin.

Jimmy was now on his way as a profes-

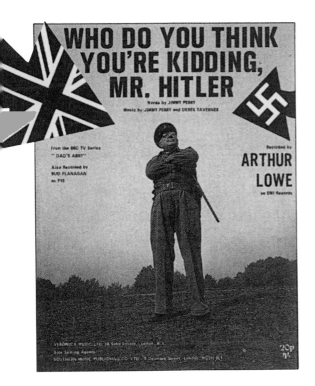

Who do you think you are kidding Mister Hitler
If you think we're on the run?
We are the boys who will stop your little game.
We are the boys who will make you think again.
'Cause who do you think you are
*   kidding Mister Hitler*
If you think old England's done?

Mister Brown goes off to town
*   on the eight twenty-one*
But he comes home each evening
*   and he's ready with his gun.*
So watch out Mister Hitler
*   you have met your match in us.*
If you think you can crush us
*   we're afraid you've missed the bus.*
'Cause who do you think you are
*   kidding Mister Hitler*
If you think old England's done?

sional performer. During the summer holidays from RADA he did seasons at Butlin's holiday camps as a singer and feed to the comics, and his experiences there were later to be the inspiration for the very successful sitcom, *Hi-de-Hi!* In 1952 he joined the cast of *Glorious Days*, which starred Anna Neagle, at the Palace theatre. Anna played Florence Nightingale, Nell Gwynn and Queen Victoria in a series of historical cameos. There was a cast of 75 and among the dancers was 19-year-old Gilda; she and Jimmy hit it off and were married in 1953. Jimmy meanwhile had a part in A.P. Herbert's *Water Gypsies* at the Winter Gardens Theatre. Repertory in Richmond and Watford followed and Jimmy and Gilda then took over the lease of the Palace Theatre, Watford. A very young pair of actor and actress/mangers now had to keep the theatre open for 52 weeks of the year with weekly rep. This they did as well as putting on an annual pantomine, the revenue of which

kept their heads above water for the rest of the year. It was from this period that Jimmy remembered a number of actors who had appeared at Watford and suggested their names for the *Dad's Army* cast. Eventually Jimmy and Gilda succeeded in persuading Watford Council to take over the Palace Theatre and to run it as a civic trust. It could then be properly funded and would not have to rely constantly on the box office to keep it open, which had always been a huge task. Watford Corporation did not want Jimmy and Gilda to be a part of the new set-up, so they were paid off.

In 1965 Jimmy and Gilda moved back to London and found a flat in Westminster. Gilda went off to do summer revues and Jimmy toured for quite a long period with John Hanson in *When You're Young*. This was followed by a tour in *Seagulls over Sorrento* in which he met author Hugh Hastings, who would later be involved with *Dad's Army*. Jimmy then spent two years with the producer/director Joan Littlewood at the Theatre Royal, Stratford East, and during this period the idea for *Dad's Army* began to develop. Jimmy had met producer/director David Croft professionally a couple of times

and his voice totally captures the atmosphere of the war years.

Jimmy also wrote the title music for *It Ain't Half Hot Mum!* and *Hi-de-Hi*. Jimmy's solo writing achievements for television series' include *The Gnomes of Dulwich* for the BBC, *Lollipop* for ATV, and *The Old Boy Network* and three series of *Turns* for the BBC. *Turns* was a compilation of film clips of some of the great variety and music hall turns of the past (a music hall performer was always known as a turn). The research involved in finding these old film clips in archives all over London and then writing the linking material was a labour of love for Jimmy. Talking to him about the music hall, one is left with the feeling that he would have liked to have been a turn on the variety circuit himself. Fortunately, however, his career went in other directions, for otherwise the viewing public would have been deprived of some outstanding television comedy.

Above: David Croft, television director, producer and writer (with Jimmy Perry) of *Dad's Army.*

and mustered courage to take his idea to him. David liked it and it was decided that they should collaborate in writing the script. That decision was the start of a long and successful partnership in which they were to create some of the most popular television productions of the 1960s, 70s and 80s which, as well as *Dad's Army*, included *It Ain't Half Hot Mum*, *Hi-de-Hi!* and *You Rang, M'Lord?* Jimmy wrote the *Dad's Army* signature tune, 'Who do you think you are kidding Mr Hitler?', with Derek Taverner; it won the Ivor Novello award in 1970 for the best signature tune. It captures the sound of the period so well that many people believe it was actually written in the 1940s; this is reinforced by the fact that it was recorded by Bud Flanagan, who was a famous music hall entertainer and recording name of the 1940s and 50s along with his partner Chesney Allen. Recording the signature tune was, in fact, the last singing engagement that Bud Flanagan undertook,

DAVID CROFT, OBE

I have often tried to think of whom David Croft reminds me and only recently have I realised who it was. As a boy I was part of a group of pranksters, scrumping apples, putting glue on bicycle handlebars and indulging in other silly activities. One of the group, Henry, was the motivator; he would set us up, then stand back when we got in a fix and laugh unashamedly. I can see him now, his shoulders heaving, the sound of his laughter 'tee-hee-hee' and the drawing in of breath with a hissing sound. We, the gang, got as much fun out of Henry's laughter as he got out of getting us into trouble.

David Croft is like Henry, because the actors and actresses in his productions are the gang who get into trouble in situations that he and his co-writers have created. He loves watching a comedy situation develop and will 'tee-hee' each time the gag is repeated at rehearsals, much to the delight of the cast.

One can be sure that millions of viewers are going to be laughing too when the programme is screened.

I have known David for 30 years and he has always had a smile in his eyes, probably because he loves comedy and, more importantly, loves life. A fairly serious illness in the late 1970s appears to have been just shrugged off as a temporary nuisance. David works hard, is disciplined, and has the good sense to surround himself with an efficient workforce. I am sure he would agree that teaming up with Jimmy Perry was another very important milestone in his life. *Dad's Army* was, after all, the beginning of a hugely successful period of writing and production for them both.

David was already a very experienced director/producer long before 1968, with the highly rated *Hugh and I, Beggar My Neighbour* and *This is Your Life* for the BBC. His experience has been gathered during a career that started with his parents, Ann Croft and Reginald Sharland (the family name), who were two big stars of the 1920s and 30s. They were both starring at the Hippodrome Theatre in London while baby David slept in the prop basket; their dressing room was his nursery. At the age of four, he wandered accidentally on to the stage at the old Shaftesbury Theatre where his parents were playing. David's mother was also a theatrical manager and at the age of 16 David himself was negotiating percentages with theatre managers on her behalf. There was, of course, no doubt that the entertainment business was to be his career and this promise was soon to be fulfilled when he took the part of the butcher's boy in the 1938 film *Goodbye Mr Chips*, starring Robert Donat. When war broke out in 1939 David became an air raid warden and in 1942 he joined the Royal Artillery in a light 'ack-ack' regiment and was posted to the 1st Army in North Africa. In 1944 he transferred to the Dorset Regiment and saw service in India and Malaya. He eventually became a major and worked with General Montgomery's staff at the War Office as hostilities drew to a close.

After the war, David was soon back on the boards with repertory at Wolverhampton and Hereford. He appeared in the London production of the musical *Wild Violets* and toured with *Belinda Fair* and *The Belle of New York*. He met his future wife Ann at the first rehearsal of *The Belle* in Mac's rehearsal studios in Windmill Street. He was playing Harry Bronson, a playboy millionaire and had to wear a lurid tail suit. Ann was understudying the leading lady. They married a year later.

At about this time David began to write in

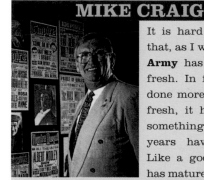

MIKE CRAIG

It is hard to believe that, as I write, **Dad's Army** has stayed so fresh. In fact it has done more than stay fresh, it has gained something as the years have passed. Like a good wine it has matured into true classic comedy. We don't just watch and laugh again and again at the catchphrases, the facial expressions, the ludicrous situations, the sheer poetry of its dialogue, we now sit and love it – and I don't think that's too strong a word to use. There can't be many people who don't feel a sense of love for the whole programme. The signature tune, our friends – the characters, the credit sequence, those talented actors who repeat after repeat never fail to bring us that special feeling of joy that good, honest laughter gives. But most of all we love it because so much love has gone into it. It is a masterpiece of writing, performance and direction and will surely live forever as a supreme example of all that is good in British comedy.

earnest with a collaborator, musician Cyril Ornadel. This union proved to be a very worthwhile partnership. David's lyrics and Cyril's music were a feature of many a lavish production at the London Palladium, the Howard and Wyndham Group, and at the Alexandra Theatre, Birmingham. The 'Alex', as it is always known, was then under the management of that fine man of the theatre (and cricket addict!) Derek Salberg, a friend to many thespians.

David sang for a while with the BBC Show Band singers and backed many international stars, both on radio and on record. He then decided to enter television and became a script editor at Rediffusion Television, then moved up to Tyne-Tees TV, which was headed at that time by the legendary George and Alfred Black. It was at Tyne-Tees TV that David learned his craft for all his future work on the small screen. Writing and directing at Tyne-Tees brought him into contact with some of the people he would be associated with in the future, including Mollie Sugden, Jack Haig, William Moore, etc.

David eventually moved back to London and for a short time became production manager for the Richard Stone Organisation (Richard was by then his agent), producing the Butlin's revue shows at their holiday camps up and down the country. A meeting with Eric Maschwitz, then one of the controllers of BBC TV, resulted in his moving over to the corporation as a television director, where he has remained ever since. He directed the early Benny Hill shows (by his own admission not very successfully) and then other programmes which set him on his present path to success. An early lesson in camera techniques and angles was demonstrated to him by a director, who used three coins on a table to represent the three cameras and moved them about in a very simple way. It is rather more complicated today but the principle remains the same and when David showed me how it is done I understood exactly what he meant.

People have said, 'He's a hard-headed businessman' or 'He understands actors, having been one' or 'He's his own best casting director', and without exception I believe they would all say that he was very good at his job.

One doesn't co-write, produce and direct 80 episodes of *Dad's Army*, 56 episodes of *It Ain't Half Hot Mum!*, 58 episodes of *Hi-de-Hi!*, 60 episodes of *Are You Being Served?* and 85 episodes of *'Allo 'Allo* without some knowledge of the business; not to mention *You Rang, M'Lord?* and *Oh Doctor Beeching!* In cooperation with just three other writers, Jimmy Perry, Jeremy Lloyd and Rob Spendlove (on *Oh Doctor Beeching!*), David has been responsible for this phenomenal output: not bad in anybody's book.

David's achievements were recognised when he won the Desmond Davis award for outstanding contributions to television, fittingly announced, at a large gathering of fellow professionals, by Arthur Lowe.

David's personal and social life is very full. He and his wife Ann have a large family, one of whom, their daughter Penny, has followed David into television script-writing. To spend time with David over a meal and a few bottles of wine is always a jolly affair and you can bet your life there will be plenty of tee-heeing going on!

Opposite above: A social evening at Thetford. Why is David Croft wearing a dinner suit? L-R: Joan Lowe (opposite her husband), the author, Ann Croft, David Croft, Arthur Lowe.

Opposite below: The launch of the first edition of the *Dad's Army* book at the Imperial War Museum in 1989. L-R: back row, Michael Knowles, David Croft, Jimmy Perry, the author; at front, Jeff Holland, Joan Le Mesurier, Kay Beck, Gladys Sinclair, Althea Ridley, Don Estelle, Felix Bowness, Frank Williams, Brenda Cowling, Hugh Hastings, Ian Lavender, Colin Bean, Harold Snoad.

CASTING THE NET

As with any period television or film production the initial research is a painstaking and arduous business, but never dull and extremely rewarding. In the case of *Dad's Army*, David Croft, Jimmy Perry and the BBC paid attention to even the smallest detail. Among the details that had to be discussed and researched before even a word of script was written were the sort of clothes that were worn in the 1940s, and vehicles of the period – cars, buses, vans and motorcycles. All the vehicles had to be obtained in a roadworthy condition as they were to be used in the programmes for real. Cigarette packets, sweet wrappers, newspapers, magazines and hairstyles of the period and the sort of food that was eaten during the war all had to be researched. Wartime recipes were found, most based on simple ingredients: beetroot, carrots, potatoes, dried egg-powder, cheese, fat bacon pieces (when they could be obtained), oatmeal, parsnips, apples, dried fish from Scandinavia (a fish cake was a real luxury) and rabbit (Flanagan and Allen has a popular song about them), and a lot in ingenuity. Most of the foods that were taken for granted before the war were rationed, becoming extremely scarce. They were obtainable only on the black market and even then in small quantities.

Typical dishes of that period included Fish in Savoury Custard, Pathfinder Pudding, Carrot Jam, Pilchard Layer Loaf, Vinegar Cake, Belted Leeks, Rabbit Surprise and, the best known of all of them, Woolton Pie. These curtailed menus obviously did no harm because it was a

ROY HUDD

One of the first films I ever saw was **Oh Mr Porter** with Will Hay, Moore Marriott and Graham Moffatt. I never thought I'd see such glorious comedy again, and then **Dad's Army** came along. The show is a throw back – a throw back to the days when comedy was innocent, character-based, beautifully acted, fun. The putting together of some of the best, and inventive, comedy actors in the business was a stroke of genius. The writing, beautifully reflecting all that was best in Britain, and based purely on the relationships between the members of the troop and their coping in adversity, was perfect: not a cheap one-liner in sight. Like Will Hay, Laurel and Hardy and Buster Keaton, Arthur Lowe and his superlative Crazy Gang are timeless. They are all these people, with a touch of Bill Shakespeare's mechanicals thrown in.

fact that many people were healthier in wartime than at almost any other period.

Much time was spent on researching the weapons the Home Guard used, from the early broomsticks and pick-axe handles, to the later American World War I P17 rifles that were sent by President Roosevelt, the Chicago

Top: Relaxing during the filming of 'Enemy at the Gates'. L-R: Arnold Ridley, Ian Lavender, Arthur Lowe, Clive Dunn, John Le Mesurier, James Beck.

Above: 'I can always find you a little something in spite of the rationing, Mr. Yeatman.' Warden Hodges makes sure the Verger gets his 'greens'.

gangster-type tommy guns, and later the British-made Sten gun, which became a great luxury even though it was in short supply. When they arrived in Britain, the American weapons were covered in layers of thick grease as they had been in store for years.

Not least of the problems to be faced by David Croft and Jimmy Perry was casting the seven main characters who would feature in the Walmington-on-Sea Home Guard. The first to be chosen was Captain Mainwaring.

David Croft: 'I had various people in mind, but hadn't given any serious thought at that early stage. Jimmy Perry was very keen at the outset for Arthur Lowe to play Mainwaring, but there were one or two people at the BBC who had doubts about it, saying "he doesn't

work for us" (a reference to his long contract in *Coronation Street* and *Pardon the Expression* for Granada TV). We arranged lunch at the BBC to discuss the idea with Arthur, but it didn't get off to a very good start. Arthur said, "I hope it's not going to be one of those silly programmes like *Hugh and I*, I can't stand it!" I had to tell him I was the director of that programme, at which he was slightly taken aback. Luckily it all resolved itself and our first casting was complete.'

Jimmy Perry: 'Michael Mills, the Head of Situation Comedy at the BBC at that time, wanted David to seriously consider John Le Mesurier for the Sergeant and with John's long experience in films this seemed a good idea. Michael also suggested Clive Dunn to play Corporal Jones. I didn't know much about Clive then, but when I see some of the videos of the programme now he makes me laugh.

'Michael was also responsible for renaming the programme. I knew my working title 'The Fighting Tigers' was not right and Michael came up with the brilliant *Dad's Army*.

'David cast Arnold Ridley, who had worked with him before in television, Ian Lavender (with the help of David's wife who had seen this "young lad" in a play), and Jimmy Beck.'

David Croft: 'It was Michael Mills again who suggested that John Laurie was available and would be great for Private Frazer who initially was a retired seafarer in the series, but later became the Walmington-on-Sea undertaker.

'Jimmy and I were both delighted to have John. After all he had been a fine stage actor in his time, and played in many prestigious films.'

Jimmy Perry: 'Very early in the series John made us both laugh when he said, "You know, I think you and David are illiterate (he was probably referring to some light hearted conversation we were having at the time). I have played every major Shakespearean role

FIONA FULLERTON

Of course, the casting was superb in **Dad's Army** and this is always a key element. The writing was without a flaw, but the brilliance of the cast is what has kept us all hooked for all these years. There wasn't a weak link, or anyone who bored you. They were all funny and charming. Sadly, though, the series was mainly about the utter hopelessness and incompetence of them all, and as we know the British love the underdog. That is why, I believe, the series was so successful.

in the theatre and I'm considered the finest speaker of verse in the country, and I end up becoming famous doing this crap!" This remark did nothing to diminish our great admiration for John!

'David cast Bill Pertwee and Edward Sinclair, and I suggested Frank Williams.'

David and Jimmy were presented with the Writers' Guild Award for three consecutive years in 1969–71 and also the BAFTA (British Academy of Film and Television Arts) Award in 1971 for Best Light Entertainment Production. In 1978 they donned morning suits for a trip to Buckingham Palance each to collect his OBE, awarded in the Queen's Birthday Honours List. The duo were further honoured on 10 May 2008 when they were presented with the prestigious Special Award from BAFTA, given at the British Academy Television Craft Awards in recognition of their great writing talents and popular success. There can be no doubt that this pair of sitcom supremos truly deserve their place in the pantheon of great comedy writers for the consistent quality of their tremendous output.

Left: Jimmy Perry and David Croft show off their OBEs.
Below: Jimmy Perry and the cast of *Dad's Army* with presenter Richard Attenborough on stage at the Society of Film and Television Arts Awards (SFTA) in 1971. SFTA became the British Academy of Film and Television Awards (BAFTA) in 1976.

Pictured on stage, from left to right, are: Arthur Lowe, Arnold Ridley, John Le Mesurier, Ian Lavender, Jimmy Beck and far right, Bill Pertwee. *Dad's Army* won the Television Light Entertainment Production award that year. On the left-hand side, Princess Anne looks on – well, the Royal Family have been fans of the show for a long time!

 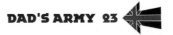

THE ACTORS

ARTHUR LOWE

During the nine-year run of *Dad's Army* I got to know everyone connected with the production very well, some more that others. Arthur Lowe fascinated me from the first day I met him. In rehearsals, you wondered how he could make everyone laugh so much, not just the rest of the cast but also the technicians, with such little effort on his part. Naturally, the script writers were involved in this laughter, for it was their job to create the funny situations, but even they could be surprised by Arthur's extra lift of the eyebrow or movement of the hand that had not been there at a previous run through. He was, you see, a natural humourist, not a manufactured actor. He had had his fair share of repertory theatre, with seasons of weekly productions up and down the country, where his natural instincts had been honed and sharpened. His dialogue in the comedy situation was punctuated by a word started in a hesitant fashion and then continued in a firmer way to make his point. Originally this was probably done to focus the audience's attention on to him – but then it had become a habit. Sometimes it seemed that he was collecting his thoughts before continuing. But whatever the reason, Arthur made it a natural part of the character he was portraying. His long pauses before he made a comment were superbly timed. Occasionally it seemed that he had paused too long, but seldom was he proved wrong. As I got to know Arthur the man more and more it became obvious that Mainwaring had been waiting for him, and Arthur for Mainwaring. The two fitted like a split screen merging into one. The first time I dined with Arthur in a restaurant, he said to the waiter, 'The Warden will sort out the bill.' This was clearly Main-waring the character overlapping with Arthur the man and he was fully aware that this remark would amuse the other diners. Off-stage, Arthur could be quite a private person. It was his belief that the mystique of the theatre should be left on the stage and that it was the public's place to observe from afar. He therefore disliked engaging in theatre chat with autograph hunters.

Not only was I sympathetic with these views, but Arthur and I had other things in common. He, like I , was a late starter in the acting profession, and we were both avid cricket fans. He knew that I liked messing about in boats, particularly in harbours, and my wife and I spent several relaxed days with Arthur and his wife Joan on board their steam yacht *Amazon*. They had bought the boat in a very rough condition and, with the aid of original plans and photographs from the National Maritime Museum at Greenwich, had set about restoring it to its original glory. During some of the early rehearsals of *Dad's Army*, Arthur would spend his spare moments pouring over the restoration plans so that he could make the necessary preparations to make the craft seaworthy. All the interior fittings were suitably chosen and the result was superb. Arthur and Joan have given some wonderful parties on board the boat and Arthur took great pleasure in walking around the deck in his yachting cap, with a gin and French in his hand, showing everyone around. He had, in fact, wanted to join the Navy, but his eyesight was not sufficiently good, so his war service was in the Army. Arthur would often chat about the Music Hall, which had always interested him, and

Right: The man and the hour: Captain Mainwaring.

some of the artists he had seen or heard about. I was convinced that some of his technique had been influenced by the great radio and variety comedian Robb Wilton who was a master at making the audience feel he was always in charge, however ridiculous the situation. Arthur had also acquired a few of Sandy Powell's mannerisms. Sandy used to make long pauses, raise his glasses slightly and then give a little cough before commenting on whatever was going on around him. When Arthur was acting though, instead of raising his glasses he would rub his hand over his face and blow a sort of silent whistle. He could also create great comic effect from just a sniff and look to acknowledge something that had been said, which either he could not be bothered to answer or did not know how to. Arthur had contradictory views about certain comic effects. He would say, 'I'm not doing that, it's pantomime stuff,' but in another scene he would perform, for example, a perfectly legitimate comic fall and then embellish it by getting up with the cap askew and his glasses in a slanting position across his face, so that effect was as near pantomime as it was possible to get.

I was touring in a play with Arthur and Joan in 1978 and I arranged a meeting between them and Sandy Powell and his wife Kay, both of whom I knew quite well. Arthur and Sandy admire each other's work and they spent a couple of hours over a few gin and tonics discussing this and that and making one another laugh. I've often wished I'd had a video camera with me that day, recording two masters of their craft in full sail.

During the tour of the play *Caught Napping*, Arthur was not sleeping well at night, although he had the odd cat nap during the day and even sometimes on stage. So he got some sleeping tablets from his doctor. One evening he mistakenly did not take them until about seven in the morning, with disastrous results. He was discovered sound asleep in his

BERNARD CRIBBINS

If you are talking about 'classic' TV shows, **Dad's Army** has to be in the top five! As an actor it's one of those shows that I would love to have been in. The quality of the writing and the direction must have made it great fun to do, and the ensemble playing is some of the best you'll ever see. If I had to name a favourite character it would have to be Captain Mainwaring, the impeccable Arthur Lowe. His hesitations and tiny double takes were wonderful, and the awful 'stupid boy'. Totally splendid!

dressing room just before curtain up and Joan and I tried to wake him by slapping his face, squirting a soda syphon on to the back of his neck and then even forcing his head out of the dressing room window. Although he was half asleep, eventually we got him on stage to the top of the stairs when he had to make his entrance down a steep staircase. As the curtain went up, Arthur in the character of Potts, the schoolmaster, dressed in shorts, tee-shirt and plimsoles, proceeded to descend the stairs. What followed next was unforgettable. He took a long time to reach the bottom step and on the way down went through the entire gambit of comic inventiveness. He may have been half asleep, but his natural talent for comedy, conjured up from the depths of a befuddled brain, soon had the audience laughing and applauding before a word had even been spoken. Arthur's natural talent for comedy had, of course, been nurtured and refined over many years. In 1946 he began his acting career at the late age of 30 in repertory in Manchester. This was not only the start of his career but also a lifelong partnership with

Top: Arthur and Joan Lowe aboard their yacht *Amazon*.
Above: A gala occasion. L-R: the Labour politician Manny
Shinwell, boxing promoter Jack Solomans and Arthur Lowe.

actress Joan Cooper. Joan takes up the story:
'Arthur was born in the very lovely village of
Hayfield in Derbyshire. His father worked for
the then London and North Eastern Railway,

and one of his duties was to arrange rail travel
for touring theatrical companies. Arthur's
early working life was spent with the Fairey
Aviation Company before joining the Army
prior to the World War II. After a not too
pleasant period in this country he was posted
to the Middle East where he began to enjoy
his service career in the Duke of Lancaster's

Own Yeomanry. In fact with a little persuasion he might have made the Army his career.

'He had a love of horses and became an expert horseman. It was while he was abroad in the Army that Arthur gained his first experience of "theatre", although this was confined to delivering books of stage plays to outposts so that the troops could enjoy play-reading to relieve the boredom (which wasn't to last too long in the Middle East). He also enjoyed himself helping to organise troop shows while he was abroad. When he came home and was demobbed he broke the news to his parent that he didn't want to go back to Fairey Aviation, but wanted to try his luck in the theatre. His mum and dad were sympathetic to his wishes, at the same time probably thinking it was best he got it out of his system and once he'd tried it he would settle down again in a "proper" job. His father gave him an introduction to Frank H. Fortescue who he knew, having done railway business with the impresario's touring theatrical companies. So it was that Arthur found himself on a cold January morning in 1946 at the Hulme Hippodrome, Manchester.

'Flare Path was the first play of the new season at Hulme, and most of the company were old friends and had worked for Fortescue before. There was one person that nobody knew. He was wearing riding breeches and a heavy Army greatcoat. He was a very thin, short, slightly bald headed man, and obviously very cold. He said he'd just come back to England after four years in the Middle East. That day my whole life was changed. From then until Arthur's death in Birmingham during the run of Home at Seven in 1982 we were seldom apart.

'At Hulme we did a new play every week, and two performances nightly, so Arthur got in a great amount of experience in a very short space of time. We talked from time to time over the next few weeks and he told me that his home was in Hayfield. That was our first

Above: Actress Joan (Cooper) Lowe.
Opposite above: A scene from Geoffrey Lumsden's *Caught Napping.* L-R: Annette Woolett, Arthur Lowe and Shelia Keith.
Opposite below: Playbill of *Caught Napping.*

bond because I was born in Chesterfield, so we were both Derbyshire people. We found we had many interests in common. My father was a cricket addict, so apparently was Arthur's. We had both been taken at a very early age to see some of the county matches at Chesterfield's ground. My dad was a church organist and choir master, and very dedicated to both, but occasionally cricket had to come first. I fell in love with Arthur during that season at Hulme, not perhaps the most romantic place to fall in love, and I think his parents were a little shocked at first; even though their son was now an actor, they looked upon stage people with a certain wariness. However, I got on famously with them and grew to adore his father. We were eventually married in 1948.'

Arthur and Joan had come to London in 1946 as they both thought for Arthur's sake

they should get into a repertory company within the London area. By 1950, after various short tours and a season at Hereford, the daily rounds of the agents in London were beginning to pay off with several small film parts and radio broadcasts, including *Mrs Dale's Diary*. Those who have seen *Kind Hearts and Coronets*, which projected even further Alex Guinness's name, may have noticed that the actor who played the reporter at the end of the film was Arthur Lowe. *Kind Hearts* was followed by another film, *The Spider and the Fly*, repertory again at Croydon and Bromley, and yet another film at Ealing Studios. In 1951 Arthur made his first television appearance. At about this time he auditioned for *Call Me Madam*, which Jack Hylton was presenting at the Coliseum. So he had arrived, as they say, in the West End, and in such a comparatively short time since that first season on the boards at Hulme Hippodrome.

Joan Cooper, by now Mrs Lowe, takes up the story again: 'We found at this time our first

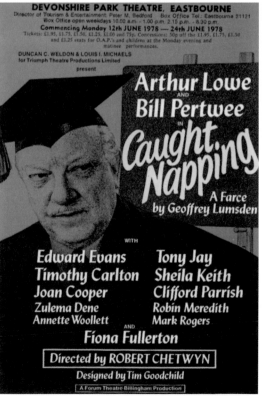

real home together, a small flat in Rutland Gate. Almost at once I found myself pregnant, much to our delight. Arthur had been such a good stepfather to my son David by my previous and young marriage, it was wonderful that he was now going to have a son of his own.' Film parts followed, then the musical *Call Me Madam* and after that he went into another Jack Hylton production, *Pal Joey* at the Prince's Theatre now renamed the Shaftesbury. More films, radio and television followed, and then he was back in the West End in 1955 in *The Pyjama Game* at the Coliseum.

While Arthur was convalescing after an appendix operation, he began to drink wine rather than the occasional beer – nothing very expensive, about 2s (10p) a bottle. By the time I first met him he was quite a wine connoisseur. His son Stephen was growing up and already at kindergarten school and David was at Hexham Grammar School near Joan's parents and had become proficient with his music studies, a talent inherited from Joan and her father. David eventually became Director of Music at Stowe School.

Soon after his operation, Arthur opened in London in *Dead Secret* with Paul Schofield. This certainly was Arthur's most important West End appearance to date. In 1960 he was offered a part in three episodes of a little series for Granada Television. He was to play Mr Swindley in *Coronation Street*. It was soon obvious that *Coronation Street* and Mr Swindley would continue, and this long-running series has, of course, become a television phenomenon. Arthur suddenly found himself being recognised in public and, being a very shy person, was shocked and frightened. Even when *Dad's Army* was fairly well established, I have heard people call out to him, 'How's Mr Swindley, then?' He would stiffen up and quietly say, 'My name is Arthur Lowe.' Although it can be galling at times, actors have to remember that, once they are on the 'box' regularly, they become public property. Why this should be so I do not know. Even now, after all these years, people will pass me in the street – and this applies to the other surviving members of the cast – and start singing, 'Who do you think you are kidding Mr Hitler?', the show's signature tune. Arthur used disguises and different voices in the hope that he would remain anonymous, but it didn't work. He was later given his own series by Granada called *Pardon the Expression* in which Mr Swindley was the main character. Arthur decided to call it a day with Mr Swindley in 1966 as he wished to move on to pastures new.

More theatre followed, then in 1967 Arthur was invited to lunch at the BBC by David Croft and Jimmy Perry. David Croft had produced many shows for the BBC and he and Jimmy wanted to talk to Arthur about a programme they were planning to write and which David would produce about the Home Guard. They wanted Arthur to play the central character of Mainwaring. In civvy street he would be the manager of the local bank. Arthur returned home and discussed the proposition with Joan who undoubtedly had a great influence on Arthur's acceptance of the role. Joan always had good judgement and advice to offer on Arthur's various projects. After all, Joan herself was an actress of long experience, having played a variety of roles in a career which began in 1939 working with the great Donald Walfit, playing pages, ladies-in-waiting, and so on, for 25s (£1.25p) a week on tour – and you had to pay your digs out of that and make sure you were always well dressed. Her later appearances were in J.B. Priestley's *Laburnum Grove* and *Beyond a Joke*, R.C. Sheriff's *Home at Seven* and

Opposite: One of the happiest periods in Arthur Lowe's career. Ian Carmichael and Arthur Lowe relaxing in Austria where they were filming the remake of the 1930s classic *The Lady Vanishes*.

Caught Napping, in which I was conscious of her acting ability as we had several scenes together in that play. Joan was featured in several episodes of *Dad's Army* and in the stage version. But to get back to Arthur's original offer from the BBC.

As much as they liked the idea, I am sure that not even Arthur and Joan could have visualised at that point just what a huge success *Dad's Army* would eventually be. As Joan has said: 'The brilliant writing team of David Croft and Jimmy Perry gave us the happiest years of our life together. To be part of that wonderful family of actors was a great delight.' It still amazes Joan, and it certainly does me, to look at Arthur's working diary and see just how much work he did prior to *Dad's Army* and during the run of the series. Most actors would have been satisfied with working in a popular television comedy series; Arthur did theatre, television and recording sessions for advertisements, voice-overs, reading children's stories and a radio series. He also managed to fit in more films, *Oh Lucky Man* being one and the very funny *The Ruling Class* with Peter O'Toole in 1971 being another. The location for this film was a huge old country mansion not far from Nottingham. Arthur and Joan used to drive out for each day's filming with Jack Hawkins, one of the most admired and loved members of our profession. Although Joan also had a small part in the film she still had time to watch some cricket at the lovely Trent Bridge ground. Arthur and Joan grew very fond of Peter O'Toole during the filming of *The Ruling Class* and this applied to the crew with whom O'Toole used to play a primitive sort of cricket during lunch-breaks. Joan told me: 'This film occasioned the only anti-fan letter that I can remember Arthur receiving. He was playing a Communist butler and had a wonderful scene shouting and swearing, breaking a family heirloom and generally being an absolute swine, before he was dragged off by the police. When the film was released, an irate letter arrived from a lady saying that she had not expected to see such behaviour from "Mr Swindley" or "Captain Mainwaring". Arthur wrote back very politely, saying, "Surely I am allowed to enjoy myself when covered by an X certificate." You see, for once he had been able to forget his almost puritanical attitude to television and family entertainment. So Arthur really enjoyed making that film.'

He then portrayed Louis Pasteur in the medical drama *The Microbe Hunters*, most of which was filmed in Paris, and still more theatre at the Old Vic in *The Tempest* with Sir John Gielgud, proving again that Arthur was not just a film comedy actor but a very good dramatic one too. Then from 1973 up until 1977 *Dad's Army* took up most of his time with the radio version, stage musical, etc, all described in more detail later. In 1977 he played Home Secretary Herbert Morrison, the Labour minister, in Granada's production of *Philby the Traitor*. This was followed with a tour of Priestley's *Laburnum Grove*. In 1978 Arthur started a new series for BBC TV called *Potter*, who was a retired suburban busybody, and a series for London Weekend TV called *Bless Me Father*. There was also a long theatre tour of *Caught Napping*. Then came the remake of the movie *The Lady Vanishes*, a spy thriller. Basil Radford and Naunton Wayne were the original cricket- loving Englishmen abroad caught up in a web of intrigue and espionage. Arthur played the Basil Radford part in the remake and Ian Carmichael the Naunton Wayne part. Arthur took Joan with him and they had a very happy time together seeing a lot of Austria and all the lovely film locations. Arthur came home to record more *Potter* and *Bless Me Father*, then had a season in a play at Shanklin on the Isle of Wight. Arthur and Joan moored the *Amazon* near Cowes and lived on her while they were there, which they greatly enjoyed. Working together and living on that

lovely boat was heaven for them both and the Isle of Wight is such a lovely place anyway. There was more to come, but not too much more. As Joan said: 'In my quieter moments I naturally miss my dear Arthur, but I do thank the entertainment business for giving us so many happy moments together, particularly Paris when he was making *Pasteur*, Austria with *The Lady Vanishes*, and all those glorious days in Norfolk and Suffolk in *Dad's Army*.'

Joan spent the last years before her death in 1989 in retirement in the village of Hayfield in the house in which Arthur spent his childhood.

Right: Arthur Lowe as a brilliant look-alike Herbert Morrison, the Labour Cabinet Minister Arthur portrayed in the Granada Television production Philby.
Below: Rehearsals of J.B. Priestley's *Laburnum Grove*. L-R: J.B. Priestley, Joan Lowe, Arthur Lowe.

 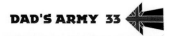

JOHN LE MESURIER

If anyone had told me before *Dad's Army* that a close friendship would develop between John and me over the years, I would have been very surprised, as we were both so different in upbringing and theatrical background; but that is exactly what happened. In the lunch-break during the first day's rehearsal for the programme at the Feathers Pub off the Hogarth roundabout at Chiswick, John came over to me and said, 'I'd like to buy you a drink.' And that was the first of many noggins we would share together during a long association. You see, John's career had encompassed many, many films, in which he had worked with some of the big names in our business and he was on first-name terms with practically all of them. He would quote people by their Christian names without any effect or desire to impress: 'I had a lovely week or two with Fred (Astaire) in Rome', or 'Noel (Coward) once said to me when we had a day together ...', and 'David (Niven) and I had a lot of laughs when he was over here last ...'. I have to admit that it did impress me and certainly made me feel that here was someone who had been around and, I felt sure, would have many interesting stories to relate. My only counter to the list of international film and stage actors that he had known and worked with was to tell him about a summer show I had done on the pier at Brighton, or about some rather dodgy weeks in variety that I had endured at West Bromwich or Cleethorpes. Our musical tastes were in one or two respects similar, but John was far more familiar with most types from jazz to light opera than I could ever be.

Against this background, it may seem surprising that we became such good mates, but there were a number of reasons why it happened. First, we made each other laugh. Just as I enjoyed his slightly sophisticated humour, he liked my far more earthly approach. John had tremendous admiration for music hall and circus folk. His lovely and vivacious wife Joan came from a circus and funfair background, so his rapport with the circus came naturally to John. He used to say that circus people had heart, and that meant a lot to him. I have some roots in the music hall and know a few stories about the greats of that profession, and I used to tell him anecdotes about Harry Tate, the eccentric comedian who worked in the earlier part of this century, Robb Wilton and Jimmy James. John would say, 'Tell me that story about Harry Tate again,' and I could hear his familiar chuckle even before I had finished. I used to go back to John's flat in Kensington for the occasional night after a long day in the studio, and we would sit up until the early hours chatting about life's eccentrics – he was rather fond of eccentrics. That slightly absent-minded attitude of his was not put on, particularly when it came to mundane things like food or organising his mail. If, however, a correspondent interested him, he would reply promptly and at length. Joan looked after the house they had in Ramsgate and where her parents also lived, and she would come up to London once or twice a week and have a good cooking session, putting all sorts of dishes into the freezer for John. One night I remember he went to the freezer and took out something that he fancied to eat, but it was at the bottom of the pile so he had to take out the other items first. When I got up in the morning all these items were still on the kitchen table, completely defrosted and therefore ruined for future use.

After a long recording session one day at Television Centre, when Ian Lavender and I had been up to the waist in a water-tank for hours on end, I had to drive up to Stamford where I had to compère a series of concerts at a caravan rally. It was pouring with rain when

Opposite: John Le Mesurier and friends on their way to Bembridge as celebrity guests at the Lifeboat Open Day.

I got into the car at about 10.30pm ready to start the long journey north. John appeared at the car window and said, 'Where are you off to, Billy?' (he always called me Billy). 'I'm off to Stamford for the weekend,' I told him and explained the reason why. He asked if he could come with me as he was not doing anything for the weekend. I replied, 'Well, OK.' He then said, 'If we pop round to the flat on the way, I'll get my toothbrush.' We headed north with a rainstorm so fierce that I lost a windscreen wiper. Half-way up the A1 we both felt a bit peckish so we pulled up at a carman's cafe – there were many of these dotted about the country at that time. Unfortunately, or fortunately, whichever way you look at it, nearly all have been replaced by neon-lit service centres, but how welcome those little 'caffs' were to weary theatricals on their journeys up and down the country. On that particular night, John and I tucked into bacon, egg, sausage, baked beans and fried bread, all washed down with a cup of steaming Camp coffee, black liquid which was poured out of a bottle. I think Camp coffee lost some of its appeal when the word 'camp' became general theatrical jargon for someone who was a bit eccentric or over the top. We were both recognised that night and John conversed as comfortably with the various lorry drivers who came up to him as he would have done with society folk at the Ritz. He used to say, 'As long as a person is interesting he deserves one's attention.' He really did not have much time for bores and, after putting up with some ridiculous conversation would say quietly, 'That fellow invented boredom.'

But back to our trip to Stamford on that wet night. I was put up at the Haycock Inn at Wansford. When we arrived at about 1am we were told that they were full up (mostly with caravan rally organisers – they were not going to spend a weekend in a caravan in a wet field!). I was told there were two beds in the room that had been booked for me and that

Above: John Le Mesurier in relaxed mood. His portrayal of Sergeant Wilson provided the perfect foil for Arthur Lowe as Captain Mainwaring.

was the best they could do. John said, 'I'm quite happy to sleep with Billy.' The receptionist gave us a funny look, but I was too tired to allay her fears about 'those theatrical people'. I was just hoping John would omit to mention the Camp coffee we had on the way up. We had a sandwich and a large Scotch sent up to the room. I dropped off to sleep straight away, but that was not surprising as not only had I spent the day in a water-tank but I had also had a

rotten drive up the A1, normally a road I enjoy driving on. At four o'clock in the morning, I woke up to find the light on, the window open, and John sitting up in bed writing.

'What the devil's going on?' I asked. 'It's four in the morning.' John replied, 'I'm writing some words to accompany that dreadful noise you've been making.' Apparently, the eggs, bacon, sausage, fried bread, baked beans, Camp coffee, late-night sandwich and the Scotch had all been too much for my digestive system and in my sleep I'd had a touch of the wind, to say the least!

I repeated this story at dear John's funeral and memorial service in London at the suggestion of Joan. I must say it brought much laughter from the congregation on both occasions, and I'm sure John wouldn't have minded. In fact, I could almost hear him say, 'Oh Billy, do be quiet,' accompanied by that quiet and infectious chuckle.

But to return to the rest of that weekend with the caravan club. When we reached the site in the morning, the previous evening's storm had all but wrecked the two huge marquees that had been erected for the concerts. The site held something like a thousand caravans. John took his coat off and, together with all the many willing hands, got down to banging in the steel pegs, hooking up the guy ropes and generally making himself useful. Once this was done, still covered in mud and obviously enjoying himself, John seemed to be invited into every caravan on the site.

John never did things by halves. He drove a not-too-new Ford car and one morning on the way to rehearsals he decided that he had had enough and didn't need a car any more, particularly in London, so he left it there and then under the Hammersmith flyover, and although he had a licence since a very early age, he never owned another car.

Some days John would arrive at the studios looking a little tired. We would ask him if he had had a bad night and he would reply, 'No,

on the contrary, a most pleasant one. I went to Ronnie Scott's Club and was so enjoying the music and meeting friends I didn't realise it was as late as it was and I didn't get home until 4am.' But late nights certainly didn't affect John's ability to learn his lines for he was always very quick at getting the words firmly in his head very early on in the rehearsal. He was a great jazz fan and knew people like Humphrey Lyttleton, Johnny Dankworth and Cleo Laine, Nat Gonella, and Ronnie Scott of course, and many more. I'm sure John would have enjoyed Clint Eastwood's movie tribute to saxophonist Charlie Parker, had he lived to see it.

When John and I drove up to filming sessions at Thetford, we avoided going via the A11 from London. We used to cut off through Royston and join the A11 later. We would stop at a small old-fashioned but extremely pleasant hotel for a drink and bite to eat. This

Above: Joan and John Le Mesurier at home in Ramsgate.

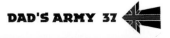

would bring memories of the 1930s flooding back to John. He used to attend various balls at the hotel, anniversaries, birthdays, etc, and those summer balls were held in the grounds of the hotel in marquees (he seems to have an affinity with marquees) where the young set would dance the night away to the music of Ambrose or Roy Fox and their bands.

On another occasion when we were going up for the annual filming at Thetford, I asked John what time he wanted me to pick him up. At the most, even with a stop for refreshment, we could do it comfortably in four hours. On this occasion we weren't needed in Thetford until Sunday night, so I thought tea-time on Sunday would be a good time to leave London. Much to my surprise, John asked if we could go up on Friday so that we could stop off in Newmarket and go to the national stud, have a look round, and also go and see a few trainers. John was on fairly intimate terms with some of the racing fraternity and was a real horse-lover and frequent visitor of race-tracks around the country when he had time. I agreed to go up on the Friday and, after a day in Newmarket, we then went on to stay at the Angel Hotel at Bury St Edmunds. This was John's home town where his father had had a most successful law business, and that evening in Bury, John and I visited practically every pub in the place before we headed back to the Angel for a late supper. At that point John was rather concerned about the stage version of *Dad's Army* that we were about to embark upon late in the summer. We were going to open in Billingham, Cleveland, before coming into the West End and few of us had heard of Billingham. 'Why do we have to go to this Billingham place, Billy? It's miles from anywhere, we shall all probably get lost.' Even the waitress came in for it during that dinner at the Angel. She was quite elderly and when she was serving the soup John suddenly said to her in an extremely loud voice, 'What about bloody Billingham!' The wait-

ress practically threw the soup at us and ran for her life. A different waitress came later to take our order for the main course. The whole Billingham saga will unfold later.

When we arrived in Thetford on that Sunday night after our two-day journey, Arthur Lowe asked John what sort of journey we'd had, and John replied, 'Fine, it took two days.' Arthur gave us that famous look of his and just said, 'Extraordinary,' and walked away. I explained to Arthur that we had spent some time in Newmarket and he said, 'Oh yes, he pats horses, you know.'

Having been born in Bury St Edmunds, John quite naturally had a long affinity with the countryside, although he lived in London for most of his adult life. He loved horses and dogs, old pubs with their local characters and village greens, preferably with a cricket match in progress. He had played cricket, in fact, for Suffolk, and was probably up to county standard in his young days. His cricketing prowess was nurtured at Sherborne School. John was fascinated by the theatre in his teens when he used to come up to London and was rather jealous of what he thought must be a terribly glamorous life. After he became an actor, he was well aware of the hard work behind the business of acting. In fact, he often said to me, 'It's not easy work, is it?'

John was 23 before he suddenly decided that he wanted to go into the theatre. Up to that time he was intent on following his father into the family law business and was in the process of travelling on his father's behalf when he decided that the legal profession wasn't for him. The urge to become an actor overtook him when he was travelling on a train from Waterloo and as he passed Sandown Park racecourse (racing and its environment seemed to punctuate his life) the decision was finalised in his mind. The fact that the day before he had been to see Adele Astaire in *Funny Face* at the Princes Theatre probably had something to do with it. At that

Top: John Le Mesurier getting a 'touch-up' from the make-up girls.

Above: 'What's to become of us all?' John Le Mesurier waiting to film on Britannia Pier, Great Yarmouth. The episode was called 'Menace from the Deep'.

time, of course, he could not have imagined that one day he would work with the great Fred Astaire. Having had a fairly easy and comfortable upbringing, it must have been something of a shock when he went into repertory earning just £4 or £5 a week.

In his highly amusing autobiography *A Jobbing Actor*, John recalls his first London engagement as 'understudy' in *Gaslight* at the Apollo Theatre. He did, however, take over one of the leading roles when the play went on tour. At the time John had met and married a young female impresario, June Melville. A female impresario was something of a phenomenon among a male-orientated business, but a pretty one was even more rare. He continued touring and June Melville continued with her job. Then came the war.

That was the start of a change of life, not just for John but for many people. He became an air raid warden in Chelsea, but there was still some touring to do. Returning with June one day, they found their house in Smith Square, Chelsea, razed to the ground by a German bomb. After this John was called up and went to do his bit for the country, but it appears that some of the military personnel had doubts as to his enthusiasm for life in the army. The answer was found by recommending him for a commission. He was posted abroad and spent much of his time in India. When he returned for demob and civvy street, his marriage to June, like so many other marriages of that period, became a war casualty.

John returned to touring with the theatre, but his sights were set on films, and before long the rounds of agents paid off. In 1947 John was taken by a friend to the famous Players' Theatre Victorian music hall under the arches at Charing Cross. It was the first of many visits and there he met actress Hattie Jacques who eventually became his second wife. Hattie was soon climbing the ladder through Tommy Handley's radio series ITMA and later in *Educating Archie*.

John's film career was also prospering and eventually he became one of the best-known faces on the silver screen with *Private's Progress, Brothers-in-Law, I'm Alright Jack*, and many others. The British film industry was in full swing and John, together with other actors like Richard Attenborough, Jack Hawkins, Peter Sellers, Norman Wisdom, Donald Sinden and all the J. Arthur Rank starlets, were becoming national names. Hattie Jacques, too, was making her way in films which led her to long association with the 'Carry On' company and eventually into the enormously popular television series with Eric Sykes. They had started a family and the two boys, Robin and Kim, were now growing up. They would eventually enter the competitive world of pop music, and make it, very successfully.

Unfortunately, John and Hattie's marriage ran into troubled waters, through no one's fault in particular, and they parted. They were still fond of one another and used to spend time together. Sunday lunch was almost a must if they were both free and everyone remained on the best of terms, even after John had married Joan. He was terribly upset when Hattie died and always remembered her with tremendous affection. I only met Hattie on a couple of occasions, once when I worked on a television episode with her, and found her to be a most charming and gracious lady.

By 1965 John had married Joan Malin. Her parents were from the fairground business and on our one and only meeting I found them delightful, perhaps quieter than their daughter, who I liked immediately when John introduced us. John was not always the easiest person to handle, but Joan was generally quick to sense the reason and find a solution. Any mood that he got into was usually the result of being bored and nothing else. He was the sort of chap who could quite happily board a place for Hong Kong at a moment's notice for a few days' filming,

Above: Clive Dunn, who played Corporal Jones, a key member of the Home Guard and the local butcher. Jones's van provided the transport for the platoon and had a vital part in several hilarious adventures. Corporal Jones's catchphrase, 'Don't panic! Don't panic!', was known throughout Britain.

armed only with a toothbrush and razor. The thought of a long run in the theatre was obviously a depressing one in his later years. Mind you it does the same to a lot of actors. It says a great deal about his marriage to Joan that they overcame certain difficulties and yet remained sweethearts until he died. Shortly before his death, John stayed at our house in Surrey for a few weeks while he was doing a play, and he would phone 'Joany', as he called her, nearly every night. We loved having him to stay. He used to have breakfast in the garden and our dog Biffa would sit at his feet as if they had been chums for years.

During the *Dad's Army* era, John worked on many other projects – as did other members of the cast – voice-overs by the dozen, other series, and the television play *Traitor* for which he won an award as Best Actor. I know that meant an awful lot to him. Just before the last series of *Dad's Army*, John went on a theatre tour abroad and was taken ill. He recovered from that, but it had taken its toll and when we arrived at Thetford for the filming of the last series, we were all told beforehand not to show surprise at his thin and strained appearance. Even though we had been warned, it still came as a shock when we met up at the Bell Hotel. A few days in East Anglia, however, back among the 'boys', soon had him somewhere near his amusing and convivial self. So it was still a shock to all of us when he finally, in his own words, 'conked out'. He'd certainly given me many laughs during a nine-year friendship and he hadn't finished then. There were even one or two surprises at his funeral.

CLIVE DUNN, OBE

How can you accurately describe someone like Clive Dunn? Clown, actor, trick cyclist, dancer, raconteur, chart topper and accomplished artist who is good enough to have his work exhibited.

Clive's experience goes back a long way. He comes from a theatrical family, and a very successful one at that. His grandfather was music hall comedian Frank Lynn, who wrote and performed his own comic songs. Clive's mother was Connie Clive, a comedienne of some note, and his father was Bobby Dunn, singer and raconteur. This family background of making people laugh influenced Clive at an early age, and his portrayal of dotty old gents on stage and television had the hallmark of music hall about them. Without that unique background I do not think any other actor could have been as inventive with those characters as Clive was. Not that he isn't a good actor, but that very useful mix of music hall and revue in his family background helped him, particularly when the script-writers sup-

plied some great situations to work with, which certainly happened to Clive as far as *Dad's Army* was concerned.

Before tackling any comedy business or routine, Clive is often hesitant and gives the impression that he is not very enthusiastic at the prospect of doing it. After a while it is obvious that this diffidence is because he wants time to think about what he is going to do and how to get the best results. When I first worked with him I really thought he was being rather off-hand with the writers and his fellow actors, but I soon realised that this was how he worked. The nervous laughter that accompanied his assessment of a situation was used as a cover for his hesitancy, a way of keeping the ball in the air, as he didn't want to isolate himself completely from those associated with it. Any other actor might have walked away and said first, 'Well, I'll think about it.' Clive's genuine laughter and good humour at all times is very infectious.

There is a story about Clive's Uncle Gordon and the salmon-and-cucumber sandwiches at Ascot races in his autobiography *Permission to Speak*. He related this story to me one day during rehearsals and he had me rolling about with laughter. I have always found him great company and look forward to meeting up with him again, which is not so often nowadays because he lives much of the time in Portugal where he lives with his family, wife Priscilla, daughters Polly and Jessica, and very young granddaughter. At whatever time of the day you dropped into the Dunn household when they lived in London there always seemed to be something to eat. Grapes, biscuits, cheese, some sort of cake he had seen in the local delicatessen, and certainly a bottle of wine. One got the impression that the whole house was run like a continental family home – with anybody welcome at any time. Connie, Clive's mother, lived in the house next door and was very independent and as lively as a cricket, despite her age. Clive

and Cilla and the girls were always very conscious of her welfare and you would generally hear a chorus of voices ringing out at odd times, 'Anyone been up to see Connie this morning?' I used to talk to Connie about the Fols-de-Rols (I have a nice postcard of her in one of the company groups), as I had also been a 'Fol' and we both knew Rex Newman, the amazing 'governor' of that show, although Connie's friendship with him had started many years before I was in the company. Rex not only owned the best concert party, the Fols-de-Rols which conquered almost every English seaside town and many inland ones as well, but in his time he was responsible for writing a lot of material for the original Crazy Gang. He also wrote a very successful 1930s musical entitled *Mr Cinders*, which was revived a few years ago in London, again to critical acclaim.

When Clive and Cilla began to put down roots in Portugal it didn't surprise me. They had both been regular visitors for years and the continental style of mixing together family and friends and different artistic talents, which they had always encouraged, in the atmosphere of a small community will give them a lot of pleasure. No doubt the Dunn home is strewn with delicacies just waiting for the first caller of the day to arrive.

Coincidence is a strange thing. One day in the early 1970s I told Clive that my family and I were moving from the coast and coming nearer to London, in fact to Surrey. I described the area and Clive told me he used to visit a composer friend 'down that way'. He started to describe the house and within minutes I know it was the one I had just bought. And would you believe it, it came to light that the composer's wife was the choreographer for a big Blackpool summer show

Opposite: 'Never mind patting it, just get up on it. My platoon is going to be a mobile platoon.' Arthur Lowe, John Le Mesurier, Clive Dunn and John Laurie in 'Man of the Hour'.

'Never mind patting it, just get up on it.'

Above: Corporal Jones: 'Here come them Jerry bombers again. I hope they don't hit my shop, I've just had a delivery of offal!'

that my wife Marion had been in when she was a professional dancer; but let's get back to Clive Dunn. It was obvious that he would go into 'the business'. His father was not keen on his following a theatrical career but eventually helped him. Almost his first job was as a boy extra in a Will Hay film *Boys Will Be Boys*, but being good theatrical parents Connie and Bobby decided that Clive should attend a stage school and they enrolled him at one of the very best, Italia Conti. With Italia Conti you had a chance to work in some professional seasonal shows which was wonderful experience. Clive was involved in some of these, and then went out into the hazardous world of commercial repertory, stage managing and playing small parts, and, as was fairly usual at that time, experiencing the

management saying, 'Sorry lads and lasses, the tour finishes on Saturday, the public aren't coming in.' Then would start the problem of paying off the landlady and finding the fare to get home, and waiting for the next engagement to come along.

Soon after this, Clive's 'next engagement' was in World War II , and his experience was far more traumatic than that of a tour closing after a few weeks. He was taken prisoner by the Germans in Greece, and although there is a humorous undercurrent to these extraordinary years in captivity, as he recalls in his autobiography, it is obvious that only a fit

person with a good sense of humour could have survived them. Other people were going through hell in Japanese captivity in the Far East or in German concentration camps, but certainly Clive's recollection of the horrendous events in his life as a prisoner make them both compulsive and humorous reading.

Clive has been described as a pro's comic actor; I wouldn't disagree with this and I don't think he would either. In the medium of television, or the Player's Theatre for instance, where he played on and off for many years, Clive would invent strange characters and originate off-beat dialogue. If this were done in the big variety theatre a throwaway line or quiet aside would have no value. So one might say he was created for the small screen, which eventually came his way in great abundance with programmes like *Bootsie and Snudge*, *It's a Square World* and various other projects, together with all the many comic lunatics who have brightened our lives over the years. It was at about this time that he met actress Priscilla Morgan, who was to become his second wife. Priscilla was already a well-established actress, having had major roles in radio and television plays, and was at that time with the Royal Shakespeare Company at Stratford-on-Avon alongside such famous actors as Albert Finney, Paul Robeson and Charles Laughton, and now she found herself being chased around by a pantomimist disguised as various old men. It must have been Clive's sense of humour that appealed to her, for Cilla telephoned her mother one day and said, 'Mummy, I'm going to marry a middle-aged comedian.' So Clive in his most athletic style 'had her up the aisle', as they say, quick as a flash.

When *Dad's Army* began, although I didn't know Clive, I realised that he had a great deal of artistic talent, and that he knew how to enjoy it. He and John Le Mesurier were already old buddies and, because of my concert party and my variety connections,

which Clive was in tune with because of his parent's earlier work in that direction, the three of us soon had some topics in common.

Clive certainly had a talent for picking the right material when he picked the song 'Granded' to record. This really was an extraordinary event, not just in Clive's life but for his family and those close to him, as we, the cast of *Dad's Army*, were at that time. During the week or two before the record's release Clive seemed to be certain that it would be fairly successful. I heard it one afternoon at about this time in John Le Mesurier's flat in Baron's Court and we liked it. It was simple and it had a good hook line (those repeating phrases that are easy for the public to pick up), but I don't think anyone realised what an impact it was going to make. Once it was released first one disc jockey started playing it, then others followed suit and before long it was being played regularly. Now came the crunch. Clive was immediately caught up in the publicity machine that only the record business knows how to use. Clive was being rushed around the country on promotional trips. There were television appearances. Managements wanted him for theatre shows and contracts were being

CLIVE DUNN

With so many repeat showings, **Dad's Army** has become part of people's lives. I had dinner with Joan Le Mesurier recently. She told me her cleaning lady, Lyn, went to see a recording of **Dad's Army** on a day Bill Pertwee was doing the warm-up. After the recording, Joan asked if she had enjoyed the evening. Lyn replied, 'I liked that Bill Pertwee, he ought to go on the stage!'

 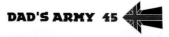

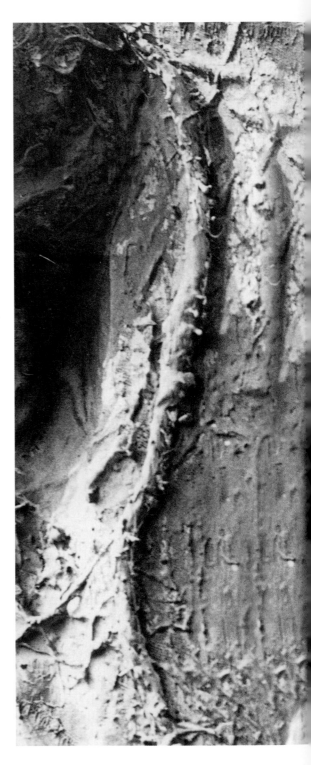

Above and Right: Clive Dunn/Corporal Jones disguised as a tree trying to capture an enemy windmill in 'Don't Forget the Diver'.

drawn up for this, that and the other. It was amazing that he coped with it all. There was also the fact that *Dad's Army* was beginning to take off in a big way, and now he had a number one hit record and appearances on *Top of the Pops* to make. His family were very supportive, of course, and also very proud of Dad – well, who wouldn't be? From an extra in a Will Hay film to *Top of the Pops* is quite something.

Clive is always good company on social occasions. In 1988 several of us went to a restaurant after appearing on the *Wogan* show and Clive was about to order a couple of dishes of Mediterranean origin when I said, 'You don't want that, you can have that in Portugal, have so and so.' Eventually he did order the things I had suggested, but after playing with the food for a bit he said, 'I don't like any of that.' Someone enquired as to why he had ordered it and Clive replied, 'The Peruvian made me have it.' (He knew I had some Peruvian ancestry on my mother's side.)

After several bottles of wine and much reminiscing about old times, we were ready for home and seeing Clive off to the airport for the return trip to Portugal. As he left, he said to the head waiter, 'I've really enjoyed myself, but don't ever employ my friend as a chef – he'll empty the place.'

ARNOLD RIDLEY, OBE

Anyone who writes 35 plays in long hand, including one blockbuster, is entitled to have writer's cramp, but when the diagnosis of loss of use of your arm and hand reveals that the nerve on the inside of that arm has died, it really is a serious business and would have made most people feel like giving up any hope of ever working again. Arnold Ridley, however, the gentle Private Godfrey of *Dad's Army*, was an exception, for beneath the surface he is very strong and determined.

Educated in his home town of Bath and nearby Bristol University, it was thought that Arnold would become a schoolteacher, but in 1914 he joined the Theatre Royal, Bristol, to take up an acting career. Later that year he enlisted in the Somerset Light Infantry and this led him into World War I and the bloody fighting in France. Arnold was eventually invalided out in 1917, his left hand and fingers badly injured, his body pitted with shrapnel, and suffering from a blow on the head from the rifle butt of a German soldier that was later to affect him with serious blackouts.

Arnold's life was equal to any adventure story. He wasn't sure what to do when he came out of the army, but decided to continue where he had left off before the war and was taken on by the Birmingham Repertory Company and later the Plymouth company, but was forced to give up acting in 1921 because of the severe injuries he had received in France. A very despondent Arnold went home to Bath and worked in his father's boot-shop. He had been a fine sportsman in his young days, playing high grade cricket and rugby for Bath. So apart from the pain and discomfort he was suffering in 1921, his frustration at having to give up his sporting activities and the problem of not being able to work properly must have been very depressing indeed. He later became the secretary of Bath Rugby Football Club and held that position for 17 years, after which he became the club's president. He was eventually made a life member. When I knew him he was always anxious to find out the latest cricket and rugby scores and particularly those of Bath Rugby Football Club.

In the early 1920s Arnold didn't know whether he would ever act again, and it was while he was working for his father that he wrote his first play. He took this to a theatrical producer in London and, although it was received with some enthusiasm, unfortunately the producer had some other important business to attend to (they always have) and could not take the project any further at that time. Arnold was desperately disappointed and after the meeting went to a theatre to see a thriller. He thought it was very ineffectual and was convinced that he could write a better one. Not long after this he was travelling by rail from the Midlands back to his home in Bath and he had to change at a country station, Mangotsfield Junction, where he had a four-hour wait. While he was sitting on the deserted platform the idea came to him for another play. The slightly eerie atmosphere of the empty station and a fairy-tale theme that he remembered sparked off the idea for *The Ghost Train*. He wrote the outline of it in about a week in his father's shop at night and decided to complete it and offer it to a management team. As a play it was not easy to produce technically. Although some very spectacular musicals had been mounted in London, it was a daring piece for a play. *The Ghost Train* was first produced in Brighton, but was not a success. It was shelved for a

while, then a tour was arranged, the result of which still did not give any real indication of the eventual success that was to come its way worldwide. After the tour it was produced at the St Martin's Theatre in London in 1925 and accompanied by a clever advertising campaign. It became a West End hit and ran for over 600 performances there. Later it transferred to the Garrick and then the Comedy Theatre. It just goes to prove that some managements who have faith in a product are prepared to gamble on their intuition even after, as was the case with *The Ghost Train*, it had had two unsuccessful attempts in the provinces. Suddenly Arnold was in the money and experiencing some notoriety as a West End author. He almost immediately wrote another play called *The Wrecker* in collaboration with another writer. Although some people thought it was even better than *The Ghost Train* and although it was produced at the New Theatre, it was not a hit.

During the rest of the 1920s and early '30s, Arnold was a prolific playwright with London productions that included *Third Time Lucky, Easy Money, Beggar My Neighbour* – all three of which were also filmed – *Glory Be, The Keepers of Youth* and *Tabitha*. Arnold adapted *Peril at End House* for the stage from an Agatha Christie thriller and certainly would have collaborated with her on future occasions had it not been for World War II, because he immediately struck up a rapport and friendship with Agatha Christie on their first meeting.

Above Right: Arnold Ridley took on the role of the gentle Private Godfrey, always needing to 'be excused'. Here he is on location in Norfolk.

Right: 'Love of Three Oranges'. Mainwaring: 'This is not a concert party you know Godfrey, this is war. You look ridiculous dressed up in a pierrot costume. We're supposed to be camouflaged for snow manoeuvres.' L-R: foreground, Arnold Ridley and Arthur Lowe; at the back, Freddie Wiles, Roger Bourne, John Laurie.

In 1935 he founded his own film company and with a partner and the backing of a bank, went to work on their first production, *Royal Eagle*. When the film was previewed it got marvellous notices, but halfway through their second movie the bank went bust. Arnold was left in serious financial difficulty, but rather than declaring himself bankrupt, he paid off all his creditors personally. It took him nearly 20 years to achieve this, but every penny was paid back. He enlisted in the army in 1939 and was sent to France with the rank of major. He became severely shell-shocked during the evacuation from France in 1940 and was reprimanded when he returned to England for failing to inform the authorities of his World War I wounds. He was invalided out of the army and decided to join ENSA (The Entertainment National Service Association). ENSA was sending companies of entertainers all over the British Isles and to His Majesty's ships in home waters. Some of these companies were made up of just two or three artists working from the back of a lorry or even solo performers at a lonely gun site. Other productions were much bigger when facilities allowed and Arnold's first assignment was to direct his own play *The Ghost Train* for a national tour.

Auditions for the play were held at Drury Lane Theatre in London, the headquarters of ENSA. One morning a lady arrived to read for one of the parts and was greeted by a small gentleman with a funny old hat who led her on to the stage. The lady thought the gentleman was the stage door-keeper, but was very soon to find out that he was, in fact, the author and director of the play. The actress was Althea Parker who had come to ENSA after driving ambulances at night during the blitz on London. Althea had heard about Arnold from a friend a couple of years previously and said, 'He sounds the sort of man I'd like to marry.' At Drury Lane, after she had got used to his funny hat, she accepted an invitation from Arnold to have a drink and decided then and there that she would marry him, and this she eventually did, but not until the war had ended. Meantime, they toured in plays together and they also did a season at the Malvern Festival.

Althea Parker had gone with her family to New Zealand when she was a very young girl and had done her initial stage-work in that country. She returned to England in 1937 and immediately got a job in the Tyrone Guthrie Company at the Old Vic, acting alongside such distinguished actors and actresses as John Mills, Vivien Leigh and Ralph Richardson. Althea was later chosen to appear in J.B. Priestley's *Time and the Conways*. After she and Arnold were married and their son Nick was born in 1947, Althea did little stage-work but some prestigious television plays.

By this time Arnold had decided to concentrate on an acting career. He loved being a father, although he had always given the impression that he wasn't too keen on having children around. Many years later he and Nick were having a chat and his son said, 'I expect I was a mistake.' Althea replied, 'You certainly weren't, I planned it,' and I'm sure she had. Nick's affection for his father was not isolated as far as children were concerned. During the run of *Dad's Army* it was very apparent who the young children would go to first when they were collecting autographs. Arnold's mailbag was always full of letters from children, which is not surprising, for 'little ones' have an instinct as to who is their 'friend'.

In about 1952 it became impossible for Arnold to use his right arm and hand because the nerve had died. This had almost certainly been caused by his lengthy period of writing, which he initially did in long hand. It was decided to operate and take the nerve from the back of the arm and graft it on to the inside –

Opposite: Actor Arnold Ridley was also a playwright with 35 plays to his credit.

an operation that had been performed only once before and not very successfully. However, Arnold went ahead with it and fortunately it proved worthwhile. While he was recovering from the surgery, Emile Littler – the well-known impresario – let it be known that he wished to stage a musical version of *The Ghost Train* at the Palace Theatre, to be entitled *Happy Holiday*, but on condition that Arnold should make over to him half the rights of the play for ever. This Arnold agreed to, but the musical was not a success. However, Arnold never regretted his decision to allow Littler to control half the rights of *The Ghost Train*, because from that time on, the impresario collected the royalties in a very business like way, which other managements in the past had certainly not done. That little idea of a train story that came into Arnold's mind on a deserted railway station in the 1920s had certainly become a money-spinner. Apart from the many productions of it all over the world, it was also made into three films, including a silent version, a second sound version starring Jack Hulbert and Cicely Courtneidge, and a third one featuring Arthur Askey and Richard Murdoch in the 1940s.

During the 1960s and '70s Arnold featured in radio's long-running series *The Archers*. He also appeared in *Coronation Street* and was a regular in *Crossroads*, playing the vicar. As with John Laurie, *Dad's Army* opened up yet another phase in Arnold's career when he was already into his seventies. It was amazing to see him picking up the laughs in the series with his quiet underplaying of the character Godfrey. In between various productions of the series he also did some more stage-work, including a long tour with Phil Silvers (Sergeant Bilko) in *A Funny Thing Happened on the Way to the Forum*, and a sell-out season at the Yvonne Arnaud Theatre, Guildford, playing the porter in *The Ghost Train*. I saw this and Arnold was marvellous, as was the play which I was seeing for the first time. It was also produced at a later

date at the Old Vic but, in Arnold's words, 'it was not a memorable production'.

Arnold always seemed to me to be a disciplined person. He was punctual at rehearsals and learnt his lines and moves quickly. During the whole run of the series I saw him cross only once and he had reason to be.

He had a little chuckle if he enjoyed hearing a joke or while telling some anecdote himself. Midway through one afternoon, when we were filming out in the country, he told David that he wasn't feeling too well. David immediately summoned a unit car and told Arnold to go back to the hotel and rest. When we arrived back much later we saw Arnold walking out of a nearby pub. We said, 'You should be resting,' and he replied, 'Well, I had a gin and tonic in the hotel and felt so much better I thought I'd go out and have another.' This was followed by that chuckle and twinkle of the eye.

In 1976 he was the subject of *This Is Your Life*. The idea of surprising him was that we were going to do a rehearsal for a scene at Marylebone Station and he was told, as we all were, to report to the station in the afternoon. Naturally, we were all in on the secret and so was Althea – in fact, she had known for several months but had kept it to herself, not always easy when you are with somebody every day. At the appropriate time Althea was hiding in the ticket inspector's office with Eamonn Andrews and once we were all lined up in front of the cameras, which had to be disguised as BBC equipment, Eamonn, in the uniform of the station master, introduced himself to Arnold and produced the 'red book'. He was stunned, and all he said was, 'Does my wife know about this?' It was certainly a relief to Althea when it all fitted into place. We were all whisked off to the studio ready to record the programme, which included not only many theatrical friends and family, but also a lot of his contemporaries from Bath Rugby Club.

In 1982, to the delight of everyone who knew him, Arnold was awarded the OBE in the

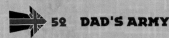

New Year's Honours List for services to the theatre. By this time, failing health was overtaking him and he was confined more and more to the flat, but was cared for in a very loving and sympathetic way by Althea. She had been a great support and strength during their whole married life in a way that perhaps only a person connected with the theatre's ups and downs, of which Arnold had his share, would understand. He died at the wonderful age of 88 in 1984.

JOHN LAURIE

When I first met John Laurie, who played the local undertaker in Walmington, and Private Frazer in the platoon, I was slightly intimidated by him – John Laurie, I mean, not Private Frazer. He breezed into the rehearsal room on that first morning and was briefly introduced to those he didn't already know, myself among them, and in a short sharp response said, 'Hello son, pleased to meet you,' and was away to the corner of the room where he had left his hat and coat and newspaper. That newspaper was almost his trademark. A copy of *The Times* was his comforter and woe betide anybody who went near it. He immediately went to work on the crossword. As the *Dad's Army* years went on it became a race between John, Joan Lowe and Ian Lavender as to who would finish the crossword first. I think that it was the crossword more than anything that really intimidated me. I don't think I had ever tried to read *The Times*, let alone dare to look at the crossword! I wondered what sort of conversation I could ever hope to have with someone who did *The Times* crossword. There was no wasting time with John – if the rehearsal wasn't going to start there and then, it was crossword time. First impressions can be deceptive and so it turned out to be with John Laurie. Once you got to know him he was, of course, just another actor – slightly eccentric perhaps, but intelligent and outspo-

Above: Walmington-on-Sea's lugubrious undertaker – Private Frazer (John Laurie). Frazer was the cynical observer of Mainwaring's foibles and had a pessimistic outlook on life: 'We're doomed, I tell you, doomed!' Below; 'Could it be an intruder after my gold pieces?' John Laurie as Frazer in 'the Miser's Hoard'.

 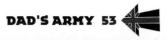

ken, which you accepted.

Very early into the first rehearsals, John said to Jimmy Perry, the co-writer, 'I hope this is going to work laddie. To my mind it's a ridiculous idea, a programme about the Home Guard.' Well, there's candour for you – and after having accepted the part he was playing too! Within a few short weeks it became obvious that *Dad's Army* was taking off and John had to retract his words. Without fear of embarrassment, he said to Jimmy, 'I never had any doubts that it wouldn't succeed.' He dismissed his first remark by making this very obvious contradiction of it. In other words, he turned it into a sort of joke, as did the writers. That little true-life incident became a comedy situation for the whole series. When Captain Mainwaring was proposing some exercise or another which seemed far-fetched to most and quite stupid to Private Frazer, he would say, 'It's folly, it'll never work, the man's mad.' When it did eventually work out in some extraordinary way, and the other members of the platoon were saying, 'I don't know how you managed it Captain Mainwaring,' or some such flattering remark, Frazer would jump straight in with, 'I never had any doubts at all that Mainwaring wouldn't pull it off.'

John Laurie came to *Dad's Army* after a long and distinguished career in theatre and films. He was born in Dumfries and was destined for a career in architecture, but then came World War I. He talked very little about this episode in his life, but from the little he did say about that war he thought that men should not have been put through such terrible experiences. He said he never expected to come out of it alive. After being invalided out of the services, he finished his war as a sergeant-of-arms at the Tower of London. Architecture, or the thought of it, seemed a thing of the past by 1919 and John decided to become an actor. He did his initial studies at Stratford-upon-Avon where he pursued his love of Shakespeare. His

Scottish single-mindedness paid off, for although he didn't play any Scottish parts for many years, as he had intended, eventually he played all the great Shakespearean roles at the Old Vic and at Stratford. His King Lear was thought to be one of the great performances on the British stage. He went into films in 1930 when he worked for Alfred Hitchcock in that director's first talkie, *Juno and the Paycock*. He worked for Hitchcock again on the memorable and original *The 39 Steps*, starring that wonderful actor Robert Donat, whose life was shortened by continual asthma attacks. Other versions of *The 39 Steps* have been filmed since then and Rupert Penry-Jones has starred as the central character Hannay in a television version, which was shown as part of BBC1's Christmas line-up in 2008. John said that Alfred Hitchcock was an extraordinary man and although he (John) never crossed swords with him, he could be very frightening to work with.

The film industry here and in the USA was expanding rapidly and John was part of it; he played the Mad Mahdi in Zoltan Korda's early classic *The Four Feathers* (the Mad Mahdi cropped up again later in *Dad's Army*). John also featured in Alexander Korda's (Zoltan's brother) *Bonnie Prince Charlie*. When the various television companies are showing some of the old classic film comedies, you will see John in one or two of them with, for instance, Will Hay, playing slightly eccentric characters. John was forever grateful that he had had the chance to work with Laurence Olivier, whom he admired tremendously, and the wonderful experience of appearing in his Shakespearean films, *Richard III*, *Hamlet* and *Henry V*. He used to say that when he watched the film of *Henry V* the battle scenes made his hair stand on end. He thought it was a masterpiece of photography and atmosphere.

It took quite a long time for me to find out anything about John. It was not that he

couldn't be bothered to talk about all the marvellous things he had done, he just thought it was all in the past and people didn't want to listen to, as he would say, 'the ramblings of an old man'. Occasionally, I did find a way to draw him out. I would tell him how much I admired all the great classical actors and that I certainly hadn't got the talent or even the inclination to tangle with that side of the 'game'. John would then be happy to tell me all about the actors he had worked with and in doing so he naturally talked about his involvement with them and the productions he had been in. However, it took me the best part of nine years to find all this out.

On the way to the studio one day from his home in Buckingham to do a recording of *Dad's Army*, John had an accident in his car. He was obviously shaken and had several cuts about the face but, being the proud Scotsman that he was, after being patched up he insisted on coming in to do the recording. He took the day fairly easily, but it still takes something out of your nervous system to do any performance, and to do it after you've been in a car crash and when you are no youngster (he was already then into his seventies) takes some courage.

On another occasion when we were filming an episode, John and I were playing a couple of desert Bedouins in a flash-back sequence that involved Corporal Jones's experiences with General Gordon and the Mad Mahdi in Khartoum. This sequence was being filmed near King's Lynn in Norfolk in some huge sandpits to simulate the desert. John and I were on horseback and had to ride at a leisurely pace into an open space beyond some high dunes. Film sequences were being prepared on the other side of the dunes, so John and I took the chance to get used to the horses. I was, and still am, very raw in the saddle (no pun) but John was an experienced horseman. However, even the most docile of animals can sometimes be disturbed and this is exactly what happened. Suddenly, a couple of practice rifle shots rang out from the other side of the dune and John's horse bolted. He managed after a time to bring it under control and pacify the animal, but I knew he was shaken by the mishap. I asked him if he would

Below: 'Whatever next?' – the Warden and Frazer disguised as tribesmen in 'Two and a Half Feathers'.

like to go back to the caravans for a rest and a cup of tea, but he said, 'No, laddie, I'll be all right, and don't mention it to the others, I don't want any fuss.' And that just about summed John up. I think he believed he might break down and not be able to carry on at all if anyone had started showing concern or sympathising with him – which would have been the case, of course, because we were such a caring company.

After rehearsals, John would dash off back to his home in Buckinghamshire, which was his anchorage. He lived very quietly there with his wife Oonah, and, when she was home, his attractive daughter Veronica. He kept horses himself and the lovely setting of that country house where he could relax in the autumn of his life and walk with his dogs had, as he said, been earned from a lifetime in acting. There is a story about John which I never heard him deny, possibly because he used to like to hear people chuckling about it, which I'm sure he quite enjoyed. On Saturday mornings he would put a notice outside his house saying, 'Manure for sale – 2s 6d a bag', and he would personally serve the customers himself because he said it boosted sales. Was this a ploy copied from the American comedian Jack Benny, whose supposed thrift served him well, as far as publicity was concerned, for many years, or was it just good business sense inherent in all Scots? Whichever way, it caused great amusement to those who knew about it. By 1968 and prior to his call up in *Dad's Army*, John would almost certainly have settled for semi-retirement, just doing the occasional radio play or a poetry reading, which he enjoyed. He always said that his new career in television was a bonus at his time of life. He was not stretched too far, and most of the time rehearsals were fairly leisurely, apart from the filming sessions in Norfolk and recording days in the studio.

One of the delights for us were his dramatic stories about a supposed experience which he would launch into if the platoon were in a tight spot on some night patrol. This would bring terror to Corporal Jones and Private Pike. With his eyes flashing he would say, 'We're doomed, I tell you. I remember the time on the lonely Isle of Barra, the wind whistling round the headland; there in the silence of the mist, it appeared. Bloodshot eyes, a huge body and a long tail, creeping nearer and nearer.' And then just as everyone was in a state of paralysed fear he would scream out, 'We're doomed, I tell you, doomed, doomed.' Of course, there would always be a perfectly simple explanation for the monster or phantom he had suggested. I shall always remember John Laurie as a larger-than-life character with a natural personality for making even the most ordinary dialogue sound extraordinary. I wish I had had the opportunity of seeing him in some of his great Shakespearean roles – it must have been quite an education.

JAMES BECK
An early theatrical idol of mine was the great comedian Sid Field. Jimmy Beck was also a fan of Sid's and I remember his surprise one day when I said to him that if the Sid Field story was ever produced, he would be a natural for the part. At times Jim looked very much like Sid, but it wasn't just the obvious parallel of one of Sid's funniest characters, the spiv 'Slasher Green', and Jimmy's Private Walker – they both, in fact, had that mischievous look of, 'What can I get up to next?' about them. Jimmy had done his preliminary training in the provinces just as Sid had before coming to London and finding fame, Sid with his very successful revues at the Prince of Wales Theatre and Jimmy through the medium of television. The similarity of coincidence did not stop there for they both died in their early forties before they had a chance to really capitalise on their potential. Sid would have been a natural for situation comedy in

Above: James Beck and John Le Mesurier during filming for 'Two and a Half Feathers'.

post-war television. Jimmy did have success in that area, but would almost certainly have gone on to other more serious aspects of the theatre, as was promised by his earlier critical acclaim in repertory.

Jimmy was born in London in 1929 in the middle of the Depression. His father was a tram driver and became one of the millions of unemployed at that time. This left Jimmy's mother to become the breadwinner; this she did by making artificial flowers, which were fashionable at that time. His great dislike of artificial flora stemmed from his early child-hood, probably because he associated them with his mother's struggle to make ends meet. Jimmy's wife, Kay, told me that if he couldn't have fresh flowers in their house he wouldn't have any. He went to art school when he was 14 and enjoyed that part of his life, which is not surprising because he became a very good

painter and sculptor. Examples of his work adorn the lovely cottage he and Kay shared for many years, and where Kay still lives. Jimmy left home at 17 and decided he wanted to go into the theatre. He had been passion-ately interested in it since he was a youngster and had compiled a scrapbook of film and stage stars, which is still intact. It is crammed full of pictures of and chit-chat about the greats in cinema and the theatre.

He was called up, as all young men were in their late teens, and he did his national service as a PT instructor. When his service was com-pleted, he started on the serious business of looking for work in the theatre. He obtained engagements with several repertory companies and it was his contract with the York Theatre

Company that was a turning point for him. He became a leading man for that company, playing in *A View from the Bridge* and Shylock in *The Merchant of Venice*, Archie Rice in *The Entertainer* (for which he received a congratulatory letter from the originator, Laurence Olivier) and other major roles.

It was while Jimmy was at York that he met his wife-to-be. The company did short seasons at Scarborough on the North Yorkshire coast and Kay was living in the resort after she had separated from her first husband. After their initial meeting, Jimmy would often cycle from York to meet her, which was no mean feat on a bicycle. Jimmy felt he had done all he could at York so decided to come back to London as soon as he and Kay were married. Further repertory seasons followed, but Jimmy still felt that he wasn't being stretched. It is perhaps essential that an actor should always feel he could do more and do it better than his or her contemporaries, particularly someone like Jimmy whose whole life was now the theatre and who became bored if he was not working. He loved watching a great performance and admired talented actors. He was well versed in opera and could quote whole passages in whichever language the particular opera was in. On holidays abroad he could pick up the language quite easily – that in itself is a gift. I do wonder whether the actor's sense of frustration, which is an understandable part of their creative talent, can sometimes be a drawback and unsettle them. I believe it did this to Jimmy more than occasionally. He did not seem to be totally satisfied with his part in *Dad's Army*, even though he was very successful in it. The general public really loved the character of Private Walker the Spiv. They remembered with great affection that sort of cheeky conman type from the war years. The spiv had an element of excitement about him and he was very useful in the black market economy, gently flouting the law. Jimmy had

the built-in excitement in his make up to make the character very believable. He was still going back into the theatre on occasions in the early days of the series and I know that John Le Mesurier and Clive Dunn went to the Palace Theatre, Watford, to see him acting in *Staircase*, and they both said he was brilliant.

By 1972 Jimmy had had several offers as a result of being seen in *Dad's Army* and they started to come to fruition in 1973. He had his own series with London Weekend Television called *Romany Jones*, he did a couple of one-off comedy hours with Ronnie Fraser, he was asked to make an LP record of Cockney songs and he was featured reading stories for *Jackanory*. At this time the BBC had made the important decision to re-record some of the old Tony Hancock scripts. Arthur Lowe was to play the Hancock character (in his own style, of course); Jimmy Beck would play the Sid James role. Ray Galton and Alan Simpson, the original writers for Tony Hancock both on radio and television, were already updating the Hancock scripts to accommodate the two actors' styles. I knew

Below: James Beck with his wife Kay and the family cat.

Arthur and Jimmy were both excited about the project but, alas, it never came about, nor did a further series of *Romany Jones* or any of the other projects destined for Jimmy, because he died in 1973. He was taken ill the day after we had been recording some BBC radio episodes of *Dad's Army* at the Playhouse Theatre in Northumberland Avenue. That Friday night was the last time any of us saw him.

There are several things I personally remember about Jimmy. He would come into the rehearsal rooms in the mornings, stand almost still, summing up the atmosphere, then flash his toothy smile and more often than not start the day with an impression of Humphrey Bogart, Edward G. Robinson or W.C. Fields. It was his way of saying, 'I'm in a good mood, I hope you are.' One night when we were away filming, John Le Mesurier met an old friend from his army days – a colonel or similar high-ranking officer – in the bar of the hotel and invited him up to his room for a nightcap, and Jimmy joined them. I decided to play a joke on him (my room was directly opposite his) and I walked across to his room stark naked except for my boots and white helmet. Realising that I had made a gaffe and that the army officer was fairly shocked, I retreated very quickly, but Jimmy Beck, who had been standing by the door, got to my room first, slammed it shut and locked me out in the corridor. We all became rather hysterical, including the officer, mostly out of sheer embarrassment. The one worry now was that Arthur Lowe, whose room was just down the corridor, would come out and see what was going on at one o'clock in the morning, so I hid in a broom cupboard for several minutes until John and Jimmy had telephoned reception to get a pass key from the night porter. When he came up, Jimmy said to him, 'The warden has just been visiting the vicar' (who was played, of course, by Frank Williams). I hoped the night porter wasn't a religious man.

Jimmy's wife, Kay, told me that one day when they were in York she and Jimmy were going into Betty's, a favourite and rather sophisticated tea room in the city. As they were going in Jimmy started talking to a tramp (they always interested him) and invited him in for tea with them. The staff at Betty's 'were not over-happy about Jimmy's new found friend'.

The family cat was certainly a friend, and on one occasion when Jimmy rang Kay at home to find out how the cat was, I asked him, 'And how's Kay?' He said, 'Fine, I think,' and after a moment's hesitation added, 'Hold on, I'll go and ring up the cat and make sure.

Kay was a truly supportive theatrical wife, the type of person who stayed behind the scenes but was always available to help Jimmy make decisions. She also gave him confidence, something so essential to an actor but something he did not have in abundance, even though he knew what he wanted. It is very easy when you're caught up in the day-to-day business of television or theatre literally to forget to eat or even to have a regular meal pattern. Kay is a smashing cook, her toasted muffins are delicious, and she always made sure that Jimmy ate well and had a secure life when he was at home. We all missed him.

IAN LAVENDER

Many people imagined that it was Warden Hodges who was on the receiving end of most of the *Dad's Army* custard pies, but if you were to sit through a selection of a dozen random episodes you would realise that it was 'Pikey' who took the greater proportion. Mainwaring, having got him into most of those ludicrous situations, would then add insult to injury with the pay-off line, 'You stupid boy'.

Ian Lavender is anything but a stupid boy. He is a dab hand at crosswords, a very good backgammon player and a real DIY fiend. I used to drop into his house for a cup of tea on occasions and was continually amazed at his

handiwork. He was born in Birmingham exactly nine months after VE-Day in 1945. It seems that his parents did rather a lot of celebrating on that day. Cadbury's Bournville Trust came into Ian's life at quite an early age. The Quaker family not only originated the famous Bournville village for Birmingham, but they also financed four technical schools that taught almost any subject. All the sports grounds were supported by Cadbury's and had better facilities than any other school in Birmingham at that time.

At the age of seven, Ian wanted to be an actor. At junior school he got the plum part of Mozart in a play because he was taking piano lessons, even though he could only play 28 bars of music. He also played Pontius Pilate in an Easter pageant, based on *A Man Born to Be King*, because his mother and father had a copy of a radio script, so it was a case of, 'It's my bat and my ball so I should have the best part' – and why not? It was all part of a childhood ambition to tread the boards.

Ian went straight from senior school to the Bristol Old Vic Drama School, a venue particularly revered by so many actors and actresses who have passed through it. Ian had obtained a grant from the City of Birmingham, a corporation that has always been generous in this direction if they believed a drama student would make good use of it. As he said, 'that was the luck of living in Birmingham.'

Ian thoroughly enjoyed his time at Bristol and when he finished there his talent and potential was quickly recognised. Almost immediately he had the offer of three jobs.

Right: Ian Lavender was cast as Pike, the youngest member of the platoon. Pike not only had to suffer the fussing of his mother, who made him wear a scarf on patrol, but also tended to jeopardise Mainwaring's plans, hence the rejoinder 'You stupid boy!' Here the two of them are in discussion. Mainwaring: 'Now listen Pike, it's my turn to man the bren gun, and I'll be covering the High Street from Timothy Whites to the Novelty Rock Emporium.'

Canterbury seemed to be the most attractive, so he began a six-month engagement at the old Marlow Theatre. After Canterbury he made his first television appearance. Ian was sent the script only the day before the first rehearsals, so assuming that it was a very small part, cast at the last minute, he didn't even bother to look at it until he arrived at rehearsals. To his astonishment, he discovered that he was playing the lead. There was no 'It's my bat and my ball' in that situation. The television play was called *Flowers at My Feet*.

Very shortly after this he was cast as Private Pike in *Dad's Army* and the first filming sequence was to be shot at Thetford. Ian arrived at BBC Television Centre to pick up the coach with all the other actors thinking they would all return that same day. When he realised that everyone had suitcases, he had to dash back home and pack a few things, because this was the first of the many location stays at the Bell Hotel in Thetford.

During filming of the first episode the dialogue was to be mute, but some of the action intended for the studio was performed instead on location. Ian had to say a few lines, so he had to study his part rapidly and find a suitable voice. To his surprise, the one he tried out first time seemed to please everyone, so the plaintive 'Mr Mainwaring' was heard for the first time. He stuck with it for the next nine years, something he doesn't regret, for it was a period in his life when he came to theatrical maturity.

The first few months of *Dad's Army* were exciting for everyone, but in particular for Ian, a young man on the threshold of a television career and in the company of some fine actors. As Ian said, 'It was a team show. Even though all the individual actors were so different in their outlook, they all got on well with each other.' John Laurie and Ian were great chums, discussing the business of acting, doing the crossword together and sometimes travelling together to locations. Ian was inclined to look after John, in the nicest possible way, and John looked on Ian as a son who was always ready to absorb the experience of John's knowledge.

The character of Pikey was never going to be easy to play, particularly for an inexperienced actor. In the bank he was a very junior clerk under Manager Mainwaring and this junior position was carried on into the Home Guard, but at the same time 'Pikey' had to emerge as a personality as far as the viewing public were concerned. Ian would be the first to agree that he had some great lines and situations which allowed him to emerge so strongly in the part.

It was inevitable that Ian would be typecast after the series finished, but he has certainly proved through a variety of roles since that he is not 'a stupid boy' and in 1989 he appeared in London alongside Dustin Hoffman in *The Merchant of Venice*. Ian was a regular in Eastenders between 2001 and 2005, playing a gay character, Derek Harkinson, and that was followed by tours of *The Rocky Horror Show* and *Donkey's Years*. In June 2009 he opened in *Sister Act, The Musical* at the Palladium. Hasn't he done well?

He has two sons, Daniel and Sam, by his first wife, Suzanne, herself an actress, and is now, along with his second wife, Michelle, hugely enjoying having a grand daughter.

FRANK WILLIAMS

Frank Williams has always been tall, certainly six foot plus, so his first professional engagement must have been very uncomfortable as he played two parts at the Gateway Theatre in London: a snail and an ant.

Born in North London where he has lived all his life, Frank had a happy childhood and his own disposition was probably responsible for this. He is fun to be with and people laugh

Opposite: Arthur Lowe to Ian Lavender: 'Don't stand there gaping boy, it's probably one of ours.'

'Dont stand there gaping, boy.'

with him even when, as Clive Dunn would comment, 'he gets in a bit of a muddle'. At the age of 12 Frank went to Ardingly College in Sussex as a boarder. He avoided all sports because he found ball games frightening; even now his comment of people who play cricket is to the point, rather like a Greyfriars pupil of the 'Bunter' ilk, 'look out chaps, they've got one of those nasty hard things they're throwing about', followed by 'come away Teddy, you'll get hurt' – some of us used to have a little practice in the lunch breaks). At Ardingly he dodged sports by joining the school Land Army, digging potatoes, etc, even on cold days. He was interested in drama, but it was not taught at Ardingly. The Junior Training Corps was compulsory for pupils, but Frank was not keen on its activities; on mock manoeuvres he said: 'You were able to get out of marching and all that stuff by getting captured early on and having a lie down in the sun until all the silly business was finished.'

Frank is very intelligent and regrets that he did not go to university. He became an inveterate cinema-goer and theatre buff and as soon as he had left school, with very good academic qualifications, he decided to enter the theatre. Not only did he perform in other writers' plays at the Gateway Theatre but in 1952 he wrote his first play which was produced there with some success. In 1955 he was cast in a television play by R.F. Delderfield (the author of *Worm's Eye View*). At about this time he also appeared in his first film. In 1957 he worked at the Palace Theatre, Watford, which was run by Jimmy and Gilda Perry. This was the start of a long association with them both. Two of his plays were produced at Watford under the Perry management.

Cast in one episode of the highly successful *Army Game* for television, Frank was brought back very quickly into the series as an army officer, Captain Pocket. He played the same role for 70 episodes in that very funny series. The *Army Game* brought Frank a certain amount of fame and security. He has performed a variety of roles in the theatre, from the classics to pantomime dame, and played both film and television productions in his own particular style. When he first joined the cast of *Dad's Army*, he immediately stamped his authority on the character of the vicar of Walmington-on-Sea.

Frank has worked mainly in the theatre in recent years, including three seasons with the English Stage Company in Vienna and frequent appearances as a dame in pantomime. Two of his many plays, *Murder by Appointment* in 1985 and a long national tour of *Alibi for Murder* in 1989, have had successful runs.

Frank is also a lay preacher and works very hard for his local church, so it is very surprising to discover that he is a gregarious character and something of an adventurer. Frank likes nothing better than to have a social evening with friends in a restaurant in the presence of amusing company, and he will make up for any jollity that is lacking in that company. He stores up stories of funny situations and laughs uncontrollably when he recalls them. For instance, there is a story that begins, 'Do you remember when John Le Mesurier, Teddy Sinclair, Bill Pertwee and I booked into a hotel in Birmingham when we were on tour with the stage show of *Dad's* and it became obvious that the hotel was used quite a lot by ladies of easy virtue and we had to tell Teddy we were going to move out? It hadn't dawned on the innocent Ted as to why, even though he did say he couldn't sleep for doors being opened and shut all night!'

When Frank is on tour he often stays with the local vicar and his family, many of whom he had become acquainted with through the Actors Church Union, a branch of the clergy that pays regular visits to theatres backstage. This custom goes back a long way to the time when in the days of low wages, the local vicar would help sort out accommodation and

other problems for the visiting actors. During his time as a committee member of Equity, the actors union, Frank had also done a great deal of work on behalf of his fellow artistes.

The partnership of the vicar and the verger, always slightly subordinate to 'His Reverence', was an inspired piece of casting. The fact that the vicar had loaned the church hall to Mainwaring on certain evenings would cause some aggravation because there would be occasions when both would want the hall for their own activities – Mainwaring's platoon with weapon training, etc, and the vicar with organising a choir practice.

One of my favourite episodes was 'The Godiva Affair'. The vicar was chairman of the committee that had to select a girl to play Lady Godiva in a pageant that was being presented to raise money for one of the wartime funds. Captain Mainwaring came out of his office at the sound of giggling and in the hall was confronted by several young ladies in bathing costumes. The air raid warden was present and Mainwaring discovered him leering at the ladies. Mainwaring admonished the warden, 'How dare you have naked girls in here, cover them up.' The vicar seemed not to be concerned by the situation and replied, 'Don't be absurd, all the fuss over a few silly girls.' The verger adds, 'Yes, if the vicar wants to have silly girls in his hall that's his affair.' Very often the vicar used the verger to spy on Mainwaring's camp. He would pretend to be dusting or doing some other ineffectual duty, but at the same time he would be peering around corners trying to pick up odd bits of information to pass on to the vicar, or if he felt particularly ill-disposed towards Mainwaring at the time, he would also inform Hodges, the warden, who would use that information to Mainwaring's disadvantage. So very often the vicar, verger and warden would all gang up against the platoon. The warden was always receptive to any idea that would give him a chance to get the better of 'Napoleon', his

Top: Frank Williams as the Vicar of Walmington-on-Sea. The vicar and his accomplice, the verger, often clashed with Captain Mainwaring over the use of the church hall. **Above:** L-R: Frank Williams, the author and Ian Lavender at the 25th Anniversary celebrations at the Imperial War Museum.

favourite term of reference for Mainwaring.

Warden Hodges believed that he should be in charge of Walmington-on-Sea in an emergency, but he never had the respect of the townspeople to do this, even if he had had the courage, which he lacked. Hodges, the target of Mainwaring's derisory remarks such as, 'What can you expect, he's a greengrocer with dirty fingernails', was basically a coward, as opposed to Mainwaring who epitomised the bulldog spirit of Britain in the 1940s. Nothing seemed impossible, and although it was more optimism than anything else, Mainwaring was convinced he could hold Walmington against a German invasion with his conviction that 'He who holds Walmington-on-Sea holds this island.'

EDWARD SINCLAIR

Known as the quiet man of *Dad's Army*, Ted Sinclair was unique. His character of the verger was a finely drawn piece of observation. Edward, or Teddy was he was known to us, only had to enter a scene in his flowing cassock with its wide belt and familiar yellow duster hanging from it, with a flat cap on his head, and the audience was immediately in the mood to laugh. Ted has a particular song in his voice that gave the verger's character an added dimension. He was meticulous, almost fussy, as an actor and that was his strength. His experience had come from years in the theatre. Ted's parents were touring repertory players until the late 1920s and he was taken on stage when he was only six months old. Ted's mother was also a pianist and singer, which obviously had a bearing on his talent for writing lyrics.

Ted realised at a very early age that acting was a precarious business, so he did the next best thing and joined an amateur company in the 1930s and played and directed for them with great success in plays as diverse as *The Admirable Crichton, Rookery Nook, The Rivals, Busman's Honeymoon* and *Twelfth Night*.

He was tempted to join the professional ranks but declined the offers he was made. He was called up into the army in 1940 and soon found himself in service concert parties playing to the troops. Demobbed in 1945, he took up where he had left off in amateur dramatics. By the 1950s Ted was married with young children and was still resisting the temptation to turn professional as he wanted to secure a future for his family. He had a very good job as a top salesman and was happy to bide his time.

When his sons Peter and Keith were firmly settled into a good education, with his wife Gladys providing a stable home life, Ted finally took the plunge and became a professional.

He appeared as Barkiss in the television serial of *David Copperfield* and then featured in various comedy programmes, including those of David Croft. Following this David cast him as the verger in *Dad's Army*.

Ted and Frank Williams became a great team in the production and their friendship spread to their off-stage activities. They would drive to film locations together in Ted's car and he would accommodate Frank's collection of books, a very heavy and almost antique video recorder, and suitcases full of clothes, etc, which would leave Ted with little room for his own belongings. One day I passed them driving up the A1 to Baldock en route to a filming session; they were doing about 25mph and Frank was trying to read a huge map which seemed to envelop them both, while at the same time he was talking non-stop to Teddy. Ted would get involved with Frank's mishaps, and Frank would complain to everyone: 'If only Teddy had listened to me, we would have been all right.' It was the perfect working combination and all was done with great good humour. Ted and

Opposite: The vicar and the verger, *Dad's Army*'s Stan and Ollie. What a partnership they made!

'What's the matter now, Mr Yeatman?'

Above: Edward Sinclair's characterisation of the verger was finely observed. He only had to enter a scene dressed in his cassock to make the audience laugh.

his wife Gladys were certainly the perfect married couple and I know that his two sons were very proud of their father. His death, just after we finished the final episode of the series in 1977, was a tremendous shock to us all, although I knew he had struggled with indifferent health for many years. Ted never made a fuss about his illness and at times it must have taken great courage for him to carry on a normal acting career which physically is always very demanding.

BILL PERTWEE, MBE

Two years ago, Actor Bill Pertwee celebrated his 80th birthday and followed it up with the publication of an updated version of his autobiography, *A Funny Way To Make a Living*. Before entering the world of show business Bill had a number of jobs: farming, factory work and making parts for Spitfire fighter planes; and for a short spell he was assistant baggage boy to the Indian cricket team, who were the first test match side to visit these shores after the war in 1946.

Next he had a year or more in the Stock Exchange as a clerk, followed by five years in the West End – as a window cleaner. Bill then stayed in the West End as a salesman in the sports department of the well-known department store, Burberry's.

He was not, therefore, following the usual route to acting, but a chance meeting with star comedienne Beryl Reid led Bill to write some sketches for a show she was doing in London and, due to the illness of one of the performers, he ended up appearing in it. After that, bitten by the theatrical bug, he got a job in a summer show in Gorlestone, Norfolk, where he met his future wife, Marion. From there, he toured the country's music halls and theatres as an impressionist, along with Marion, and then worked for nearly two years at London's Windmill Theatre, doing six shows a day, seven days a week.

Round about this time, he managed to break into radio, working with some of the big stars of that medium, such as Jack Warner, Max Miller, Ted Ray, Charlie Chester and his hero, Kenneth Horne. Bill appeared regularly in *Beyond Our Ken* and then Round *The Horne. Bill* is naturally probably best known for his role of ARP Warden Hodges in *Dad's Army* and he appeared in the very first episode and over 60 more, not to mention the radio versions, the stage show and the film.

In more recent years Bill has appeared in many West End plays, including the hugely successful farce, *Run For Your Wife* by Ray Cooney. He also went to Canada with it, and

Above: Bill Pertwee and his dear son Jonathan, celebrating Bill's investiture by Her Majesty the Queen in 2007 – a special day indeed.

has toured all over the UK in many plays.

He was delighted to be included in Jimmy Perry and David Croft's terrific series, *You Rang, M'Lord?*, which ran from 1988 to 1992, and he felt it had great costumes and scenery and a super cast.

Bill started writing in the late 1970s, and has produced several books on a variety of subjects. When he's not writing, Bill spends his time after-dinner speaking (and what a story he has to tell!), and organising charity events. In 1999 he was the subject of *This Is Your Life* and in 2007 he was awarded the MBE in the Queen's Birthday Honours List for his services to charity, radio, television and theatre. Not bad for a window cleaner!

by Tony Mulliken, Literary Agent, Midas Public Relations.

THE BACK ROW, BACKROOM BOYS AND WELCOME GUESTS

It was obvious from the outset that there would have to be regular platoon personnel in the Walmingon-on-Sea Home Guard. After all, it would be strange if new faces kept cropping up, which certainly would not have happened in reality as most males had been called up for service in the armed forces during the war, leaving behind the fairly old and the young. The same had to apply to the television platoon and it became essential to find male actors who would be available for several series – if the programme ran that long – actors who for most of the time would have little or no dialogue but who would regularly be involved in the action. It was necessary that these actors should be able to take the odd line when needed, so they had to be actors of experience. The final selection was very interesting.

Hugh Hastings had earned high plaudits in the theatre as a playwright with his very successful West End production of *Seagulls over Sorrento*, a naval play which starred John Gregson, Ronnie Shiner (star of the long running *Worm's Eye View*), Bernard Lee (M in the James Bond films), William Hartnell (the first Dr Who) and Nigel Stock (Dr Watson in various Sherlock Holmes stories). *Seagulls over Sorrento* ran for hundreds of performances in London and had some success in America where it starred Rod Steiger. The play was eventually adapted by Hugh Hastings into a musical, *Scapa*, which opened at the Adelphi

Theatre in London and starred Pete Murray and Edward Woodward.

Hugh came to England from Australia in 1936 and followed his parents' musical tradition by playing a piano in a band at Blackpool; later he went into repertory at Dundee, where Charlotte Frances taught him most of what he knows about the theatre.

Hugh joined the Royal Navy at the outbreak of World War II and had the worst day of his life on 19 August 1942 when he took part in Operation 'Jubilee', the abortive raid on Dieppe when only 2,300 Allied soldiers out of the 7,000 who took part in the mission returned to England.

After the war Hugh went into revue with Hermione Gingold and then went on to enjoy astonishing success with *Seagulls over Sorrento*. The euphoria of this production, even though it lasted for some time, did not sustain him forever, and he became a cabaret artiste in night clubs, where he played the piano and sang his own songs (Hugh had been writing lyrics since the age of 15 when he was working on a sheep farm in Australia). He then accompanied Sarah Churchill on cabaret dates and later became my accompanist in concerts after I had met him in *Dad's Army*. During the run of the series he had had the good fortune to appear in John Osbourne's *Sense of Detachment* which brought him to the notice of Frank Dunlop's Young Vic Company, with

whom he toured all over the world.

Colin Bean (who played Private Sponge) began as one of the back row of the chorus but gradually assumed a more prominent role. Jimmy Perry arrived at the name for the character when he saw the word 'Sponge' over a shop and thought it was unusual and attractive. Colin Bean was trained at the Northern School, Bradford, where some of his classmates included Robert Stephens, Tom Bell and Bernard Hepton. He made his initial radio appearances in Japan, where he was stationed with the British forces. Colin returned home to seasons of repertory at Sheffield in the company of Paul Eddington and Bernard Archard, before he moved on to a long stint with Harry Hanson's Court Players. Colin first met Jimmy Perry at Watford's Palace Theatre, and later Jimmy remembered the hardworking affable Colin and invited him to join the television platoon. Colin's arthritis curtailed his theatrical career and in his final years he spent more time involved in radio work.

Michael Moore was a well-known radio and theatre actor in the 1940s and '50s, mainly because of his appearances in the radio programme *Ignorance is Bliss*, which also included Harold Berens and Gladys Hay and introduced the Chairman Eammon Andrews, to the listening public.

Leslie Noyes, an ex-variety performer and a good-natured stooge to Arthur Haynes in stage and television productions, was another asset to the platoon, as were: **George Hancock**, a retired opera singer who could still sing an aria in his deep bass voice; **Richard Jacques**, actor, director and pianist; **Ewan Evans**, singer with a

Below: Sponge: 'Look out! Here comes the Captain!' Colin Bean (left) as Private Sponge with Ian Lavender as Pike.

Above: Felix Bowness was a guest star and went on to become a regular character in *Hi-de-hi*.

store of Welsh anecdotes; **Jimmy Mac**, with the irresistible smile and a gag a minute recalled from a vast experience in music hall and pantomime; **Roger Bourne**, Jimmy Perry's old friend from Collins Music Hall; **Hugh Cecil**, a children's entertainer who had brought many happy hours to youngsters of all ages, particularly at the seaside; **Vernon Drake**, part of a famous music hall double act, Connor and Drake; **Frank Godfrey**, formerly manager of the Palace Theatre, Watford; **Freddie Wiles**, **Freddie White** and **Desmond Callum-Jones**, a big man with a big car and a little financial independence tucked away in the form of property. All these men made up a marvellous and friendly group of lads who were determined to help stop 'Hitler's army' from landing. The amount of entertainment that these professionals could jointly have provided would have enabled them to put on a show in their own right. They did lose **Vic Taylor**, who died in the early days of the series, but even in the short time that he was with the platoon, he

proved a tremendous asset, particularly with all the filming sequences.

HAROLD BENNETT

Harold quite regularly made guest appearances as the old Mr Bluett, who was not going to fall in with all the alarmist notions that were put about in Walmington-on-Sea. Mr Bluett would show great impatience at being aroused in the middle of the night just to please Mainwaring's mob in search of a lost gun or at the warden's excitable warnings and bangings on the door because he believed that German bombers were approaching. In real life Harold appeared to be a frail old gentleman, but when it came to playing his part, he was dominating and forthright without any sign of hesitancy. Harold went on to play 'Young Mr Grace' for the entire run of the comedy series *Are You Being Served?* Although Harold Bennett was a senior citizen himself, he played regularly in the London theatres.

FELIX BOWNESS

Many thousands of people who have been part of a television studio audience over the years will probably have experienced the disjointed volley of quips, jokes, racing tips and general audience participation from Felix Bowness, as he warmed up an audience. The first appearance he had in a small role in *Dad's Army* was just as frenetic and caused us to wonder whether he was wound up in the morning with a key and let loose on the world like a clockwork toy.

Felix had been an entertainer for nearly 40 years in variety and summer shows all around the country (very often in his favourite resort on the Isle of Wight), playing in pantomime and cabaret and giving after-dinner speeches. It was Benny Hill who suggested that Felix would make a good warm-up man, or studio host as they are now called, and he has warmed up something like 5,000 television productions, working for as many as 15 different

studio shows a week. On one particularly fraught evening, he began by warming up the audience for *Wogan* at the BBC Theatre in Shepherd's Bush at 7pm and then jumped on a motorbike to dash down to the Thames Television studios at Teddington in Middlesex to warm up the audience for the Des O'Connor show at 8pm. Although studio hosting can be a difficult job at times, Felix's professional approach has earned him the admiration of many top professional actors and the eventual reward of appearances in their shows. After making dozens of small guest appearances in various productions, a regular character was eventually found for him as the jockey Fred Quilley in Jimmy and David's successful *He-de-Hi!* series.

In 1986 Felix was warming up the audience for *This is Your Life*. It is not an easy job because the audience must be kept amused for a long time while the guest celebrity is brought from wherever he or she has been surprised, and then sent to the make-up department or to change their clothes. On one such occasion, while Felix was amusing an audience waiting for the guest to arrive, the late Eammon Andrews came on stage, tapped Felix on the shoulder and said, 'Felix Bowness, this is your life.' It was a memorable night for him as his show-business and racing friends came in to offer congratulations.

Felix's career began when he won a talent contest at the old Palace Theatre, Reading. Shortly afterwards Vera Lynn heard him singing and was impressed by his voice. Although she offered to coach him personally at her London home, Felix was determined to make a career as a comedian, so the Atomic Comic, as he called himself, was launched, without a song. In his teens he was ABA (Amateur Boxing Association) champion for London and Southern Counties three years running. He still has a great interest in sport.

Felix has a son (a detective in the Hampshire Constabulary), three grandchildren and he still lives in the Reading area with his wife, Mavis. When agent Richard Stone took Felix on his books 30 years ago, he said, 'I'll make you a star one day.' Although Felix never became a big star, he has won many friends in show business and the racing world. He certainly had more than a few in *Dad's Army*. Long may he continue to warm us all up with his humour.

JOHN CLEGG

John Clegg became a regular member of the cast of *It Ain't Half Hot Mum!* after he featured in a *Dad's Army* episode entitled 'The Great Big Wheel'. This episode was based on some true facts. During the war an inventor suggested the idea that huge wheels, similar to those at fair grounds, could have rockets fixed to them, and in the eventuality of a German invasion force landing in this country, the wheels, which would be radio-controlled, would be manoeuvred into position and then directed across the beaches firing their rockets at the enemy landing forces. Members of the wartime Cabinet and high-ranking military personnel attended the demonstration, but it went slightly wrong. The huge wheels could not be controlled properly and went into reverse, scattering the on-lookers. The events of this story became the basis of the *Dad's Army* episode in which John Clegg played the absent-minded radio operator.

Apart from appearing in all 56 episodes of *It Ain't Half Hot Mum!* as la-di-dah Gunner Graham, John has guested in many other television programmes and is also equally well known in the theatre. I have played with him on more than one occasion on stage and he has great command as an actor. His one-man show, *In the Eye of the Sun* on Rudyard Kipling's Indian writing, is also a testament to his stagecraft. John's most recent film appearance was in *Bridget Jones's Diary*. John's wife, Mavis Pugh, who went on to play many grand ladies, most notably in *You Rang, M'Lord?* started down that particular avenue with her first tele-

Above: After *Dad's Army* John Clegg appeared in all 56 episodes of *It Ain't Half Hot Mum!* as la-di-dah Gunner Graham and is also well known in the theatre.

vision appearance, which was in an episode of *Dad's Army*, playing Lady Maltby, who loaned Captain Mainwaring her Rolls Royce.

BRENDA COWLING

Brenda's role as the farmer's widow in the episode 'All is safely gathered in', where she is helped by Private Godfrey (an admirer from her youth) and backed by the platoon in gathering in the annual harvest, was pitched at just the right level, sympathetic and friendly.

I had the pleasure of working with Brenda again for four years in Perry and Croft's television series *You Rang M'Lord?* from 1988 to 1992. Again Brenda put just the right characterisation into the Meldrum household cook in that series. She has a wealth of theatre work behind her, and may I say is charming company off stage.

PAMELA CUNDELL

My first meeting with Pam Cundell was in 1955 in East Anglia when I was in a very small concert party near Great Yarmouth and Pam was in a smart and sophisticated seaside revue called *Between Ourselves* at nearby Lowestoft. *Between Ourselves* was produced by Bill Fraser, who later made quite a name for himself in films, television and on the West End stage, including the National Theatre. At a later date Pamela became Mrs Fraser.

It was a pleasant surprise to know that she would be playing Mrs Fox in the series, a character who was to become a fairly regular visitor. The sight of Mrs Fox would make Corporal Jones, who ran the butcher's shop in Walmington, become weak at the knees. She played on his romantic emotions for a little favour or two – an extra lamb chop or sausage over and above her weekly meat ration. In spite of her little wiles, Mrs Fox was a homely and endearing lady which made the character real. Pam Cundell's portrayal of the character was very convincing because she herself is a sincere and warm-hearted person.

In one episode, Mrs Fox is invited to the Marigold tea-rooms by Captain Mainwaring who wants to talk to her about Corporal Jones. Jones is infatuated with her and is not concentrating on his Home Guard duties because he believes that Mrs Fox is flirting with someone else, something she is inclined to do on occasions. However, Mrs Fox thinks that Mainwaring has invited her to the tea-rooms to engage in pleasantries himself, perhaps to ask her to take a port and lemon with him one evening and to make some sort of flirtatious advances towards her. The playing of this scene could have been very heavy handed, but with Arthur Lowe's usual deft touch as Mainwaring and the misreading of the situation by Mrs Fox as played by Pam, it became a joy to watch.

Pamela Cundell was trained at the Guildhall School of Music and Drama. She has had a varied career in all departments of the enter-

'Arthur, you know he's got a weak chest.'

tainment business, making her West End debut in revue at the London Palladium. Film appearances include *Half a Sixpence* and she's been in television programmes with Benny Hill, Frankie Howard and Harry Worth. Pam has also guested in *Eastenders*, playing Nora Swann, and no doubt her cry of 'Hello darlings' when she arrived for rehearsals cheered up the other inmates of Albert Square considerably!

JANET DAVIES

Janet looked like a pretty housewife, someone you would want to come home to, which was exactly what she was intended to be when she was cast as Mavis Pike, mother of Frank Pike, and in a very discreet way the comforter of Sergeant Wilson. Mrs Pike's continual concerns that Frank should not get cold on night duty, that he should have enough to eat and that he should always have his scarf with him were typical of any fussy mother. Mavis would burst

into the church hall on parade nights and let fly at Mainwaring with, 'My boy is not be out all night and then get up for work at the bank in the morning. I mean, what about his chest, he's always been delicate since he had the croup,' and then quietly say to Sergeant Wilson on her way out, 'And what about you, Arthur? Will you be in for your cocoa at the usual time?' This would bring the familiar response from Wilson of 'Please, Mavis', and then he would dismiss her with a wave of his hand.

The way that the situation between Wilson and Mrs Pike was handled appeared to leave little to the imagination, but it was written so well and played so skilfully by Janet that it took some time for the people to realise the significance of their conversation. When they did,

 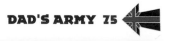

everyone was part of the secret; the viewers at home liked to think that they had discovered a clandestine relationship, although it was never confirmed. Mainwaring occasionally referred to it when he and Wilson were having a quiet tete-a-tete, but even then there was only a slight suggestion in his questioning and certainly no conclusions were drawn from it.

Born of a Welsh father and Cockney mother, Janet Davies's career began in repertory at Northampton, Watford and Leatherhead, and she was also a popular member of the Theatre Clwdd company. Her London theatre seasons included *The Love Match* with Arthur Askey at the Victoria Palace and *Saturday Night at the Crown* at the Garrick Theatre. Janet was also very proud to have been featured in the film version of *Under Milk Wood* with Richard Burton. Although she had guested in other comedy productions such as *The Last of the Summer Wine* and the *Dick Emery Show*, I am sure she will be best remembered for her appearances as Mrs Pike in *Dad's Army*.

DON ESTELLE

A very little man walked into the first day's rehearsal for the episode 'Big Guns', but nobody knew him, apart from Arthur Lowe, and then only as a passing acquaintance. This quiet man, who was later to show great entrepreneurial flair, was Don Estelle. Don's climb from north of England club singer and carpet salesman to television fame is extraordinary.

Don was playing one of the extras in 'the crowd' in a costume drama at Granada Television which starred Arthur Lowe and Jim Dale. Wanting to better his lot in show business, and being a fan of *Dad's Army*, Don followed Arthur Lowe around the studios in Manchester, constantly asking him how he could get into *Dad's Army*. Arthur eventually told Don to write to David Croft, which he did. David, who was always on the look-out for a character, asked Don to come down to London for an

Above: Don Estelle appeared in several episodes of *Dad's Army* but became famous as Lofty in *It Ain't Half Hot Mum!*. He went on to have a hit record with Windsor Davies with the song 'Whispering Grass'.

interview. The result was a small part as a removal man in 'Big Guns'.

This was Don's first speaking part in television, but he learned quickly, although the dialogue bothered him slightly in those early days. He appeared in a number of other episodes, including 'The Test' and 'Under Fire'.

In 1972 Don was cast as Lofty in the new series of *It Ain't Half Hot Mum!* and Don's acting career really began in earnest. His television appearances affected his cabaret club dates in the north; he was able to ask for more money for his singing spots, which had always satisfied his audiences, and his biggest break came when he combined with the Sergeant-Major (Windsor Davies) in *It Ain't Half Hot Mum!* to record an old favourite, *Whispering Grass*. This record went to number one and brought not only more fame to Don and Windsor but also added to the growing popularity of the television series.

Don had his own music publishing company and wrote and recorded his own songs. In the '80s, he did some 'serious' television acting, playing Starveling in *A Midsummer Night's Dream* and Crook-Fingered Jack in *The Beggar's Opera*, directed by Jonathan Miller, and had a brief return to comedy, appearing in two early episodes of *The League of Gentlemen* in 1999. Of his days in *Dad's Army* he said that he was always very grateful for the help he received from everyone and that he would never forget the social occasions that sometimes accompanied the filming sessions in Norfolk. Don said with sincerity: 'I am only one of many performers who should be grateful to David Croft and Jimmy Perry for giving us a career that otherwise would probably never have happened and just left us scratching a living where we could.'

JACK HAIG

Jack Haig , who played Lerclerc (the clerk) in the tremendously successful television series *'Allo, 'Allo!*, featured in several episodes of *Dad's Army*. These include 'The Day the Balloon Went up', in which he appeared as a hedge-cutting gardener, and in another as a publican who is faced by a group of German soldiers – in actual fact they were Mainwaring's 'boys' in disguise. As usual this led to hilarious complications when Jack contacted the police with the news that 'the Germans have landed'.

Born of parents who had a very successful music-hall comedy double act known as Haig and Escot, Jack (like his parents before him) had played every variety house in the country, excluding the London Palladium. That omission was rectified as the former comedian and dancer spent a record-breaking season at the world's premier theatre as part of the stage production of *'Allo 'Allo!*

Jack progressed from the music hall to television via contracts with Tyne-Tees Television where he first met David Croft. Jack appeared

Above: Another guest who went on to star in a later comedy series: Jack Haig, Leclerc in *'Allo, 'Allo.*

in a very successful children's series called *Whacky Jacky* for seven years and then spent a number of years in *Crossroads* and, of course, made regular appearances in the TV version of *'Allo, 'Allo!*

NIGEL HAWTHORNE

Nigel played a tramp in an early episode of the series. No one needs reminding of his very successful career in the theatre, cinema (*The Madness of King George*) and particularly television, as the indomitable Sir Humphrey in the hugely popular series *Yes Minister*.

MICHAEL KNOWLES

Michael Knowles played Regular Army Captain Coutts in various episodes of *Dad's Army* and this led to his being cast as the silly Captain Ashwood in *It Ain't Half Hot Mum!*, which began in 1972 and ran for several years,

Above: Michael Knowles was so successful as Regular Army Captain Coutts that he went on to play the silly Captain Ashwood in *It Ain't Half Hot Mum*.

Right: A scene from the episode 'Battle of the Giants'. At the bar, L–R: Geoffrey Lumsden, Robert Raglan and Arthur Lowe.

including two stage productions. He served *Dad's Army* in a very different capacity at a later date – as a writer – and he was one of several actors whose television careers blossomed after working at the Palace Theatre, Watford.

GEOFFREY LUMSDEN

Geoffrey Lumsden was more than a welcome guest to *Dad's Army*. Captain Colonel Square was full of enthusiasm and blustering energy. Square's cry of 'Mainwaring' (pronounced 'Mainwaring' as far as he was concerned) would always put a certain amount of fear into the platoon, and more often than not he would be happy to catch Mainwaring out on some point of order.

At this point the reason for the double ranking used by Square of 'Captain Colonel' should be explained. Ex-World War I officers who joined the Home Guard and were thought to be of sufficient knowledge and competence were given command of a platoon. This was the case with Square. As far as *Dad's Army* was concerned, the character was given command of the Eastgate Platoon with the rank of captain, just as Mainwaring was given

command of the Westgate Platoon. In the series, Square had finished at the end of World War I with the rank of Colonel, so he decided to title himself 'Captain Colonel Square'.

The habit of repeating certain lines such as 'What's Mainwaring up to now? What's he up to now?' was very much part of Geoffrey's personal approach to a conversation. Arthur Lowe and I went out on a long tour in 1978 in one of Geoffrey's plays, *Caught Napping*, and

there was a character of a major-general in the play which Geoffrey himself had played several years before in the West End, and this character was always repeating his lines just as Square did in the series, with very amusing results.

One had to have a sense of the ridiculous to write a play like *Caught Napping* and we, the cast, really enjoyed every moment of that wonderful tour. One of the many wonderful comic moments in the play is when the dotty butler

Above: Fulton Mackay (left) with John Laurie in 'The Miser's Hoard'.

announces that the Aga Khan has come to visit the house. The visitor is, in fact, a bookmaker dressed as a plumber, so bears no resemblance to the Aga Khan. After the plumber has left, the major-general, who is also rather dotty, says quite casually and as a matter of course, 'Funny I always thought the Aga Khan was a much taller man.'

The seed for the play and the end-of-term frolics in school concerning a horse, a bath, a dotty master's butler and the major- general's hard-of-hearing wife was sown in Geoffrey's mind while he was at Repton College.

After leaving college, Geoffrey spent some time working at a colliery, but as he said later, 'After nine months the output of coal fell so alarmingly that I was handed my hat and a cheap tie pin from Woolworths. Deciding on a career in the theatre was the best thing I ever did.' His acting career began at London's Cambridge Theatre in 1933 and from then on Geoffrey was rarely out of London, except when he was working abroad in Canada, South Africa and New York, among other places. Eventually television claimed much of his time, but he was always happy to return to the stage; one memorable experience was when he played at the Prince of Wales Theatre with James Stewart in *Harvey*, the story of an invisible white rabbit. An actor of the old school, Geoffrey was a most convivial person. Whether he was filming or having a drink at the end of the day, he always had a story to tell about people he had known or worked with during his long career. The theatrical world was deprived of a talented actor when Geoffrey died a few years ago.

FULTON MACKAY

This fine, talented Scottish actor featured in more than one episode of the series. Fulton's wealth of experience was apparent in his performances, not only in *Dad's Army* but in many television plays. Millions of viewers saw him as prison officer 'Mackay' in the long-running comedy series *Porridge*. Theatre audiences had always know of his talents and with a similar acting background to John Laurie, they had plenty to talk about during the filming sessions at Thetford.

PHILIP MADOC

Philip appeared in the very funny episode 'The Deadly Attachment'. It was a wonderful piece of situation comedy. A German U-boat had sunk and the crew, including its commander (Philip Madoc), was drifting towards the coast at Walmington-on-Sea in a rubber dinghy. Eventually they were captured by Mainwaring and 'our gallant boys' and marched under armed guard to the church hall to await a full military escort to a secure prisoner-of-war camp. It should have been a straightforward operation, until that is, the air raid warden started to interfere. Mainwaring was told by his commanding colonel to keep the prisoners in the church hall for the night and to give them some food. 'Send out for some fish and chips if you haven't got any food in the hall.' This led to the hilarious scene in which Private Walker was ordered to go to the fish and chip shop. Walker had to take the orders for the prisoner's meals and the U-boat commander said that he wanted plaice and nothing else. Walker said, 'Right, I've got seven cod and one plaice so far.' He then asked who wanted vinegar, etc. The commander replied that he wanted nice crispy

 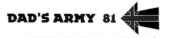

chips, not soggy ones. Mainwaring suddenly realised that the situation was getting out of hand and said, 'You'll have what you're given. If I say you'll eat soggy chips, you'll eat soggy chips.' The air raid warden then entered and completely confused the situation as he always did. The performance of Philip Madoc was a lesson in underplaying, which made the character of the German U-boat commander even more sinister. Philip has made numerous other television appearances over the years and played the lead detective in a series for Channel 5, entitled *A Mind to Kill*. His sonorous Welsh tones can also be heard on many voice-overs.

WILLIAM MOORE

Anyone who described one of his performances as similar to a frantic ferret, which was how William Moore thought of himself in the episode entitled 'The Royal Train', must be able to make people laugh. We had a great deal of fun filming that episode at Sheringham and Weybourne stations on the North Norfolk Railway. William, who lived near me at that time, was my driving companion on a sunny Sunday journey up to Cromer where we were scheduled to stay for that filming session. We stayed at the Grand Hotel and at the time the hotel was in the hands of the receivers and the BBC had to advance them some money to buy the next day's food. I remember the jolly Irish barman saying to us, 'The more you drink tonight, gentlemen, the bigger the breakfasts in the morning.' With a number of thirsty BBC actors and technicians staying at the hotel, the breakfasts were, in fact, quite substantial.

The filming of this famous episode required a considerable amount of physical effort and William's part as the station master required that he should dash about like a madman, checking the signalbox and making sure the station was spick and span, etc. As is usually the case, however, the person who thinks he's in charge generally is not and expends a lot of wasted energy.

Above: William Moore, another fine comedy actor who made a guest appearance in *Dad's Army* before moving on to the successful BBC series *Sorry!*. William was married to the actress Mollie Sugden.

William's character as Ronnie Corbett's father in *Sorry!*, with his catch-phrase 'Language, Timothy', was a much more staid performance. Bill enjoyed a varied career in television, including two years in *Coronation Street* as Police Sergeant Turpin and in a 13- part series of Charles Dickens' *Dombey and Son*.

Before the long-running series *Sorry!*, William's theatrical roots were in the theatre, as is the case with many actors who have succeeded in the medium of the small screen. Trained as an engineering draughtsman, he would probably have stayed in that profession had he not had an inclination to get involved in amateur dramatics in his home town of Birmingham. Transition to professional acting was

not difficult because the old and famous Birmingham Repertory Company used amateurs in the crowd scenes of some of their productions and William so enjoyed the occasions he worked for them that he decided the theatre was where his future lay. Before long he had made his mark as a professional. He won an award for his performance in *Great Expectations* and then took part in the Pitlochry Festival in Scotland for a number of seasons where he played and directed. Teaching at the Bristol Old Vic Theatre School was another departure for this jolly and talented actor.

William related an amusing story of an event that happened when he was with J.B. Priestley's comedy *When We Are Married* at the Strand Theatre in London. Fred Emney, that larger-than-life cigar-smoking actor, was playing the photographer and J.B. Priestley himself came to watch the final dress-rehearsal. At the end of the rehearsal one of the cast said, 'He didn't laugh,' referring to the playwright, and Fred Emney said, 'If he didn't think it was funny he shouldn't have written the bloody thing.'

William, who was married to actress Mollie Sugden, was a great family man, and very proud of his twin sons and their families.

GORDON PETERS

Gordon played a fireman in a scene that was never televised. In the very first episode of the series there was a scene that involved a fireman who in true Chaplinesque fashion became tangled up in his hoses and got in everyone's way. The episode was already over running-time in rehearsals and the fireman's scene had to be edited out of the transmission. Gordon returned in several episodes of *Dad's Army*, but not as a fireman. He eventually had his own series of six programmes for BBC TV and over the years has guested in several other series. He is also familiar with pantomime and cabaret, and tours all over the country with his one-man shows on jesters, called *Cap N' Bells*.

Above: In the first episode of the series Gordon Peters played a fireman, in a scene that was never televised.

ROBERT RAGLAN

Bob Raglan, who played the colonel in charge of the Counties Home Guard in many episodes, was a very affable man. His own character came across in his portrayal of the colonel who had to deal with all the various eccentrics who made up the platoons under his command. Although his patience was sorely tried at times, his job was to try to keep everyone happy and not to dampen their enthusiasm, which occasionally tended to get out of hand, while at the same time maintaining some semblance of army discipline. Robert was a find stage and film actor, but he also had just the right technique for the small screen to make any character he played very believable.

WENDY RICHARD

Anyone who remembers a chart-topping pop-song called *Come Outside* might also remember that the singer was Mike Sarne and the girl who answered his invitation in the negative was Wendy Richard.

Now of course Wendy will be chiefly remembered for her role as Pauline Fowler, as

she spent over twenty years in *Eastenders*, starting with the very first episode. Her appearances in *Dad's Army* were numerous, as she played Private Walker's girlfriend. I know we all loved having guests in the programme. As some folks used to say, 'It makes a change from listening to a lot of old buffers yackity-yacking to one another.'

Her other major TV role was Miss Brahms in *Are You Being Served?* but her many other television credits include *Dixon of Dock Green*, *Z Cars*, *Up Pompeii*, *On the Buses*, *Please Sir!*, *No Hiding Place* and *Danger Man*. She was also a guest on almost every quiz or game show on television. Several film appearances included the *Carry On* productions, *Doctor in Clover* and *No Blades of Grass*.

Wendy was trained at the Italia Conti stage school after completing her general education at the Royal Masonic School at Rickmansworth. She was a very friendly person, who often talked about her love of Chinese, Japanese and Italian food, and was a great cook herself. I must say one of her hobbies worried me a bit – collecting frogs; she also collected clowns and pierrots.

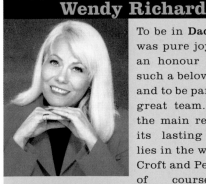

Wendy Richard

To be in **Dad's Army** was pure joy! It was an honour to be in such a beloved show, and to be part of that great team. I think the main reason for its lasting success lies in the writing of Croft and Perry. And of course, the casting was sheer genius – to bring these actors together (and they were not all known as 'comic' actors) and turn them into a team which will be remembered for generations to come. They don't have talent like that nowadays.

Wendy appeared in several pantomimes and in stage versions of well-known television productions, and I used to look forward to going to one of her first nights as I knew I'd be offered a glass of her favourite beverages afterwards: champagne!

CARMEN SILVERA

Carmen prominently featured in the episode entitled 'Mum's Army'. She and Captain Mainwaring struck up a friendship which developed into a brief encounter. This brought out the worst in the gossipy Private Frazer and one or two other members of the platoon and rumour of a romance between them was rife in Walmington while it lasted. As usual the molehill had become a mountain in no time at all. This was one of several episodes that had pathos as well as the usual content of comedy. One of the strengths of *Dad's Army* scripts was that the situation and ideas were consistently varied.

Carmen worked with David Croft for many years, most notably on the eight-year run of the very successful series *'Allo, 'Allo!*, which firmly established her in situation comedy, although her range of acting went very much deeper. She appeared in *Compact*, one of television's first soap operas, which was set in the publishing offices of a woman's magazine, and also acted in a fine BBC2 drama series based on the events of World War II in Italy, although the series was filmed in Yugoslavia.

Carmen was born in Canada, of a Canadian mother. Her father was born in Jamaica and ran his own rum distillery and banana plantation on the island. The family then moved to England and Carmen became fascinated with the idea of going on the stage. She enrolled at a dancing school near Leamington Spa and by the time she was 11 had passed all the major dancing examinations. During World War II, she was evacuated to Montreal and was given her first chance to join a professional ballet company in that city.

After the war, by which time Carmen had returned to England, she went to drama school and was so enthusiastic and hard working that in one day she sat and obtained the bronze, silver and gold medals from the London Academy of Music and Dramatic Art.

Carmen's theatre work included twice-nightly repertory seasons with Harry Hanson's Court Players and Scotland's Pitlochry Festival. For five years she was assistant director at the Thorndike Theatre in Leatherhead under Hazel Vincent Wallace. Carmen was also casting director at the Thorndike.

TALFRYN THOMAS

An omission in the first edition of this book was entirely my fault. If I had had all the details of each series to hand then I would naturally have remembered Talfryn's contribution to the series. He came into *Dad's Army* after James Beck (Private Walker) died. There of course was no question of casting another actor in the role of Walker. Talfryn's

Below: Talfryn Thomas played the role of the local newspaper photographer.

character was that of the local newspaper photographer attached to Mainwaring's platoon. It is not easy for an actor to come into a well-established series, but Talfryn need not have worried; he got stuck into the character and his keeping close to Mainwaring and his continued buttering up to the 'Captain' was very good. 'Oh yes Captain Main-waring, oh yes, that's good boyo, just another one,' was a pleasure to watch. Mainwaring of course was thrilled and flattered by the attention he was receiving and made remarks such as, 'I think this is my best side, don't you', or, 'do I look authoritative enough?'. The photographer was well to the fore in the episode 'My British Buddy' and provided some very funny moments. Talfryn was in only one series, but his characterisation hit just the right note. Talfryn's background was theatre and radio, both in Wales and nationally; he was very experienced in both.

FREDDIE TRUEMAN

As most of the cast were cricket fans, it was a great thrill when we opened our scripts for the episode 'The Test' and found among the extra characters was E.C. Egan, to be played by Freddie Trueman, one of England's great fast bowlers. Fred arrived in Thetford for the exterior sequences on one of the very few rainy days we encountered. The character E.C. Egan had been engaged by the air raid wardens to play in their team in the challenge match against Mainwaring's Home Guard unit; he was their secret weapon. The match was played and filmed on a disused army sports field, complete with pavilion. Although the ground was rough, Freddie made the ball come through at an alarming rate and we all felt that we were lucky not having to face him in his heyday. During his career he had been the first bowler ever to have taken 300 test match wickets.

During his stay with us at Thetford the cast were invited to the Colman's Mustard head

office in Norwich for a social evening and presentation of prizes to their staff. A coach was laid on to take us the 20 miles or so after a day's filming. Plenty of drinks were available as Coleman's were promoting their wines from a bottling plant they had taken under their umbrella of companies. On the return journey to Thetford in the coach, Don Estelle, who was also in the episode, Freddie and Arthur Lowe led the cast as they sang bawdy North Country songs. What with the motion of the coach, a certain amount of alcohol, and a general atmosphere of abandon, most people finished up on the floor with Don Estelle at the bottom of the heap, but still singing, mostly a rude version of *Goodbye* from White Horse Inn.

In 1976 when we were at the Alhambra Theatre in Bradford, on tour with the stage version of *Dad's Army*, Freddie and his wife Veronica came to see the show and invited John Le Mesurier and myself to spend the day with them at their lovely Yorkshire home. It was a day for talking cricket and viewing Fred's mementoes from cricket grounds all around the world. You felt it was a great privilage to be in Yorkshire when you spoke to Fred Trueman, one of the proudest 'tykes' to put on a pair of cricket boots.

EDWARD UNDERDOWN

This tall, elegant actor was cast as a staff officer in a few episodes of the series and it was a pleasure to welcome this gentle man of stage and films who had been so popular during the 1940s and '50s. Edward starred above the title in the film *The Rocking-Horse Winner* and the beginnings of his stage career went back even further: he played in several of Noel Coward's stage successes in the 1930s.

An extraordinary coincidence that occurred in *Dad's Army* centred on Edward. Some of the filming for the first episode in Norfolk took place among some stables that belonged to a country house within the Stamford battle area, which was by then War Department property.

Nothing was left of the house except a large patio and verandah, and the stables. As soon as the cast and crew arrived at his venue John Le Mesurier realised that it was familiar to him and said, 'I used to come here for weekend parties in the 1930s when it was all private property and the house belonged to Edward Underdown's parents.'

So it was that Edward found himself working in a television series that had featured part of his old home. In later years he worked as a steward at Newbury Racecourse, which is fitting for a man who not only loved horses but was also an expert rider. John Le Mesurier and I visited him on several occasions at his delightful cottage in the Berkshire countryside.

ERIC LONGWORTH

Eric appeared in several episodes, playing the officious town clerk. He was bitten by the acting bug while out in India during the war, where he was a member of the Bombay Light Opera and the Bombay Players. His professional career began after he was demobbed at Oldham Rep, where he remained for several years, eventually becoming the theatre manager. From there he went on to become the manager of the old Guildford Theatre and he stayed there, acting as well as carrying out management duties, until the theatre unfortunately burnt down in 1963. He then decided to concentrate on acting and worked as a jobbing actor for many years. In more recent times he was a familiar face at *Dad's Army* events and he thoroughly enjoyed his trips to Norfolk and elsewhere. Eric died in 2009, four weeks after his 90th birthday.

Opposite: A very special guest star; former England fast bowler, Freddie Trueman, enjoys a cup of tea in 'The Test'. Freddie made the ball come through at an alarming rate and we all felt that we were lucky not having to face him in his heyday.

'Make sure you knock Napoleon's block off.'

HAROLD SNOAD

Harold Snoad was not only responsible for finding all the filming locations for *Dad's Army* but worked hard to run a tight ship, keeping tabs on our wonderful back room boys and girls, of which there were many, including camera and sound crews, wardrobe and make-up departments. All these people played a huge part in the success of the production.

Harold went on to direct seven of the episodes and, in 1969, the BBC promoted him to the role of Producer/Director; in those days he was one of the youngest in the business. Over the years he then produced and directed numerous comedy series' starring, amongst others, Ronnie Barker, Derek Nimmo, John Inman, Eric Sykes, John Cleese, Leslie Phillips, Marti Caine, Francis Matthews, Geraldine McEwan, Susan Hampshire and Dick Emery, with whom he worked for eight years.

His credits include *Oh Brother*, *Are You Being Served?*, *His Lordship Entertains*, *Sykes and a Big, Big Show*, *Rings On Their Fingers*, *Casanova '73*, *The Dick Emery Show*, (59 episodes including four Christmas specials, plus a seven-part comedy thriller, *Legacy of Murder*, filmed entirely on location in the U.K., Paris and Tunisia), *Tears Before Bedtime*, *The Further Adventures of Lucky Jim*, *Partners* and *Hilary*.

In 1983 Harold was promoted to Executive Producer/Director and was twice offered the role of Head of Comedy but declined because he loved producing and directing programmes so much. Then followed the six series' of *Don't Wait Up*, starring Tony Britton, Nigel Havers and Dinah Sheridan; *Ever Decreasing Circles* starring Richard Briers, the Ray Cooney farce *Wife Begins at Forty* and *Keeping Up Appearances* starring Patricia Routledge. He made five series' (40 episodes) of the latter, plus four specials for Christmas.

Harold has also directed a feature film, a Ray Cooney farce starring Leslie Phillips, Roy Kinnear, Michele Dotrice, Ian Lavender, June

Whitfield and its author, and, as a writer, he, along with Michael Knowles, re-wrote 66 episodes of Dad's Army for radio before writing two original comedy series for that medium, starring Hugh Paddick and Michael Robbins and John Le Mesurier respectively, and a series for television starring Richard Wilson and Bernard Cribbins.

He is the author of *Directing Situation Comedy* and a book shortly to be published about the making of *Keeping Up Appearances*. Harold is now enjoying a well-earned retirement!

CHARLES GARLAND

When Charles Garland joined the BBC, his second week was spent on location with David Croft, as part of the production team on *Hi-De-Hi!* – principally in charge of providing tea. He continued to join David's office whenever a production was imminent, as an Assistant Floor Manager through five series' of *'Allo 'Allo!* and into *You Rang, M'Lord?* as Production Manager. In between Croft productions, Charles directed many light entertainment programmes and wrote and directed several comedy pilots. He was Assistant Producer for the first series of *Oh, Dr. Beeching!*, David Croft's last comedy series, and when the second series was commissioned, David invited him to be the Producer.

When the BBC decided that they wanted to repeat a series of *Dad's Army*, they asked David Croft for permission to re-edit the programmes, in order to reduce them to a uniform 29 minutes' duration. He agreed, on condition that only Charles should be responsible for the edits. David felt that Charles' knowledge of Croft and Perry's vast archive, combined with army service and experience as an actor, director and writer, provided him with a unique blend of skills which would enable him to carry out this difficult task sympathetically and without losing any essential elements. Once the process was underway, David generously sug-

gested that Charles should add his name to the credits as Series Editor, to acknowledge the complexity of the task.

In addition to shortening most of the episodes, Charles used this opportunity to improve the quality of the pictures, removing camera faults, scratches and losses of colour where they occurred, utilising the facility of 21st-century equipment in the hands of the BBC's talented senior editor Steve Jamison. Following this, each episode was re-mastered in a sound studio by Michael McCarthy, who was Sound Supervisor on most of David Croft's programmes, and whose skill was legendary. There is a way to tell very quickly whether the version of the show you are watching is one of these improved episodes. The signature tune, written by Jimmy Perry – the famous 'Who do you think you are kidding Mr Hitler?' – contained two more lines in its original version, as recorded by Bud Flanagan. Unfortunately this complete version was just too long, so those lines were edited out – but the edit was not perfect, and left a very slight 'bump' in the soundtrack, which you can hear on older recordings of the show, just after '… and he's ready with his gun, so …'. At this point the original went on to 'watch out Mr Hitler ….' But the broadcast version goes, of course, to 'who do you think …' again. During the remedial work on the programmes, Michael ingeniously removed this bump, so that the music flows completely smoothly. Much better! Charles has now left the BBC, is a full time writer and composer, and lives with his family in rural Suffolk.

Paul Joel

The happiest years of my 30- year career in the BBC were the five I spent designing **Dad's Army**, from 'Museum Piece' in 1968 to 'The Recruit' in 1973 – 52 episodes out of 80 over the nine series. Amongst the fondest memories are playing bar billiards with Ian Lavender in the film location hotel in Thetford (he and I were usually the youngest of the cast and crew); being asked by Arthur Lowe if I could give him advice on the design for the renovation of his boat; watching Jimmy Beck drawing doodles and caricatures of the other cast members; being introduced to the studio audience by Bill Pertwee – 'Paul designed these sets – I bet you thought they were real rooms on your telly at home'; and getting the thumbs up from Clive Dunn when he first saw his Butcher's Shop interior. However, I do regret not being able to design the movie and even more importantly the final episode. I retired from the BBC in 1994 and now live in the beautiful Cornish harbour village of Mousehole where my wife Judy and I have an art gallery. I'm an honorary member of the Dad's Army Appreciation Society and try to keep in touch with friends from **Dad's Army** whenever possible. Ian Lavender opened one of Judy's solo art exhibitions, and we've been to reunions in London and the Steam Museum in Bressingham where there is a permanent **Dad's Army** exhibition. Recently Bill Pertwee visited us in Mousehole and we introduced him to our friend who doesn't miss a single repeated episode, whatever channel it's on. Meeting Bill was the highlight of his year! Over the past few years I have been asked to contribute to several publications about **Dad's Army**, including the DVD collection, and am proud to have worked on such a timeless series and to be included in Bill's book.

WALMINGTON · ON · SEA

Walmington-on-Sea was set as a seaside town on the Kent coast, about 20 miles from Dover, with all the characteristics one would associate with such a place in the 1940s. Although it was not a fashionable resort, it had always been popular with the great number of holiday-makers who stayed in the many guest houses that line Coast Road and the roads leading from it, catering for all tastes. There were numerous streets of small houses or bungalows which accommodated the large number of retired people who had come to this genteel town to enjoy the peace and quiet.

The Marigold Tea Rooms, managed by Miss Fortescue, where customers were entertained by Miss Rowland's Trio, provided light refreshment for the visitors, as did the Dutch Oven and Ann's Pantry, well known locally for its Devonshire teas. More substantial refreshment was available at the British Restaurant, where a set meal could be had at a very reasonable cost, although more traditional food could be obtained from Charlie's Cafe or one of several fish-and-chip shops in the town.

Walmington Station (SR), situated to the north adjacent to the local bus garage, was the site of the busy Saturday market, where anything for the home could be bought from stalls that frequented the towns of the south coast. The majority of shops could be found on Alexandra Parade and West Street, with the remainder on the High Street. The seafront played host to a small pier with a pavilion, and was a favourite spot for the local fishermen. All the trappings of a traditional seaside town were to be found here, including the Novelty Rock Emporium, the Jolly Roger Ice Cream Parlour, Stone's Amusement Arcade and the Beach & Souvenir Shop.

When war was declared in 1939, the town became the 'forefront of the Allied defences', or so the captain of the Local Defence Volunteers would have you believe. In fact the town was altered little. The beach was covered with the usual barbed wire, mines and tank traps. Pillboxes were situated on the main roads, and the pier was blown in half to prevent an enemy landing, although this was after it was severely damaged by a royal Navy corvette one foggy day!

With the onset of war, many of the amusements associated with peacetime closed down. People could not afford the luxury of a holiday, so the businesses that remained lived off the local inhabitants with limited resources.

AUTHOR'S NOTES

The idea for the town plan came from the desire to put together all the clues given in the programme and construct a completely new, fictional town. All conflicting movements have been eliminated; you are quite welcome to trace the platoon's progress during the programmes without fault (I hope!).

The town plan is dated from the very start of the war, when all of the towns' facilities were still open and most of the wartime measures put in place. I do not think I have left anything off: all roads, public houses, streets, shops, building and facilities, etc, mentioned within the TV and radio series' have been

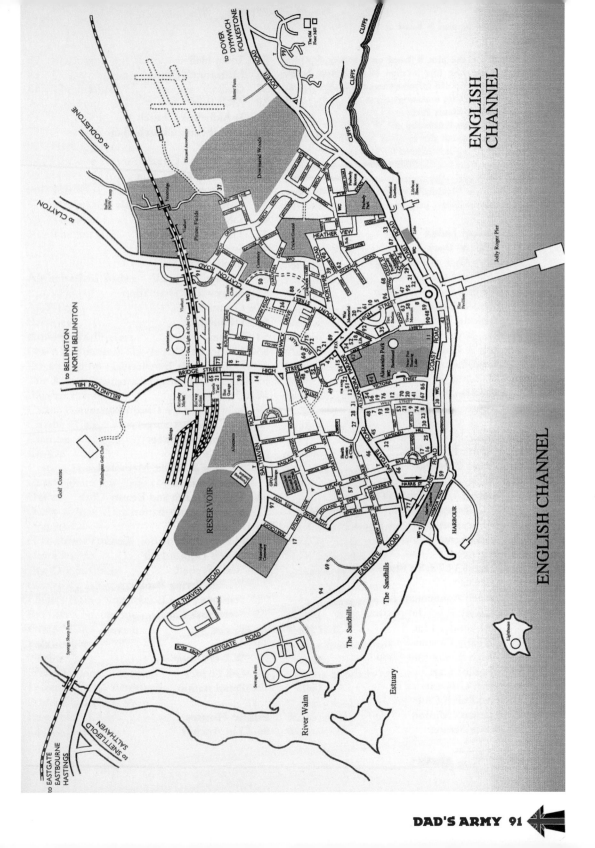

ENGLISH CHANNEL

ENGLISH CHANNEL

included, with suitable additions (e.g. newsagents, bakeries, etc). Some exceptions include the North Bellington Turkey Farm (from 'Turkey Dinner'), the boat-house and windmill ('Don't Forget the Diver') and Mrs Prentice's farm ('All Is Safely Gathered In'), all of which were sited too far from the town to be included on the map. It is surprising how much information about the town is contained within the scripts: most of the main characters acquired addresses, work colleagues and families. Although a few errors of continuity did emerge, they were not noticeable.

The keen eyed will notice some familiar road names in the town. I make no excuse for including them. For the curious, the plan is based on Chalfont St Giles, Buckinghamshire (the location of the feature-length film), and transposed to 'somewhere on the Kent coast'.

Whilst the plan is an original piece of work, I must acknowledge Messrs Perry and Croft, M. Knowles, H. Snoad, J. Burke, P. Ableman and, of course, the BBC.

Finally, I would like to thank Jack Wheeler for his support during this project, for checking and double checking all the locations illustrated on the map and for his many useful suggestions. These comments are based on his article 'Wartime Walmington' in the Dad's Army Appreciation Society magazine.

Numerical Index

1 Swallow's Bank
2 Jones High Class Butcher
3 Hodges Greengrocer
4 Frazer Funerals' Director
5 Stead & Simpson
6 Timothy White's
7 The British Restaurant
8 Fish & Chip Restaurant
9 Ann's Pantry
10 Marigold Tea Rooms
11 The Dutch Oven
12 Woolworths
13 Marks &Spencer
14 Frazer Funerals' Workshop
15 Elliott's Radio Store
16 Carter Patterson's
17 Dairy
18 Barbers/hairdressing shops
19 H.E. Drury funerals
20 Off licences
21 Newsagents
22 Bakery
23 Frazer's Philatelist Shop
24 Co-Op
25 Stone's Amusement Arcade
26 Novelty Rock Emporium
27 Girl Guide Hut
28 Embassy Cinema
29 Beach & Souvenir Shop
30 Charlie's Cafe
31 Swan Groceries
32 Free Polish Club
33 Seamen's Mission
34 Police Station
35 Town Hall
36 Magistrate's Court
37 Godfrey's Cottage
38 ARP Post
39 St Aldhelm's Church
40 St Aldhelm's Church Hall
41 Milk Bar
42 St Mathews Church
43 Harris Orphans' Hut
44 Sea-Scout Hut
45 Darby & Joan Club
46 Salvation Army Hall
47 Tiffany Cinema
48 Sweet Shop
49 Bugden Printers
50 Cottage Hospital
51 Sedgewick's Shoe Shop
52 Chemists
53 Fishmonger
54 Draper
55 Methodist Chapel
56 Cunningham Jewellers
57 Harris Orphanage
58 Dry Cleaners
59 Jolly Roger Ice Cream Parlour
60 McCleavedy's Surgery
61 Maxwell Solicitors
62 Vicarage
63 Victoria & Albert Memorial Rose Garden
64 Ladies' Health and Beauty Club
65 Electricity Sub-station
66 Jubilee Hall
67 Holiday Information Centre
68 British Legion Hall

69 Walker's shed
70 Trustee Savings Bank
71 Stationers and Bookshop
72 Newman's Car Accessories
73 Florist
74 Taxi Garage and Rank
75 Walker's 'shop'
76 Gill Taylor's
77 Petrol Station

Public Houses
86 The Anchor
87 Black Lion
88 Dog & Partridge
89 The Feathers
90 The Fox
91 Fox & Pheasant
92 Goat & Compasses
93 Hare & Hounds
94 Horse &Groom
95 Horse & Hounds
96 The King's Head
97 Marquis of Granby
98 The Red Lion
99 The Six Bells

Alphabetical Index

Above: Weybourne station as in 'The Royal Train'.   **Below:** Thetford Guildhall as the Town Hall.

Above: Honington School was used for the exterior of St Aldhelm's Church Hall.
Left: Nether Row was used in various episodes.
Below: The bridge at Sanlon Downham featured in 'Brain versus Brawn'.

FILMING THE TELEVISION SERIES

When we went up to Thetford for our annual filming sessions we would tell our friends and relations beforehand to book their holidays at the same time. In nine years of filming in Norfolk we only had three or four days of bad weather, which included one day of snow. So the sunny days and weeks became known as 'Croft's weather'.

It was always a joyous occasion to make the journey to Thetford where we were based for the exterior work. A coach was laid on at the BBC Television Centre in Wood Lane, London, to accommodate anyone who was not going up under their own steam. A number of the cast took their own cars and a few went by train (from Liverpool Street Station, changing at Ely). The wardrobe girls and boys, make-up assistants, most of the extras and two or three principals usually travelled by coach. The rest of us took our own vehicles, except John Le Mesurier who travelled with Clive Dunn or me. Everyone took their time, generally leaving on Sunday morning and stopping for lunch on the way. Often we would pass each other en route and sometimes stop and have a chat on a country road to admire the lovely scenery and exchange pleasantries. The production crew (cameramen, lighting and sound technicians) and the special effects department would all have gone on earlier.

The gathering of the cast and crew at the hotel in Thetford was a noisy, bustling affair. The wardrobe department had to get the costumes out of the caravans that had previously arrived from London, towed by Land Rovers. A room was set aside at the hotel for the use of the wardrobe department and the make-up girls. The hotel reception area seemed to be full of bodies: actors asking questions, sorting out their room numbers, ordering hot buttered toast to accompany the tea which they could make in their own rooms. Frank Williams (the vicar) was usually enquiring whether Teddy (the verger) had brought everything out of the car, and sorting out volumes of books and suitcases and other impedimenta he had packed into Teddy's car for the journey from London. Arthur Lowe would immediately enquire if the 'corner shop' still sold Craven A cigarettes, as that was the only brand he and his wife Joan smoked. Jimmy Perry would be telling everybody that he had brought his well-worn medicine chest with him, which included indigestion tablets, Aspro, throat spray, senna pods, diarrhoea tablets, malaria pills, snake bite ointment, shark poison antidote and a selection of plasters, splints and spare sets of false teeth should they be needed by anyone. Other people would ask if their rooms overlooked the river, because they did not want to face the court yard as they did last time because it was very noisy at night.

With a general chorus of 'See you in the bar before dinner' the eager actors mounted the stairs brandishing their room keys, while the

Above: Members of the Senior Citizens' Club, Thetford, used as extras.
Below: The Anchor Hotel, Thetford.

Above: The Anchor Hotel, Thetford.

girls behind the reception desk breathed a sigh of relief. However, they would quickly receive calls from various rooms in the hotel with complaints of minor inconveniences.

Early on in the series, before the Bell Hotel had tea-making facilities in the rooms, Arthur Lowe would come out on to the landing early in the morning and ask, 'Where's the tea-boy? He's put two tea-bags in my pot again and he knows I only have one.' The Bell was the main dormitory for the principal actors and guest artistes, and the Anchor Hotel, which was just across the river, the secondary accommodation. Both hotels had to cope with many early morning breakfasts and in some cases at the Bell serve it in the rooms, as actors would be going to the make-up girls in their tee-shirts and trousers and only completing their wardrobe call after breakfast. Those of us in the dining-room would discuss the news of the day or what scenes we would be filming. Arthur Lowe was generally in deep conversation with the waiter, telling him how he wanted his kippers cooked, or sometimes asking if the cold ham was tender.

Location instructions for 'Knights of Madness'

Sunday 12th June

LOCATION:	GRANGE FARM
	SAPISTON
	HONINGTON, SUFFOLK
CONTACT:	MR MUDD
	TEL: 03596 227
DIRECTION:	A.1088 FROM THETFORD - AT HONINGTON
	TURN LEFT THROUGH VILLAGE TOWARDS
	SAPISTON CROSSING OVER RIVER - INTO LAMPITT
	WAY ½ MILE UP THE ROAD
PARKING:	MAKE-UP AND WARDROBE CARAVAN AND
	MOBILE TOILET TO PARK AND FARMYARD - THE
	REST BEHIND HOUSE AS DIRECTED
UNIT CALL:	9.00 AM
ARTISTS:	FRED MCNAUGHTON - THE MAYOR
	ERIC LONGWORTH - TOWN CLERK
	EDWARD SINCLAIR - VERGER
	OLIVE MERCER - MRS. YEATMAN
	& PLATOON

ALL EXTRA, INCLUDING LADIES KEEP-FIT TEAM, MORRIS DANCERS, AND BOY SCOUTS, TO BE READY TO LEAVE THE BELL HOTEL AT 8.30 AM

ARTHUR LOWE - CAPTAIN MANWARING
JOHN LE MESURIER – SGT. WILSON
CLIVE DUNN – L/COL. JONES
JOHN LAURIE – PRIVATE FRAZER
ARNOLD RIDLEY – PRIVATE GODFREY
IAN LAVENDER – PRIVATE PIKE
COLLIN BEAN –PRIVATE SPONGE
BILL PERTWEE – ARP WARDEN HODGES
FRANK WILLIAMS – VICAR

TO LEAVE BELL HOTEL AT 10.00AM FOR COSTUME AND MAKE-UP ON LOCATION

N.B IAN LAVENDER NEEDED FIRST

Suddenly a production assistant would announce that the coach was leaving in five minutes, and, in an instant, actors and crew from both hotels would be congregating in the reception area of the Bell with their equipment, newspapers and other possessions, waiting to start the day. It was the job of the production assistant to make sure that everyone got on to the coach for the drive to the location. Those who were not needed for a few hours would be told to relax and that the coach or a unit car would be back to pick them up later. Getting everybody on to the coach was a military operation in itself. Someone had generally forgotten something – for example, a pair of boots they thought the dressers had, but now remembered they had left in their room, or a spare tee-shirt they wanted to change into at lunchtime.

The early morning drives out to the Stamford battle area were always sunny and we would see all sorts of wildlife, including a few dozen rabbits looking up from the grass verges, obviously saying to themselves, 'what's that silly old bus doing waking us up this early'. The freshness of the dew-covered grass and the scent of the pine needles was quite exhilarating.

Once we had arrived at our destination, which would be marked by the earlier arrival of the wardrobe van, catering bus and the all-important honey wagon (toilets), not to mention various cars, technical equipment and even, if necessary, Jones's butcher's van and period vehicles of all descriptions. David Croft, who had bought a house nearby, would already have arrived in his car and be in the process of looking for the right spot to set up the cameras and equipment for the first shot of the day. It is worth mentioning that the whole of the Stamford battle area had once consisted of small estates that were generally made up of the main house of the local gentry with perhaps a small farm, and a general store, pub and, in some cases, their own church. This is now, and has been for a long time, War Department property, and nearly all the buildings had been used for

HAROLD SNOAD

As Production Manager it was part of my job to find any locations called for in the making of a series. When it came to **Dad's Army** the main requirement was for an area we could use freely and without the usual problem of members of the public putting in an appearance in the back of a shot either on foot or, worse, in a vehicle (which wouldn't be in period anyway) right in the middle of a 'take'. In other words we needed somewhere private – especially with a show that called for a large degree of location work. Thinking about this problem it occurred to me that a suitable place might well be an area under the control of the Ministry of Defence. With that in mind, I contacted the MoD who were very helpful. One of their suggestions didn't appeal to me because it seemed that it was used rather too often for military manoeuvres, so I decided to visit the other one – the Stamford Practical Training Area near Thetford, Norfolk. I was given a contact, the CO of the camp (Col. Cleasby-Thompson) and, on 5 March 1968, I drove down there. The CO made us very welcome and told us to drive about and have a good look around. We did so, and I immediately knew that it would be ideal. Not only was there some lovely countryside but there were some proper roads (which would pass as public roads – indeed, originally they had been). There were also various buildings which had originally been part of small hamlets, but which had then been taken over by the MoD when they acquired the whole area, including cottages and a church. Some of the buildings had suffered somewhat, having been used for target practice, but on the whole there was enough left to provide most of what we needed. There was also a river (with gates that allowed us to flood the surrounding area when filming Pike's rescue from a bog) and a bridge. The CO was extremely helpful and we were virtually given a free hand to do anything we needed. He and I liaised on a daily basis to ensure that, on the whole, we weren't using an area they were planning to use, and vice versa.

 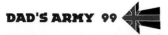

army exercises in which battle conditions were simulated with live ammunition, so very little was left of them. Harold Snoad was the first production assistant on the series and it was he who had found and selected the battle area as the main location for the exterior filming. He explained some of the filming techniques as follows: 'The Stamford Practice Training Area was a large area of countryside of several square miles, used by the Ministry of Defence for training our own and NATO forces. I had a very simple arrangement with the army officer commanding the area (Colonel Cleasby-Thomson). I gave him a schedule showing where we wanted to film each day and he kept any troop training away from us. However, I do remember one occasion when things went slightly wrong. We were at a stables (disused but it still looked OK) filming a complicated sequence with the platoon trying to learn how to ride (Captain Mainwaring had decided that with strict petrol rationing the platoon's transport would be equestrian), when suddenly there was a rustle in the bushes alongside our camera and a young officer in full camouflage uniform (blackened face, the lot) politely informed me that he and his men had orders to blow up this area in 10 minutes! At this a large degree of frenzied conversation ensued and, after I had made an urgent telephone call to the authorities, it was agreed, with only three minutes to go, that they could come back and blow it up the next day! I also remember we once had to film a sequence in the battle area involving Pike falling into a bog. To achieve this under controlled conditions consistent with the artiste's safety, I arranged for some soldiers to dig a pit seven feet by five and six feet deep alongside a river which ran through the area, and which one could flood slightly by dropping some sluice-gates. We did this, allowing the pit to fill up and also giving us about an inch of water over the surrounding terrain. Once we had floated some cork chips and peat on the surface, our 'bog' was just what David wanted for the scene.

'We started by putting some rostra in the bottom of the pit and then, as Pike was supposed to be sinking deeper and deeper (while Mainwaring and the rest of the platoon performed fruitless attempts to try and rescue him) we gradually reduced the height of the rostrum, allowing Pike to sink lower and lower, but we'd reduced it a bit too quickly and suddenly poor Ian Lavender was standing on tip-toe on the bottom of the pit with water up to his neck. Then the hapless Private Pike let out a terrible yell and screamed hysterically asking to be pulled out. When we had done as he had bid, we discovered that a large frog had somehow worked its way up his trouser leg. We all thought it was very funny, but Ian didn't find it quite so amusing.

'The final stage of the 'bog' sequence came that evening after we had all gone back to the Bell Hotel. I hadn't realised, but it was the habit of the helpful army officer in charge of the battle area (the aforementioned Colonel Cleasby-Thomson) to walk his dog by the river every evening. He was the sort of man who wore tough knee-high boots and so thought nothing of strolling alongside his river. Unfortunately he had forgotten that we had been filming the 'bog' sequence and suddenly disappeared up to his neck in dirty water. When I went to see him the next day to tell him that the 'rushes' were OK and that the hole could be filled in, he was not in quite his normal cheery mood, but I invited him and his wife to join us for diner at the Bell Hotel that evening and all was forgiven.'

Some of the chase sequences that involved a lot of vehicles were very tiring for everyone concerned, but the results were usually good and in the tradition of the old Mack Sennett comedies. It generally finished with Warden Hodges being flung into a lake or being pushed off a bridge into the river; on one occasion he had a mushy type of custard-coloured liquid poured over him from a great height. In this sequence the warden was trying to guide the spotter plane which was carrying the custard liquid over to the place

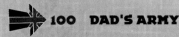

where he knew Mainwaring and his men were hiding; however, the plane dropped its load on top of Hodges by mistake. This sequence was filmed first with the aeroplane flying overhead and then dustbins full of the liquid were filmed as they were emptied from the top of a high crane to simulate aerial movement. Unfortunately, the liquid quickly went solid and filled Hodges' ears.

'I (Hodges) was taken in a fast unit car to Thetford Cottage Hospital for treatment. When we arrived, however, a notice on the gate informed us that it was half-day closing. We eventually found a doctor who dealt with the problem using various instruments and a syringe. I also needed a long soak in the bath to get the rest of the liquid off my body.'

In another episode Hodges was riding the familiar 1940s motorbike with the vicar on the pillion and the verger in the side-car. It was a fairly fast ride into the camera shot but suddenly a mechanical failure caused the machine to go out of control and the camera and sound crew had to jump for their lives. The vicar's only comment was 'I hope the verger didn't have his usual roughage for breakfast.'

On another occasion when we were filming at Lowestoft, the warden, having seen the lighthouse illuminated and guessing that Mainwaring's platoon had had something to do with it (in fact, they had been guarding it and Corporal Jones had touched the on switch), decided to row out to them. He cut loose a pedallo boat which had been tied up on the beach at the outbreak of war and paddled towards the lighthouse. He didn't know that the boats had been holed to stop them from being used by an enemy landing force. The idea for the film sequence was that the warden should get halfway to his objective and then slowly sink. David Croft and the camera crew were on the jetty, filming the action. Suddenly, an enveloping mist descended and nothing was visible - the camera crew, Hodges in the boat or the shore. The only sound – and it was an eerie sound at 2

o'clock in the morning – was of the sirens of fishing-boats that were trying to find the harbour. Luckily, Hodges, who was far out to sea by now, was picked up by a diver and guided in to the shore. Harold Snoad was on hand to administer large doses of Scotch and to get the luckless Hodges back to the hotel in Yarmouth.

Very early the next morning Warden Hodges was rehearsing the boat scene again off the Britannia Pier. Although the water looked very calm from high up on the pier, when the warden was put into the water wearing only his flesh-coloured jock strap, the waves knocked him back on to the girders beneath. The scene required that Hodges should be chased by a sea mine that was attached to his steel helmet. It was quickly decided to use a strunt double for the scene, and Hodges had only to fall in the water – although it was very cold!

The warden was also in some peril during the 'Royal Train' episode. The mayor of Walmington, the vicar, the verger and warden were crowded on to a pump truck trying to stop a runaway railway engine that was carrying Mainwaring and his lads. The pump truck is a small platform with two levers which, when hand-pumped, simply propel it along. The truck was in a small cutting and going very fast in pursuit of the engine when one of the handles caught in my trouser pocket, tore it and began to lift me up in the air. I managed to save myself, but I could easily have gone over the side. The cast of the platoon also had to take care because more of them were crawling about on the engine complete with camera crew.

Clive Dunn had some hair-raising sequences to do as Corporal Jones. On one occasion he had to climb out on to the town hall roof and try to pull in a German pilot who had bailed out of his aircraft and been caught on the hands of the town hall clock. Some of this was done with trick photography, but the final result was excellent. Harold Snoad recounts another Jones escapade: 'The sequence called for Corporal Jones to get caught up on the sails of a large

 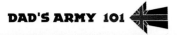

windmill and fly round several times on same. We found a huge windmill which looked very impressive, but of course it only went round if there was almost a gale force wind (unlike some others it hadn't been converted to other turning systems). As we couldn't possibly film in those conditions I suddenly hit upon the idea of putting what looked like a small timber hut on the ground between the camera and the sails of the windmill. In fact the hut didn't have a back and two strong scene boys stood behind it and once we'd got it going they kept the sails turning by giving each of them a shove as the bottom end came past them. It worked extremely well.'

Another difficult episode to make was entitled 'The Day the Balloon Went Up'. The story revolved around a barrage balloon that had broken loose from its moorings and was hovering above the church hall. Mainwaring organised everybody, even the reluctant Warden Hodges, to take the guy ropes and walk the balloon into open country and to wait for the Army to come and pick it up. In the exterior filming sequences, the whole platoon, plus the warden, vicar and verger, are seen holding the ropes. Captain Mainwaring managed to get his legs caught up in one of the ropes and he goes up with the balloon as it rises when the others panic and let go of their ropes. The journey of Mainwaring skimming over the treetops (in fact, a stunt-man was on the end of the rope) was quite hilarious, and the final scene in which he is caught under a railway bridge in the path of an approaching train before he is rescued by the rest of the platoon, was in the best traditions of screen comedy.

Much of the filming was done in Thetford itself and this gave us all a chance to get to know the people of this little Norfolk town. Jean Bishop, who owned the Anchor Hotel at that time, became a real friend to us all and made us feel most welcome when we met there for dinner or a drink before eating at the Bell. Jean threw a few parties for us and was a good hostess. The staff at the Bell Hotel were most helpful and always made sure we were well looked after. In the early days, the rushes (rough cut) of the day's filming would be put on the train to London and returned next day for us to see. These we viewed at the little local cinema in Thetford (see illustration on page 91) after the regular film show finished at night. At 10.30pm, a group of actors could be seen walking up the road to the cinema and waiting for the 'late' doors to open. Sequences of the filming were greeted with 'Look at the warden, over-acting again' or 'So and so could have done better then'. A funny sequence would be greeted with spasmodic applause or laughter. Arthur Lowe would generally fall asleep but wake up at just the right moment to make a cryptic remark. We would then return to our respective hotels for a night-cap or two. Harold Snoad continues: 'Whenever we had to do any filming in the streets of Thetford it was necessary for the windows of any houses we saw in the background (and this could be quite a large number in some of the platoon marching sequences) to look correct – i.e. criss-crossed with sticky tape as they would have been during the war. When we first started filming the series we used to spend many a long hour trudging up the road, visiting each house with tolls of sticky tape, explaining what we wanted and often having to do the job ourselves. We very quickly decided that this was far too time-consuming, so when the second series came along we duplicated copies of a letter explaining what we wanted, with a diagram of a typical finished window, and these were dropped through the letter boxes in envelopes along with a roll of brown sticky tape and a pound note for their trouble. And everybody obliged!'

There were certainly some magical moments that I shall never forget. Several old vehicles were lined up in the street one day ready for

Opposite: 'He's pinched my uniform, Captain Mainwaring'; a scene from 'Don't Forget the Diver'. L-R: Bean, Laurie, Ridley, Lowe, Beck, Lavender, Le Mesurier, Taylor.

 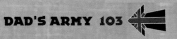

filming when a traffic warden appeared and told David Croft that he couldn't park the vehicles on a yellow line. David explained that we were filming and would be as quick as possible. The traffic warden looked at one of the old vehicles (an Austin Seven – and said, 'And by the way, the tax disc is out of date; it's showing 1940.'

At breakfast one morning at the hotel, we learned from the newspaper that Clive Dunn had been awarded an OBE. Clive was already in make-up and we would not be able to see him until we got on the coach. Arthur Lowe was tucking into his breakfast and someone asked him what he thought about Clive Dunn being awarded an OBE. Arthur looked up, put down his knife and fork, adjusted his glasses and said, 'Very good, but when it comes to my turn I don't want any of that bargain basement stuff.' I hope I'm not speaking out of turn when I say that I think Arthur was overdue for some recognition at the end of the series.

John Le Mesurier always amused me. On one occasion he said to me, 'I don't want to eat in the hotel tonight, let's go and get some fish and chips.' So we drove out of Thetford and found a fish-and-chip shop. I told him that we couldn't eat them in the car as they would leave a terrible smell. We drove on until we found a bus shelter on a lonely stretch of road. Sitting in the shelter eating our fish and chips in the fading light of the evening, John turned to me and said, 'Our programme's watched by twenty million people. Such is fame, if only the public could see us now, up to our elbows in batter in a bus shelter in Norfolk."

Harold Snoad remembers an instance when we were filming on a very hot day and John looked at his watch and found that it had stopped. He said, 'This heat is really exhausting. Could someone wind up my watch for me, please.

Harold Snoad knew exactly what David Croft wanted in the way of filming sequences, etc, and was obviously destined to go further within the BBC. This he has done, as the pro-

ducer/director of some of their top comedy programmes such as *The Dick Emery Show*, *Don't Wait Up*, *Ever Decreasing Circles*, *Brush Strokes* and the very popular *Keeping Up Appearances*, now a big success in America too.

The social highlight of our stay in Thetford was a visit, sometimes more than one, to David and Ann's house for a large Sunday lunch. David and Ann were the ideal hosts and the table would groan under the weight of food and wine, all of which was accompanied by great conviviality. We swam in the pool, played cricket with the youngsters, watched the girls riding their ponies around the field and chatted. We, of course, tried to reciprocate by inviting David and Ann to dinner with us at the Bell when they were free to do so, but it was a poor return for the wonderful times we spent under their roof.

Below: The warden enjoys a break in filming.
Opposite above: 'Man Hunt'.
Opposite below: 'Brain versus Brawn'.

Above: The warden in the drink again.

Below: Setting up the filming of 'The Royal Train' at Weybourne Station.

Above: Another moment from 'The Royal Train'.
Below: Filming 'Two and a Half Feathers' in the King's Lynn sandpits.

Above and Left: Sales of Lledo's models of Jones's and Hodges's vans contributed to the Motor and Allied Traders' Benevolent Fund. A sizeable cheque is seen being handed over at the Birmingham Motor Show.
Below: 'Everybody's Trucking'.
Opposite above: Captain Mainwaring's nightmare as Napoleon in 'A Soldier's Farewell'.
Opposite below: Don Estelle (left) making a guest appearance in 'The Test' with Edward Sinclair and Arthur Lowe.

THE TELEVISION SERIES EPISODE BY EPISODE

SERIES ONE (B/W, BBC1)
(Recorded/Broadcast: 1968)
Series One newsreel narration: E.V.H. Emmett.
Series One titles were preceded with an episode number.

1. THE MAN AND THE HOUR
Wednesday 31/7/68, 8.20–8.50pm
Studio recording: Monday 15/4/68
In which our heroes band together to form a platoon of Local Defence Volunteers to defend our island home.
With: Janet Davies (Mrs Pike), Caroline Dowdeswell (Janet King), Bill Pertwee (the ARP Warden), John Ringham (Bracewell) and Neville Hughes (the Soldier).

2. MUSEUM PIECE
Wednesday 7/8/68, 7.00–7.30pm
Studio recording: Monday 22/4/68
In which our heroes go to great lengths in their endeavours to equip themselves as a fighting force powerful enough to repel a ruthless enemy.
With: Janet Davies (Mrs Pike), Caroline Dowdeswell (Janet King), Eric Woodburn (Museum Caretaker), Leon Cortez (the Milkman) and Michael Osborne (the Boy Scout).

3. COMMAND DECISION
Wednesday 14/8/68, 8.20–8.50pm
Studio recording: Monday 29/4/68
In which our poorly-armed heroes receive an offer of rifles and horses. All Mainwaring has to do to secure their delivery is to hand over command of the Walmington-on-Sea platoon to the supplier – the blustery Colonel Square.
With: Caroline Dowdeswell (Janet King), Geoffrey Lumsden (Colonel Square), Charles Hill (the Butler) and Gordon Peters (the Soldier).

HUGH HASTINGS

The episode 'Command Decision' involved six of the platoon volunteering as horsemen. I had not been astride a nag's back since working as a cowhand outside Sydney, Oz, when I was 16. I asked the handler whether I might have lost my 'seat' and he assured me that it was like riding a bike. I mounted my animal, which I can only describe as a fiery steed. No matter; I found myself comfortably 'seated', there being no problem except for David [Croft] who explained that he wanted me to give the impression I'd never ridden before. This made it marginally more difficult to control the headstrong creature. A gap in the fence surrounding the paddock was plugged by the handful of handlers on duty. In the storyline it emerges that the stable of walk-on quadrupeds, characterised by their stubborn refusal to do anything more than trot in a circle, was circus-trained. Once the shot was in the can I asked the lady handler why the attendant grooms had stood where they did, also mentioning that I had found my particular chestnut to be something of an equine prima donna. 'Oh, I should have warned you: it's a racehorse,' she informed Private Hastings, whose jaw dropped by a nose!

4. THE ENEMY WITHIN THE GATES
Wednesday 28/8/68, 8.20–8.50pm
(Postponed from 21/8/68)
Studio recording: Monday 22/4/68
*In which our heroes capture two German airmen.
However, Private Godfrey complicates matters
when he releases them from his charge to go for a
tinkle.*
With: Caroline Dowdeswell (Janet King), Carl
Jaffe (Captain Winogrodzki), Denys Peak and
Nigel Rideout (German Pilots), Bill Pertwee (the
ARP Warden) and David Davenport (Military
Police Sergeant).

5. THE SHOWING UP OF CORPORAL JONES
Wednesday 4/9/68, 8.20–8.50pm
(Postponed from 28/8/68)
Studio recording: Monday 13/5/68
*In which Corporal Jones is tested and our heroes
ensure that he is not found wanting.*
With: Janet Davies (Mrs Pike), Martin Wyldeck
(Major Regan), Patrick Waddington (the
Brigadier), Edward Sinclair (the Caretaker) and
Therese McMurray (the Girl at the Window).

6. SHOOTING PAINS
Wednesday 11/9/68, 8.20–8.50pm
(Postponed from 4/9/68)
Studio recording: Monday 20/5/68
*In which our heroes use their rifles and their wits
to compete for the honour of guarding a VIP.*
Guest star: Barbara Windsor (Laura La Plaz).
With: Janet Davies (Mrs Pike), Caroline
Dowdeswell (Janet King), Martin Wyldeck
(Major Regan), Jimmy Perry (Charlie Cheeseman)
and Therese McMurray (the Girl at the Window).

SERIES TWO (B/W, BBC1)
(Recorded 1968, Broadcast 1969)
Episodes marked (*) no longer exist in the BBC
Archives.

7. OPERATION KILT (*)
Saturday 1/3/69, 7.00–7.30pm
Studio recording: Sunday 13/10/68
*In which Mainwaring's brave Home Guard
platoon endures a trial of strength with the
regular Army.*

MICHAEL KNOWLES

Jimmy Perry, his wife Gilda and my wife Linda had worked together at the Palace Theatre, Watford, when Jimmy was in management there. I always feel rather privileged that although I wasn't actually present at the conception of Dad's Army, I was certainly there during its gestation! In the late 1960s, Jimmy was living in London, not far from what was known as the 'Actors' Labour Exchange' (mainly because most of the London-based actors registered there). Having 'signed on', my wife and I would often drop into Jimmy's flat in London. He was at that time working on what would become the pilot of Dad's Army and while Gilda gave us coffee, Jimmy would come dashing in from his study and read out the latest draft of a scene. So we were actually the first people to hear it. (Michael did eventually play a silly-ass captain in several episodes which led to regular characters in two more Perry and Croft series – **It Ain't Half Hot, Mum** and **You Rang, M'Lord?**)

With: Janet Davies (Mrs Pike) and James
Copeland (Captain Ogilvy).

8. THE BATTLE OF GODFREY'S COTTAGE (*)
Saturday 8/3/69, 7.00–7.30pm
Studio recording: Sunday 20/10/68
In which the bells ring for invasion.
With: Janet Davies (Mrs Pike), Amy Dalby, Nan
Braunton (Miss Godfrey), Bill Pertwee (the ARP
Warden) and Colin Bean (Private Sponge).

9. THE LONELINESS OF THE LONG DISTANCE WALKER
Saturday 15/3/69, 7.00–7.30pm
Studio Recording: Sunday 27/10/68

In which Private Walker is called up for National Service.
With: Anthony Sharp, Diana King (the Chairwoman), Patrick Waddington (the Brigadier), Edward Evans, Michael Knowles (Captain Cutts), Gilda Perry, Larry Martyn and Robert Lankesheer.

10. SGT WILSON'S LITTLE SECRET
Saturday 22/3/69, 7.00–7.30pm
Studio Recording: Friday 15/11/68
In which Sergeant Wilson finds it difficult to concentrate on Home Guard activities as he has a little problem of his own.
With Janet Davies (Mrs Pike) and Graham Harboard (Little Arthur).

NIGEL HAWTHORNE

I remember that we were just about to open **The Marie Lloyd Story** at Stratford East directed by the legendary Joan Littlewood. The stage manager told me that another of the actors was unhappy in his dressing room and could he share with me. Hardly had he sat down than Jimmy Perry began to regale me with stories of his script-writing attempts. One script in particular, he told me, was being given a second look by the BBC. It was all about the Home Guard, and I remember thinking in my ignorance at the time 'not many laughs here'! The rest is history. I met Jimmy some years later, when the series had become a much-loved favourite, on the platform of Notting Hill underground. I was very out of work while he was glowing with success. He asked me if I'd like to be in the series. My heart leapt. A regular, perhaps! No, just one line. I was the Angry Man in 'The Armoured Might of Lance Corporal Jones' and said ' 'ere! that's my bike' when someone tried to nick it. But at least I was in **Dad's Army**, and very, very proud to be so.

11. A STRIPE FOR FRAZER (*)
Saturday 29/3/69, 7.00–7.30pm
Studio Recording: Friday 15/11/68
In which Captain Mainwaring is told to promote one of our heroes to the rank of corporal.
With: Geoffrey Lumsden (Captain-Colonel Square), John Ringham (Captain Bailey), Gordon Peters and Edward Sinclair (the Caretaker).

12. UNDER FIRE (*)
Saturday 5/4/69, 7.00–7.30pm
Studio Recording: Wednesday 27/11/68
In which our heroes suspect a local resident of signalling to the enemy. If there's one thing the heroes of the Home Guard are constantly alive to, it's the ever-present danger of the enemy within – the dreaded Fifth Column. So when it appears that a local is in treasonable communication with the enemy ...
With: Janet Davies (Mrs Pike), Geoffrey Lumsden (Captain-Colonel Square), John Ringham (Captain Bailey), Ernst Ulman (Sigmund Murphy), Bill Pertwee (the ARP Warden), Queenie Watts (Mrs Keane), June Petersen and Gladys Dawson.

SERIES THREE (COLOUR, BBC1)
(Recorded/Broadcast 1969)

13. THE ARMOURED MIGHT OF LANCE CORPORAL JONES
Thursday 11/9/69, 7.30–8.00pm
Studio Recording: Sunday 25/5/69
In which our heroes add an armoured car to their fighting strength.
With: Janet Davies (Mrs Pike), Bill Pertwee (the ARP Warden), Frank Williams (the Vicar), Pamela Cundell (Mrs Fox), Jean St Clair (Miss Meadows), Nigel Hawthorne (the Angry Man), Queenie Watts (Mrs Peters), Oliver Mercer (Mrs Casson), Harold Bennet (the Old Man) and Dick Haydon (Raymond).

14. BATTLE SCHOOL
Thursday 18/9/69, 7.30–8.00pm
Studio Recording: Sunday 1/6/69
In which our heroes practise the art of war with a rare chance to use live ammunition.
With: Alan Tilvern (Cpt Rodrigues), Alan Haines (Major Smith) and Colin Bean (Private Sponge)

15. THE LION HAS PHONES

Thursday 25/9/69, 7.30–8.00pm
Studio Recording: Sunday 8/6/69
In which an enemy aircraft crash lands in the town reservoir and our heroes make the crew surrender.
With: Janet Davies (Mrs Pike), Bill Pertwee (the lARP Warden), Avril Angers (the Telephone Operator), Timothy Carlton (Lt Hope Bruce), Stanley McGeagh (Sgt Waller), Richard Jacques (Mr Cheesewright), Pamela Cundell, Bernadette Milnes and Olive Mercer (the Ladies in the Queue), Linda James (Betty), Gilda Perry (Doreen), Colin Daniels and Carson Green (the Boys).

16. THE BULLET IS NOT FOR FIRING

Thursday 2/10/69, 7.30–8.00pm
Studio Recording: Sunday 22/6/69
In which our heroes use up their ammunition on a passing aircraft and Captain Mainwaring calls a Court of Enquiry.
With: Janet Davies (Mrs Pike), Frank Williams (the Vicar), Tim Barrett (Captain Pringle), Michael Knowles (Captain Cutts), Edward Sinclair (the Verger), Harold Bennett (Mr Blewitt), May Warden (Mrs Dowding) and Fred Tomlinson, Kate Forge, Eilidh McNab, Andrew Daye and Arthur Lewis (the Choir).

17. SOMETHING NASTY IN THE VAULT

Thursday 9/10/69, 7.30–8.00pm
Studio Recording: Sunday 15/6/69
In which our heroes discover an unexploded bomb in the vault of Captain Mainwaring's bank.
With: Bill Pertwee (the ARP Warden), Robert Dorning (the Bank Inspector), Norman Mitchell (Captain Rogers) and Janet Davies (Mrs Pike).
This episode won the SFTA (now BAFTA) Award for Best Light Entertainment Production and Direction.

18. ROOM AT THE BOTTOM

Thursday 16/10/69, 7.30–8.00pm
Studio Recording: Sunday 29/6/69
In which Captain Mainwaring discovers that he is not a commissioned officer.
With: Anthony Sagar (Drill Sergeant Gregory), John Ringham (Captain Bailey), Edward Sinclair (the Verger) and Colin Bean (Private Sponge).

19. BIG GUNS

Thursday 23/10/69, 7.30–8.00pm
Studio recording: Sunday 6/7/69
In which our heroes receive some heavy artillery.
With: Edward Evans (Mr Rees), Edward Sinclair (the Verger), Don Estelle (the Man from Pickfords) and Roy Denton (Mr Bennett).

20. THE DAY THE BALLOON WENT UP

Thursday 30/10/69, 7.30–8.00pm
Studio Recording: Thursday 23/10/69
In which our heroes capture a runaway barrage balloon.
With: Bill Pertwee (the ARP Warden), Frank Williams (the Vicar), Edward Sinclair (the Verger), Nan Braunton (Miss Godfrey), Jennifer Browne (the WAAF Sergeant), Andrew Carr (the Operations Room Officer), Therese McMurray (the Girl in the Haystack), Kenneth Watson (the RAF Officer), Vicki Lane (the Girl on the Tandem), Harold Bennett (Mr Blewitt), and a fleeting appearance of Jack Haig (as the Gardener).

 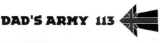

21. WAR DANCE

Thursday 6/11/69, 7.30–8.00pm
Studio Recording: Thursday 30/10/69
In which Captain Mainwaring decides to lift the morale of the troops by giving a platoon dance.
With: Frank Williams (the Vicar), Edward Sinclair (the Verger), Janet Davies (Mrs Pike), Nan Braunton (Miss Godfrey), Olive Mercer (Mrs Yeatman), Sally Douglas (Blodwen), The Graham Twins (Doris and Dora), Hugh Hastings (the Pianist) and Eleanor Smale (Mrs Prosser).

FRANK WILLIAMS

Memories for me tend to centre round those wonderful days on location in Norfolk, marching across the fields hanging on to a runaway barrage ballon, hurtling up and down a railway track on a hand trolley at breakneck speed, watching Bill Pertwee as ARP Warden Hodges falling into yet another river or lake – one could go on forever. Then, usually at the end of the day, enjoying each other's company over dinner and drinks at the Bell Hotel in Thetford. (We did actually like each other and got on well together, probably another secret of the programme's success.) Then there were the idyllic days when we were on tour with the stage show, during the hottest summer for years. Often I would go out with Bill Pertwee, Edward Sinclair and Ronnie Grange (who as well as being a singer and dancer, played a number of characters in the stage production) and we would explore the countryside round the town where we were playing that week. Sometimes we would be accompanied by John Le Mesurier who would entertain us all by singing rude words to the songs from the show through the open window of the car. **Dad's Army** was a great experience, and above all a happy one. I shall always be grateful that I was part of it.

22. MENACE FROM THE DEEP

Thursday 13/11/69, 7.30–8.00pm
Studio Recording: Friday 7/11/69
In which our heroes are very nearly blown to kingdom come.
With: Bill Pertwee (the ARP Warden), Stuart Sherwin (the 2nd ARP Warden), Bill Treacher (the 1st Sailor) and Larry Martyn (the 2nd Sailor).

23. BRANDED

Thursday 20/11/69, 7.30–8.00pm
Studio Recording: Friday 14/11/69
In which the bravery of Private Godfrey is called into question.
With: Bill Pertwee (the Chief Warden), Nan Braunton (Miss Godfrey), Roger Avon (the Doctor), Stuart Sherwin (the 2nd ARP Warden).

24. MAN HUNT

Thursday 27/11/69, 7.30–8.00pm
Studio Recording: Friday 21/11/69
In which our heroes enlist a recruit with four feet.
With: Bill Pertwee (the Chief Warden), Janet Davies (Mrs Pike), Patrick Tull (the Suspect), Robert Aldous (the German Pilot), Robert Moore (the Large Man), Leon Cortez (the Small Man), Olive Mercer (the Fierce Lady), Miranda Hampton (the Sexy Lady) and Bran the dog (as himself).

25. NO SPRING FOR FRAZER

Thursday 4/11/69, 7.30–8.00pm
Studio Recording: Friday 28/11/69
In which Frazer loses a vital part.
With: Frank Williams (the Vicar), Edward Sinclair (the Verger), Harold Bennett (Mr Blewitt), Joan Cooper (Miss Baker) and Ronnie Brandon (Mr Drury).

26. SONS OF THE SEA

Thursday 11/12/69, 7.30–8.00pm
Studio Recording: Friday 5/12/69
In which our heroes acquire a platoon boat.
With: Michael Bilton (Mr Maxwell), John Leeson (the 1st Soldier), Jonathan Holt (the 2nd Soldier) and Ralph Ball (the Man on Station).

SERIES FOUR (COLOUR, BBC1)

(Recorded/Broadcast 1970)

Above: Preparing to film 'Sons of the Sea' on the Norfolk broads.

27. THE BIG PARADE

Friday 25/9/70, 8.00–8.30pm
Studio Recording: Friday 17/7/70
Captain Mainwaring decides that Walmington-on-Sea Home Guard should have a mascot to lead them on parade. But he soon discovers that trusting Private Walker to supply one was a serious error judgement.
With: Bill Pertwee (the ARP Warden), Janet Davies (Mrs Pike), Edward Sinclair (the Verger), Colin Bean (Private Sponge) and Pamela Cundell (Mrs Fox).

28. DON'T FORGET THE DIVER

Friday 2/10/70, 8.00–8.30pm
Studio Recording: Friday 24/7/70
The ingenuity of Walmington-on-Sea's Home Guard is put to the test as they attempt a daring manoeuvre which doesn't quite go according to plan.
With: Bill Pertwee (the ARP Warden), Frank Williams (the Vicar), Edward Sinclair (the Verger), Geoffrey Lumsden (Captain Square),

Robert Raglan (the Home Guard Sergeant), Colin Bean (Private Sponge), Don Estelle (the 2nd ARP Warden) and Verne Morgan (the Landlord).

29. BOOTS, BOOTS, BOOTS

Friday 9/10/70, 8.00–8.30pm
Studio Recording: Friday 31/7/70
The Walmington-on-Sea Home Guard are instructed in the three I's – all of which, it seems, involve feet. And so begins a gruelling programme of exercises and route marches to toughen up their metatarsals.
With: Bill Pertwee (the ARP Warden), Janet Davies (Mrs Pike) and Erik Chitty (Mr Sedgewick).

30. SERGEANT – SAVE MY BOY!

Friday 23/10/70, 8.00–8.30pm
Studio Recording: Saturday 27/6/70
When Private Pike is trapped in a minefield, Private Godfrey risks his life to save him.
With: Bill Pertwee (the ARP Warden), Janet Davies (Mrs Pike), and Michael Knowles (the Engineer Officer).

31. DON'T FENCE ME IN

Friday 23/10/70, 8.00–8.30pm
Studio Recording: Friday 10/7/70
The men of Walmington-on-Sea's Home Guard are sent to watch over the local Italian POW camp.
With: Edward Evans (General Monteverdi), John Ringham (Captain Bailey) and Larry Martyn (the Italian POW).

32. ABSENT FRIENDS

Friday 30/10/70, 8.00–8.30pm
Studio Recording : Friday 7/8/70
Our heroes take advantage of Captain Mainwaring's absence and undermine his authority. But Mainwaring receives help from an unexpected quarter.
With: Bill Pertwee (the ARP Warden), Janet Davies (Mrs Pike), Edward Sinclair (the Verger), J.G. Devlin (Regan), Arthur English (the Policeman), Patrick Connor (Shamus), Verne Morgan (the Landlord), and Michael Lomax (the 2nd ARP Warden).

CARMEN SILVERA

I was very honoured to be asked by Bill Pertwee to contribute to this book. It is with fond affection that I recall being invited by David Croft to play in the episode entitled 'Mum's Army' playing the part of Mrs Gray, a role which David told me he had written especially for me, and which he said afterwards was one of his very favourite episodes.

I had always loved the series, and was a little in awe of the stars of the show when I turned up for the first rehearsal. I needn't have worried, however, since every one was so kind and friendly towards me. I was quite nervous on the day of transmission because it was the first time I had done a television show in front of a live audience – my previous TV work had been mainly in drama or in the soap **Compact** and none of them had live audiences. The show went very smoothly and my nerves soon disappeared, thanks to the support and encouragement of the marvellous cast.

The two writers, Jimmy Perry and David Croft, were quite brilliant at creating truly distinctive characters and casting them so cleverly, and I feel sure that it is for that reason that **Dad's Army** will remain forever fresh, humorous and compulsive viewing. Like millions of other viewers, I never tire of seeing it again and again.

33. PUT THAT LIGHT OUT
Friday 6/11/70, 8.00–8.30pm
Episode based on an idea by Harold Snoad
Studio Recording: Friday 30/10/70
Walmington-on-Sea's Home Guard are sent to guard the local lighthouse but end up accidentally turning the light on the town – making an inviting target for enemy planes overhead.
With: Bill Pertwee (the ARP Warden), Avril Angers (the Telephone Operator), Stuart Sherwin (the 2nd ARP Warden), and Gordon Peters (the Lighthouse Keeper).

34. TWO AND A HALF FEATHERS
Friday 13/11/70, 8.00–8.30pm
Studio Recording: Friday 6/11/70
The glorious history of Lance Corporal Jones comes under a cloud when an old comrade-in-arms dredges up their service in the Sudan.
With: Bill Pertwee (the ARP Warden), John Cater (Private Clarke), Wendy Richard (Edith), Queenie Watts (Edna), Gilda Perry (Doreen), Linda James (Betty), Parnell McGarry (Elizabeth) and John Ash (Raymond).

35. MUM'S ARMY
Friday 20/11/70, 8.00–8.30pm
Studio Recording: Friday 13/11/70
Captain Mainwaring involves the ladies of the town for the local war effort and becomes involved himself with one of their number ...
With: Carmen Silvera (Mrs Gray), Janet Davies (Mrs Pike), Wendy Richard (Edith Parish), Pamela Cundell (Mrs Fox), Julia Burbery (Miss Ironside), Rosemary Faith (Ivy Samways), Melita Manger (the Waitress), David Gilchrist (the Serviceman), Eleanor Smale (Mrs Prosser), Deidre Costello (the Buffet Attendant) and Jack Le White (the Porter).

36. THE TEST
Friday 27/11/70, 8.00–8.30pm
Studio Recording: Friday 20/11/70

The wardens challenge the Home Guard to a cricket match.
With: Bill Pertwee (the ARP Warden), Frank Williams (the Vicar), Edward Sinclair (the Verger), Don Estelle (Gerald), Harold Bennett (Mr Blewitt) and the special appearance of Freddie Trueman (as E.C. Egan).

37. A WILSON (MANAGER)?

Friday 4/11/70, 8.00–8.30pm
Studio Recording: Friday 27/11/70
Captain Mainwaring is left smarting when he is informed that promotion is in the air for Sergeant Wilson – both at Swallow's Bank and in the Home Guard.
With: Frank Williams (the Vicar), Edward Sinclair (the Verger), Janet Davies (Mrs Pike), Blake Butler (Mr West), Robert Raglan (Captain Pritchard), Arthur Brough (Mr Boyle), Colin Bean (Private Sponge) and Hugh Hastings (Private Hastings).

38. UNINVITED GUESTS

Friday 11/12/70, 8.00–8.30pm
Studio Recording: Friday 4/11/70
After the ARP Headquarters is damaged in an air raid, Hodges moves his wardens into Mainwaring's HQ at the Church Hall, much to the Home Guard platoon's irritation. A battle for territory ensues which leads to a blazing climax on the roof.
With: Bill Pertwee (the ARP Warden), Frank Williams (the Vicar), Edward Sinclair (the Verger), Rose Hill (Mrs Cole) and Don Estelle (Gerald).

39. FALLEN IDOL

Friday 18/12/70, 8.00–8.30pm
Studio Recording: Friday 11/12/70
An officers' drinking session at the weekend Battle School leaves Captain Mainwaring more than a little the worse for wear. Only an heroic action can restore his wounded reputation in the eyes of his men.
With: Geoffrey Lumsden (Captain Square), Rex Garner (Captain Ashley-Jones), Michael Knowles (Captain Reed), Anthony Sagar (the Sergeant-Major), Tom Mennard (the Mess Orderly) and Robert Raglan (Captain Pritchard).

Above: Jones: 'Take no notice of him Captain Mainwaring, the verger's a spy working for Captain Square.' L-R: John Laurie, Frank Williams, Clive Dunn, Arthur Lowe, Edward Sinclair, John Le Mesurier in 'Battle of the Giants'.

SPECIAL EPISODE FOR CHRISTMAS
(Colour, BBC1) (Recorded/Broadcast 1971)

40. BATTLE OF THE GIANTS

Monday 27/12/71, 7.00–8.00pm
Studio Recording: Sunday 19/10/71
Captain Mainwaring's Walmington-on-Sea platoon takes part in an initiative test against old rivals – the Eastgate platoon. The contest is umpired by the warden, the vicar and the verger.
With: Bill Pertwee (the ARP Warden), Geoffrey Lumsden (Captain Square), Frank Williams (the Vicar), Edward Sinclair (the Verger), Robert Raglan (the Colonel), Charles Hill (the Sergeant), Colin Bean (Private Sponge) and Rosemary Faith (the Barmaid).

SERIES FIVE (COLOUR, BBC1)
(Recorded/Broadcast 1972)

41. ASLEEP IN THE DEEP

Friday 6/10/72, 8.30–9.00pm
Studio Recording: Friday 26/5/72
The platoon is trapped in an underground room at the Water Works. They happily await rescue – until a main begins to leak.
With: Bill Pertwee (the ARP Warden), and Colin Bean (Private Sponge).

42. KEEP YOUNG AND BEAUTIFUL

Friday 13/10/72, 8.30–9.00pm
Studio Recording: Friday 9/6/72
The ARP was formed long before the Home Guard and has the younger, fitter men; the Home Guard has more than its share of veterans. So when the powers suggest an exchange of personnel, Mainwaring's outfit sets out to thwart it with the young look.

COLIN BEAN

One particular day filming 'A Soldier's Farewell' on location in Norfolk I had set my alarm especially early as this was to be the day when I would be exchanging my normal rough serge battledress for the far more colourful one of a French officer, Marshal Ney in fact, alongside Mainwaring's Napoleon. Warden Hodges had been known, on more than one occasion, to call the good Captain 'Napoleon'. This was a dream sequence after the platoon's visit to the cinema and Mainwaring's cheese supper which followed. After the fitting out of my ceremonial costume as Ney (which I hope wasn't as tight on him as it was on me that morning), I was to be mounted on a horse for the sequence, and I had never been on one before, even in my service days. Once in the saddle I was then instructed to move 'over there' which meant the horse had to move, and obviously me with it. It was only about 20 yards, but to me it was like a glimpse into the Grand National. Of course Arthur Lowe was an experienced horseman and was busy exercising his horse in between filming takes. The filming went well, but at the end of the day a very grateful Colin Bean was relieved to shed Marshal Ney, have a hot bath, and a couple of pints in the hotel bar. It had certainly been a different day for all of us, but the result seems to have been enjoyed by viewers ever since.

With: Bill Pertwee (the ARP Warden), Robert Raglan (the Colonel), James Ottaway (the 1st Member of Parliament), Charles Morgan (the 2nd Member of Parliament) and Derek Bond (the Minister).

43. A SOLDIER'S FAREWELL

Friday 20/1/72, 8.30–9.00pm
Studio Recording: Friday 2/6/72
Mainwaring dreams that he is Napoleon.
With: Bill Pertwee (the ARP Warden), Frank Williams (the Vicar), Robert Gillespie (Charles Boyer), Joan Savage (Greta Garbo), Colin Bean (Private Sponge) and Joy Allen (the Clipper).

44. GETTING THE BIRD

Friday 27/10/72, 8.30–9.00pm
Studio Recording: Friday 19/5/72
Walker arranges for Jones to get some off-ration pigeons, but did they come from Trafalgar Square?
With: Bill Pertwee (the ARP Warden), Frank Williams (the Vicar), Edward Sinclair (the Verger), Pamela Cundell (Mrs Fox), Olive Mercer (Mrs Yeatman), Seretta Wilson (the Wren) and Alvar Liddell (the Newsreader).

45. THE DESPERATE DRIVE OF CORPORAL JONES

Friday 3/11/72, 8.30–9.00pm
Studio Recording: Friday 16/6/72
Mainwaring's platoon is sitting in a barn which is the target for some 25-pounders; only Jones knows of the danger.
With: Bill Pertwee (the ARP Warden), Frank Williams (the Vicar), Edward Sinclair (the Verger), Robert Raglan (the Colonel), Larry Martyn (the Signals Private) and James Taylor (the Artillery Officer).

46. IF THE CAP FITS...

Friday 10/11/72, 8.30–9.00pm
Studio Recording: Friday 30/6/72
One way to deal with a grumbler is to let him take over – so Mainwaring tries it with Frazer.
With: Bill Pertwee (Warden), Campbell Singer (Major General Menzies), Robert Raglan (the Colonel), Edward Sinclair (the Verger), Alex McEvoy (the Sergeant) and Dennis Blanch (2/Lt).

47. THE KING WAS IN HIS COUNTING HOUSE

Friday 17/11/72, 8.30–9.00pm
Studio Recording: Friday 23/6/72
A bomb falls on the strong room of Mainwaring's bank. He insists that the platoon counts the money and guards it.
With: Bill Pertwee (the ARP Warden), Frank Williams (the Vicar), Edward Sinclair (the Verger), Wendy Richard (Shirley) and Colin Bean (Private Sponge).

BRENDA COWLING

I was delighted to be offered the part of Mrs Prentice in 'All is Safely Gathered In'. I loved being part of the programme and enjoyed working with all the members of the wonderful cast. One particular memory I have was when we were filming in a Suffolk field. The platoon had just finished a harvest festival meal and had imbibed quantities of Mrs Prentice's home-brewed poteen and were about to attend an open-air thanksgiving service. John Laurie and John Le Mesurier were sitting shivering in the October sunshine waiting for the filming to begin, proving how hardy they were.

It's always a pleasure to work on any David Croft/Jimmy Perry production so it was a particular honour to be asked to create the part of Mrs Lipton in **You Rang, M'lord?** in 1988; another series of great quality.

48. ALL IS SAFELY GATHERED IN

Friday 24/11/72, 8.30–9.00pm
Studio Recording: Friday 3/11/72
The platoon helps a widowed lady friend of Private Godfrey to gather the harvest.
With: Bill Pertwee (the ARP Warden), Brenda Cowling (Mrs Prentice), Frank Williams (the Vicar), Edward Sinclair (the Verger), Colin Bean (Private Sponge), April Walker (Judy) and Tina Cornioli (Olive).

49. WHEN DID YOU LAST SEE YOUR MONEY?

Friday 1/12/72, 8.30–9.00pm
Studio Recording: Friday 10/11/72
Jones can't remember where he put the £500 that was collected for the canteen fund, so the platoon tries to jog his memory.
With: Bill Pertwee (the ARP Warden), Frank Williams (the Vicar), Edward Sinclair (the Verger), Harold Bennett (Mr Blewitt) and Tony Hughes (Mr Billings).

50. BRAIN VERSUS BRAWN

Friday 8/12/72, 8.30–9.00pm
Studio Recording: Friday 17/11/72
The members of the platoon disguise themselves as firemen during an initiative exercise, but are called on to tackle a real fire.
With: Bill Pertwee (the ARP Warden), Robert Raglan (the Colonel), Edward Sinclair (the Verger), Anthony Roye (Mr Fairbrother), Maggie Don (the Waitress), Geoffrey Hughes (the Bridge Corporal) and David Rose (the Dump Corporal).

51. A BRUSH WITH THE LAW

Friday 15/12/72, 8.30–9.00pm
Studio Recording: Sunday 26/11/72
A light is left burning from the Church Hall so the Chief Warden puts Mainwaring in court.
With: Bill Pertwee (the ARP Warden), Frank Williams (the Vicar), Edward Sinclair (the verger), Geoffrey Lumsden (Captain Square), Jeffrey Gardiner (Mr Wintergreen), Stuart Sherwin (the Junior Warden), Marjorie Wilde (the Lady Magistrate), Chris Gannon (the Clerk of the Court) and Toby Perkins (the Usher).

52. ROUND AND ROUND WENT THE GREAT BIG WHEEL

Friday 22/12/72, 8.30–9.00pm
Studio Recording: Friday 1/12/72
The platoon is chosen for special duties during the test of a secret weapon which runs amok.
With: Bill Pertwee (the ARP Warden), Geoffrey Chater (Colonel Pierce), Edward Underdown (Major-General Sir Charles Holland), Michael Knowles (Captain Stewart), Jeffrey Segal (the Minister) and John Clegg (Wireless Operator).

53. TIME ON MY HANDS
Friday 29/12/72, 8.30–9.00pm
Studio Recording: Friday 8/12/72
An enemy pilot bales out and becomes tangled up with the town clock – and so does Mainwaring's platoon.
With: Bill Pertwee (Warden), Frank Williams (the Vicar), Edward Sinclair (the Verger), Harold Bennett (Mr Blewitt), Colin Bean (Private Sponge), Joan Cooper (Miss Fortescue), Eric Longworth (Mr Gordon) and Christopher Sandford (the German Pilot).

SERIES SIX (COLOUR, BBC1)
(Recorded/Broadcast 1973)

54. THE DEADLY ATTACHMENT
Wednesday 31/10/73, 6.50–7.20pm
Studio Recording: Friday 22/6/73
Captain Mainwaring's platoon are detailed to guard a captive U-boat crew landed from a fishing vessel.
Featuring: Philip Madoc (as the U-boat Captain).
With: Bill Pertwee (Warden Hodges), Edward Sinclair (the Verger), Robert Raglan (the Colonel) and Colin Bean (Private Sponge).

Below: A famous scene: chasing 'The Royal Train'.

55. MY BRITISH BUDDY
Wednesday 7/11/73, 6.50–7.20pm.
Studio Recording: Friday 8/6/73
The first contingent of American troops arrive in Walmington-on-Sea. The platoon makes arrangements to welcome them.
With: Bill Pertwee (Warden Hodges), Alan Tilvern (the US Colonel), Frank Williams (the Vicar), Edward Sinclair (the Verger), Janet Davies (Mrs Pike), Wendy Richard (Shirley), Pamela Cundell (Mrs Fox), Verne Morgan (the Landlord), Talfryn Thomas (Mr Cheeseman), Suzanne Kerchiss (Ivy), Robert Raglan (the Colonel) and Blain Fairman (the US Sergeant).

56. THE ROYAL TRAIN
Wednesday 14/11/73, 6.30–7.00pm
Studio Recording: Friday 29/6/73
HM King George VI is passing through Walmington by train. The platoon provides a guard of honour.
With: Bill Pertwee (Warden Hodges), Frank Williams (the Vicar), Edward Sinclair (the Verger), William Moore (the Station Master), Freddie Earlle (Henry), Ronnie Brody (Bob), Fred McNaughton (the Mayor), Sue Bishop (the Ticket Collector) and Bob Hornery (the City Gent).
NB: This episode was broadcast in an earlier

timeslot than other episodes in Series Six as part of a special day's schedule to celebrate the Royal Wedding of HRH Princess Anne and Captain Mark Philips, 14/11/73.

57. WE KNOW OUR ONIONS
Wednesday 21/11/73, 6.50–7.20pm
Studio Recording: Friday 15/6/73
Captain Mainwaring and the platoon take part in a Home Guard Efficiency test.
With: Fulton Mackay (Captain Ramsey), Bill Pertwee (Warden Hodges), Edward Sinclair (the Verger), Alex McAvoy (the Sergeant), Pamela Manson (the NAAFI Girl) and Cy Town (the Mess Steward).

58. THE HONOURABLE MAN
Wednesday 28/11/73, 6.50–7.20pm
Studio Recording: Sunday 8/7/73
A relation of Sergeant Wilson dies. This puts Wilson on the outer fringes of the aristocracy, much to Mainwaring's annoyance.
With: Bill Pertwee (Warden Hodges), Frank Williams (the Vicar), Edward Sinclair (the Verger), Eric Longworth (The Town Clerk), Janet Davies (Mrs Pike), Gabor Vernon (the Russian), Hana-Maria Pravda (the Interpreter), Robert Raglan (the Colonel), Pamela Cundell (Mrs Fox) and Fred McNaughton (the Mayor).
The studio sequences in this episode represent James Beck's last work on the TV *Dad's Army*. He recorded two radio episodes – 'Sergeant Wilson's Little Secret' and 'A Stripe for Frazer' – the following Friday night and died after a short illness on Monday 6/8/73.

59. THINGS THAT GO BUMP IN THE NIGHT
Wednesday 5/12/73, 6.50–7.20pm.
Studio Recording: Sunday 15/7/73
Jones's van, carrying the platoon, breaks down outside an apparently deserted house where Mainwaring decides they should spend the night.
With: Jonathan Cecil (Captain Cadbury) and Colin Bean (Private Sponge).
NB: This episode features James Beck in location film work, shot prior to the studio recording of 'The Honourable Man', and is, in transmission order, his final appearance in the TV series.

60. THE RECRUIT
Wednesday 12/12/73, 6.50–7.20pm.
Studio Recording: Sunday 22/7/73
Captain Mainwaring is temporarily in hospital; during his absence Sergeant Wilson allows the Vicar to join the platoon.
With: Bill Pertwee (Warden Hodges), Frank Williams (the Vicar), Edward Sinclair (the Verger), Susan Majolier (the Nurse) and Lindsey Dunn (the Small Boy).

SERIES SEVEN (COLOUR, BBC1)
(Recorded/Broadcast 1974)

61. EVERYBODY'S TRUCKING
Friday 15/11/74, 7.45–8.15pm
Studio recording: Sunday 27/10/74
Mainwaring's platoon is to signpost the route for the big exercise. They discover a steam engine obstructing the road.
With: Bill Pertwee (Warden Hodges), Frank Williams (the Vicar), Edward Sinclair (the Verger), Pamela Cundell (Mrs Fox), Harold Bennett (Mr Bluett), Olive Mercer (Mrs Yeatman), Felix Bowness (the Driver) and Colin Bean (Private Sponge).

62. A MAN OF ACTION
Friday 22/11/74, 7.45–8.15pm
Studio Recording: Tuesday 7/5/74
A bomb drops on the outskirts of Walmington-on-Sea. Mainwaring declares Martial Law.
With: Bill Pertwee (Warden Hodges), Talfryn Thomas (Mr Cheeseman), Frank Williams (the Vicar), Edward Sinclair (the Verger), Eric Longworth (the Town Clerk), Harold Bennett (Mr Bluett), Arnold Peters (Fire Officer Dale), Jay Denyer (Inspector Baker), Robert Mill (Cpt Swan) and Colin Bean (Private Sponge).

63. GORILLA WARFARE
Friday 29/11/74, 7.45–8.15pm
Studio Recording: Sunday 27/10/74
During an exercise, Mainwaring casts himself as a highly important secret agent. The regular Army tries to prevent him from completing his mission.
With: Bill Pertwee (Warden Hodges), Talfryn Thomas (Private Cheeseman), Edward Sinclair (the Verger), Robert Raglan (the Colonel), Robin Parkinson (Lieutenant Wood), Erik Chitty (Mr

FELIX BOWNESS

My Days in **Dad's Army** were just wonderful. Although I'd done TV before, I had never been away on location, filming and it opened my eyes to the fun that was to be had.

Bill Pertwee had been a 'turn' before he became an actor and we knew each other through summer shows in many seaside towns. Bill warned me, as did Jimmy Perry, that I was doing an acting part now, and was not playing as a comic in a summer show, and pointed out that David Croft was very strict when filming. I turned to Jimmy and David a great deal for advice and they were a great help to me in how I should play my part. David was so pleased with my efforts that I was re-booked for other episodes. I found it difficult not to laugh out loud when they were filming, especially at Clive Dunn, so they asked me to keep well away. One day, when I was up a tree well out of the way, I started to do some bird impressions and Bill came rushing over and said 'stop whistling, the sound boys will pick it up on their mikes.' When the episode come out, there was this lovely country scene with birdsong in the distance. Only Bill and I ever knew who the bird was, and he's never given me away yet!

Clerk), Rachel Thomas (the Mother Superior), Michael Sharvell-Martin (the Lieutenant), Verne Morgan (the Farmer) and Joy Allen (the Lady with the Pram).

64. THE GODIVA AFFAIR
Friday 6/12/74, 7.45–8.15pm
Studio Recording: Sunday 3/11/74
Captain Mainwaring's platoon decide to perform a Morris Dance in the Walmington-on-Sea Spitfire Fund Carnival.

With: Bill Pertwee (Warden Hodges), Talfryn Thomas (Private Cheeseman), Frank Williams (the Vicar), Edward Sinclair (the Verger), Janet Davies (Mrs Pike), Pamela Cundell (Mrs Fox), Eric Longworth (the Town Clerk), Peter Honri (Private Day), Rosemary Faith (the Waitress), Colin Bean (Private Sponge) and George Hancock (Private Hancock).

65. THE CAPTAIN'S CAR
Friday 13/12/74, 7.45–8.15pm
Studio recording: Sunday 17/11/74
Captain Mainwaring is offered the use of a Rolls-Royce. On the way to be camouflaged, it gets mixed up with the Mayor's car.
With: Bill Pertwee (Warden Hodges), Talfryn Thomas (Private Cheeseman), Frank Williams (the Vicar), Edward Sinclair (the Verger), Robert Raglan (the Colonel), Eric Longworth (the Town Clerk), Fred McNaughton (the Mayor), Mavis Pugh (Lady Maltby), John Hart-Dyke (the French General) and Donald Morley (Glossip).

66. TURKEY DINNER
Monday 23/11/74, 8.00–8.30pm
Studio recording: Sunday 10/11/74
The platoon decide to give a turkey dinner to the old-age pensioners of Walmington-on-Sea.
With: Bill Pertwee (Warden Hodges), Talfryn Thomas (Private Cheeseman), Frank Williams (the Vicar), Edward Sinclair (the Verger), Harold Bennett (Mr Bluett), Pamela Cundell (Mrs Fox), Janet Davies (Mrs Pike), Olive Mercer (Mrs Yeatman) and Dave Butler (the Farmhand).

ERIC LONGWORTH

There was great rejoicing in the Longworth household when my agent rang to say **Dad's Army** required a town clerk. Already in its fourth year, I was a fan and so was excited at the prospect of joining a well-established series. This can also be a bit frightening but I soon felt at home. Of all the characters the one that intrigued me most was Pike. What was Ian like in real life? And the answer? Completely the opposite to his brilliant interpretation of the part. I shall always remember one moment in particular in 'The Godiva Affair' (my favourite episode) having previously slavered over the word 'fleshings' (the town clerk, Mr Gordon had to select a lady Godiva) prompted by the thought of the luscious Mrs Fox riding through the streets of Walmington-on-Sea wearing long golden tresses. Ian Lavender shortly afterwards repeated the word 'fleshings' with even more fervour and one of his very own facial expressions.

SERIES EIGHT (COLOUR, BBC1)
(Recorded/Broadcast 1975)

67. RING DEM BELLS
Friday 5/9/75, 8.00–8.30pm
Studio Recording: Thursday 3/7/75
Captain Mainwaring and the platoon play the
part of Nazi soldiers in a training film.
With: Bill Pertwee (Warden Hodges), Frank Williams (the Vicar), Edward Sinclair (the Verger), Jack Haig (the Landlord), Robert Raglan (the Colonel), Felix Bowness (the Special Constable), John Bardon (Harold Forster), Hilda Fenemore (Queenie Beal), Janet Mahoney (the Bariad) and Adele Strong (the Lady with Umbrella).

68. WHEN YOU'VE GOT TO GO
Friday 12/12/75, 8.00–8.30pm
Studio recording: Friday 6/6/75
Private Pike receives his call-up papers and, to the
great alarm of his mother, he is passed A1.

IAN LAVENDER

With the passing of a few years I find that my memories of **Dad's Army** are guided by thoughts of personal comfort and so I can say quite categorically that my favourite episode is not the one with the Germans but the one where we were the Germans in 'Ring Dem Bells'. We made this episode in 1975, so after eight years of wearing singularly ill-fitting and uncomfortable uniforms, Sgt Wilson and Pte Pike were to play German officers in the proposed propaganda film. This meant that John Le Mesurier and I had several days of filming and a whole day in the studio in comfortable tailored German officers' uniforms not to mention the joy of speaking lines like 'Seventeen bitter shandies mit der ginger beer', when we all decided to have a drink in the pub – much to the consternation of the publican – who immediately phoned the police and told them that the invasion had started. Running close is of course 'The Deadly Attachment'. It has always been a continuous source of amazement to me that whereas catchphrases usually take months of repetition to establish themselves, David and Jimmy achieved what must be the fastest catching on of a catchphrase with: U-boat captain: 'Your name will also go on ze list. Vat is it?'
Mainwaring: 'Don't tell him Pike!'
Every time I watch an episode the more I realise that each one has some moments in it that would make it a candidate for 'favourite'. They all conjure up a joyous memory or two.

With: Bill Pertwee (Chief Warden Hodges), Frank Williams (the Vicar), Edward Sinclair (the Verger), Janet Davies (Mrs Pike), Eric Longworth (the Town Clerk), Freddie Earlle (the Italian Sergeant), Tim Barrett (the Doctor), Colin Bean (Private Sponge) and Frankie Holmes (the Fish Fryer).

69 IS THERE HONEY STILL FOR TEA?
Friday 19/9/75, 8.00–8.30pm
Studio Recording: Thursday 26/6/75
Private Godfrey's cottage is condemned to be bulldozed because a new airstrip is to be built.
With: Bill Pertwee (Chief Warden Hodges), Gordon Peters (the Man with the Door), Robert Raglan (the Colonel), Campbell Singer (Sir Charles McAllister), Joan Cooper (Dolly) and Kathleen Saintsbury (Cissy).

70. COME IN, YOUR TIME IS UP
Friday 26/9/75, 8.00–8.30pm
Studio Recording: Thursday 10/7/75
Mainwaring's platoon discovers a German aircraft crew in a dinghy on a lake and endeavours to bring it to shore.
With: Bill Pertwee (Chief Warden Hodges) Frank Williams (the Vicar), Edward Sinclair (the Verger), Harold Bennett (Mr Bluett) and Colin Bean (Private Sponge).

71. HIGH FINANCE
Friday 3/10/75, 8.00–8.30pm
Studio Recording: Friday 30/5/75
Mainwaring decided that Jones's bank account has been in the red too long ...
With: Bill Pertwee (Chief Warden Hodges), Frank Williams (the Vicar), Edward Sinclair (the Verger), Janet Davies (Mrs Pike), Ronnie Brody (Mr Swann), Colin Bean (Private Sponge) and Natalie Kent (Miss Twelvetrees).

72. THE FACE ON THE POSTER
Friday 10/10/75, 8.00–8.30pm
Studio Recording: Thursday 17/7/75
Mainwaring starts an advertising campaign to increase recruiting but Wilson mixes up the photographs for the poster.
With: Bill Pertwee (Chief Warden Hodges), Frank Williams (the Vicar), Edward Sinclair (the

Verger), Peter Butterworth (Mr Bugden), Harold Bennett (Mr Bluett), Gabor Vernon (the Polish Officer), Colin Bean (Private Sponge), Bill Tasker (Fred) and Michael Bevis (the Police Sergeant).

SPECIAL EPISODE FOR CHRISTMAS
(Colour, BBC1) (Recorded/Broadcast 1975)

73. MY BROTHER AND I
Friday 26/12/75, 6.05–6.45pm
Studio Recording: Friday 23/5/75
Captain Mainwaring gives a sherry party for local dignitaries. Unfortunately, an unwelcome guest turns up...
With: Bill Pertwee (Chief Warden Hodges), Frank Williams (the Vicar), Edward Sinclair (the Verger), Arnold Diamond (the Major-General), Penny Irving (the chambermaid) and Colin Bean (Private Sponge).

SPECIAL EPISODE FOR CHRISTMAS
(Colour, BBC1) (Recorded/Broadcast 1976)

74. THE LOVE OF THREE ORANGES
Sunday 26/12/76, 7.25–7.55PM
Studio recording: Friday 10/10/76
Walmington-on- Sea's Home guard platoon decides to help the Vicar with his bazaar to raise money for comforts for the troops.
With: Bill Pertwee (Chief Warden Hodges), Frank Williams (the Vicar), Edward Sinclair (the Verger) Pamela Cundell (Mrs Fox), Janet Davies (Mrs Pike), Joan Cooper (Dolly), Eric Longworth (the Town Clerk), Olive Mercer (Mrs Yeatman) and Colin Bean (Private Sponge).

SERIES NINE (COLOUR, BBC1)
(Recorded/Broadcast 1977)

75. WAKE-UP WALMINGTON
Sunday 2/10/77, 8.10–8.40pm
Studio Recording: Friday 8/7/77
The people of Walmington are no longer taking the threat of invasion seriously. The platoon, therefore, masquerades as Fifth Columnists to test the town's reaction.
With: Bill Pertwee (Chief Warden Hodges), Edward Sinclair (the Verger), Geoffrey Lumsden (Captain Square) Sam Kydd (the Yokel), Harold

Bennett (Mr Bluett) (sic), Robert Raglan (the Colonel), Charles Hill (the Butler), Jeffrey Holland (the soldier), Barry Linehan (the Van Driver), Colin Bean (Private Sponge), Alister Williamson (Bert), and Michael Stainton (Frenchy).

76. THE MAKING OF PRIVATE PIKE
Sunday 9/10/77, 8.10–8.40pm
Studio Recording: Friday 1/7/77
Captain Mainwaring is given a staff car. It breaks down when Private Pike and his girlfriend borrow it to go to the pictures.
With: Bill Pertwee (Chief Warden Hodges), Frank Williams (the Vicar), Edward Sinclair (the Verger), Jean Gilpin (Sylvia), Anthony Sharp (the Colonel), Jeffrey Segal (the Brigadier), Pamela Cundell (Mrs Fox), Janet Davies (Mrs Pike) and Melita Manger (Nora).

77. KNIGHTS OF MADNESS
Sunday 16/10/77, 8.10–8.40pm
Studio recording: Friday 22/7/77
To help 'Wings for Victory' Week, Mainwaring and the platoon stage the Battle of St George and the Dragon.
With: Bill Pertwee Chief Warden Hodges), Frank Williams (the Vicar), Edward Sinclair (the Verger), Colin Bean (Private Sponge), Janet Davies (Mrs Pike), Olive Mercer (Mrs Yeatman), Eric Longworth (the Town Clerk) and Fred McNaughton (the Mayor).

78. THE MISER'S HOARD
Sunday 23/10/77, 8.10–8.40pm
Studio Recording: Friday 24/6/77
Frazer keeps his savings in gold sovereigns. Mainwaring thinks the money should be in a safe place, such as a bank – his bank!
Special Guest Appearance: Fulton Mackay (as Dr McCeavedy).
With: Bill Pertwee (Chief Warden Hodges), Frank Williams (the Vicar), Edward Sinclair (the Verger) and Colin Bean (Private Sponge).

79. NUMBER ENGAGED
Sunday 6/11/77, 8.10–8.40pm
Studio Recording: Friday 15/7/77
The platoon is guarding a vital telephone line.

Above: We do like dressing up: 'Knights of Madness'.

They awake to find a bomb emmeshed in the wires.
With: Bill Pertwee (Chief Warden Hodges), Frank Williams (the Vicar), Edward Sinclair (the Verger), Ronnie Brody (the GPO Man), Robert Mill (the Army Captain), Kenneth MacDonald (the Army Sergeant), Felix Bowness (the Van Driver), Colin Bean (Private Sponge), Stuart McGugan (the Scottish Sergeant), Bernice Adams (the ATS Girl).

80. NEVER TOO OLD (*)
Sunday 13/11/77, 8.10–8.45pm
Studio recording: Friday 29/7/77
Love comes to Corporal Jones in this, the final episode of Dad's Army.
With: Bill Pertwee (Chief Warden Hodges), Frank Williams (the Vicar), Edward Sinclair (the Verger), Pamela Cundell (Mrs Fox), Janet Davies (Mrs Pike), Colin Bean (Private Sponge), Joan Cooper (Dolly) and Robert Raglan (the Colonel).

*Repeated on 8/5/95 as part of BBC programmes celebrating the 50th Anniversary of VE-Day.

PAMELA CUNDELL

I have two very different recollections of my life in **Dad's Army**. Perhaps my favourite moment happened in my favourite episode, the last of the series. I am marrying Jones (at last!), and I have asked Captain Mainwaring to give me away. Come the rehearsals, and as usual, lots of fun. Arthur and myself had to go through a door arm in arm. Well, as we went through we got stuck. No one noticed in the rehearsal, so Arthur whispered to me 'don't do it again until the actual transmission and everyone will be in stitches – it's a good piece of business.' Of course he was right; David, Jimmy, the crew, audience, everyone, fell about – it was the best moment! The other recollection concerns Clive. We were doing an episode ('My British Buddy') about the American Army joining in a social evening we were having. One GI flirts with me, and gives me a pair of nylons, much to Jones' chagrin. Anyway, there was one line I just couldn't get right so Clive said, 'Write it on the palm of your hand, nobody will see it but you, and all will be well'. Lovely, I thought. Come the transmission I had the line safely written in my palm, so off we went. At the said line I held up my hands in joy to read it. No lines! With the heat and nerves the line had run, to leave only a runny inky mess! But fate came to my rescue, and I found the line came perfectly.

I just adored Arthur. He was such fun to be with, and what a lesson for us all in timing. I still miss him.

Dear Clive comes to London every now and then, so I see him occasionally and we always have a good time and lovely 'natters' together.

TELEVISION PRODUCTION CREDITS

GUIDE TO ABBREVIATIONS:
S = Series
BG = 'Battle of the Giants'
MB = 'My Brother and I'
L3 = 'The Love of Three Oranges'

Signature Tune:

Words by Jimmy Perry
Music by Jimmy Perry and Derek Taverner
Sung by Bud Flanagan (all episodes)

Closing Theme: Band of the Coldstream Guards conducted by Director of Music, Captain (later Major) Trevor L. Sharpe, MBE, LRAM, ARC, psm. (all episodes)

Costumes: George Ward (S1,4); Odette Barrow (S3); Michael Burdle (S3); Barbara Kronig (S4); Judy Allen (BG); Susan Wheal (S5-7); Mary Husband (S8-9, MB, L3).

Make Up: Sandra Exelby (S1); Cecile Hay-Arthur (S3), Cynthia Goodwin (S4-5); Penny Bell (BG); Anna Chesterman (S4-5); Ann Ailes (S6); Sylvia Thornton (S7-9, MB, L3).

Visual Effects: Peter Day (S3-6,8); John Friedlander (S4); Ron Oates (S4); Len Hutton (BG); Tony Harding (S5); Jim Ward (S7); Martin Gutteridge (S9).

Studio Lighting: George Summers (S1, 2, 4): Howard King (S3-9, BG, MB, L3).

Studio Sound: James Cole (S1, 2); Michael McCarthy (S3-8, L3); John Holmes (S3-4); John Delany (S5); Alan Machin (S8, MB); Laurie Taylor (S9).

Film Cameraman: James Balfour (S3, 5-6); Stewart A. Farnell (S4-5, BG); Len Newson (S7); Peter Chapman (S8-9).

Film Sound: Les Collins (S4-5, BG); Ron Blight (S5); John Gatland (S6-7); Bill Chesneau (S8); Graham Bedwell (S9).

Film Editor: Bob Rymer (S3, 5-6, BG); Bill Harris (S4-7); John Stothart (S8); John Dunstan (S9).

Production Assistant: Bob Spiers (S7); Jo Austin (S8, MB, L3); Gordon Elsbury (S9).

Design: Alan Hunter Craig (S1): Paul Joel (S1-6, BG); Oliver Bayldon (S2); Ray London (S3); Richard Hunt (S3); Bryan Ellis (S7); Robert Berk (S8, MB); Geoff Powell (S9); Tim Gleeson (S9).

Director: Harold Snoad (S2-4, selected episodes); Bob Spiers (S9, selected episodes); David Croft (all other episodes).

Producer: David Croft (all episodes).

Studio Material recorded at BBC Television Centre, Wood Lane, Shepherds Bush, London.

Location Material filmed at (among other places):
The Guild Hall, Thetford, Norfolk – as Walmington-on-Sea's Town Hall (many episodes); Nether Row, Thetford, Norfolk – a street in Walmington-on-Sea (many episodes); Palace Cinema (Interior), Thetford, Norfolk – 'A Soldier's Farewell', 1972; Stamford Practical Training Area (MOD), near Thetford, Norfolk (many episodes); Britannia Pier, Lowestoft, Suffolk – 'Menace from the Deep', 1969; the North Norfolk Steam Railway, including Weybourne Station, Weybourne, Norfolk – 'The Royal Train', 1973; Lynford Hall, Lynford, Norfolk – 'Wake Up Walmington'; All Saints' Church Honington and Honington V.C. Primary School, Honington, Suffolk – the church and Church Hall exteriors (many episodes); Drinkstone Mill, near Woolpit, Suffolk – 'Don't Forget the Diver', 1970.

Below: John Laurie, John Le Mesurier and the Author in 'A Soldier's Farewell'.

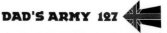

THE TALKING WIRELESS

Recording the radio version of *Dad's Army* was never going to be easy, but it was a very enjoyable experience and the end result was received with a great deal of pleasure by the listening public. On several occasions we recorded on our day off from the television studios, and there was one spell of about a fortnight when we did two recordings a day.

Writing for radio is just as difficult as writing for television. You have 50 or 60 blank pages to fill up for a half-hour programme, and in the case of *Dad's Army* it was no easier to write for radio than it was for television. Naturally the characters had been established in the public's mind for some time, but a great deal of thought had to be put into replacing the visual situations with the spoken word and making sure that they would still be funny. One or two episodes were completely rewritten because adaptation just was not possible. Not every member of the cast was used in each programme simply because there would not have been enough for everyone to do in a particular episode. Harold Snoad and Michael Knowles did the excellent adaptation for this very long radio series. Michael Knowles takes up the story.

'The BBC commissioned Harold Snoad and myself to adapt *Dad's Army* for radio. They liked the pilot programme and we went on to adapt some 70 episodes.

'They were recorded first at the old Playhouse Theatre in Northumberland Avenue and later at the BBC Paris Studios in Lower Regent Street. By its very nature *Dad's Army* is very visual and it required a lot of work to translate this visual element into purely sound terms. Characters were required to ascend in barrage ballons, risk death from unexploded bombs and runaway giant wheels spitting fire, commandeer trains and negotiate raging rivers while defending their country against the ever-present threat of Nazi invasion!

'The producer, John Dyas, was terribly enthusiastic about the project and sometimes got a little carried away by his enthusiasm. For example, one episode had the platoon adrift in an open boat. In an attempt to simulate sitting in a rowing boat on radio, John had arranged all the actors' chairs in the rough shape of a boat on the stage of the Paris Studio. This was fine in theory, but it had one drawback – the microphones, which were fixed, were all on the port side of the 'boat' as it were. This meant the actors sitting on the starboard side couldn't be heard, or had to scramble over the person next to them in order to reach the microphones! This resulted in some chaos as the actors got tangled up with each other, and even, in one or two cases, finished up on the floor muttering mild oaths. It was then decided to go back to the more conventional broadcasting methods.

'Another episode called for Corporal Jones to cycle through the streets of Walmington-On-Sea. John Dyas decided it would be a good idea if Clive Dunn actually rode a bicycle on stage. Clive's enthusiastic response to this was immediate. "I should like to volunteer to ride a bicycle round the stage sir!" With that he leapt astride the bike and tried several circuits of the stage before the idea was abandoned as

being not only too dangerous for the cast but also for the audience! As it turned out, it worked better when Clive walked between microphones. Such is the magic of radio!'

The late John Dyas, the producer of the radio series, said at the time:

'Radio cannot hope to reproduce the visual gag, nor should it try, but when this element has been removed from any original *Dad's Army* script, there remains enough dialogue for the actors to create good radio comedy. Of course, the scripts cannot be performed just as they are. The visual gags have to be replaced by written lines. This was the job of the two writers. Incidentally, the two involved in this production were well known to *Dad's Army*: Harold Snoad, who began as a production assistant with the television series, and Michael Knowles, who took part in several episodes of the programme. They both understood the characters (and the actors playing them), created by Jimmy Perry and David Croft, well enough to make their job easier than it normally would have been. Recreating their television roles for the radio was no worry to the cast, but the techniques of having to use the static microphone to create a sense of distance and atmosphere, combined with all the sound effects which have to be allowed for, took quite a little time to get the hang of; but once mastered our merry band of Home Guards got down to the real business of entertaining, which they all did terribly well, as always.'

Below: A parody of Arthur Askey's 'Big-hearted Arthur' went: 'Big-Helmet Wilkie they call me, 'Big-Helmet Wilkie, that's me. Now they've made me a warden, I get my torch batt'ries free! Big-Helmet Wilkie they call me, Wilkie the Warden that's me!

 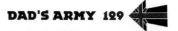

THE RADIO SERIES EPISODE BY EPISODE

ARTHUR LOWE as Captain Mainwaring
JOHN LE MESURIER as Sergeant Wilson
CLIVE DUNN as Lance Corporal Jones
JOHN LAURIE as Private Frazer
JAMES BECK, GRAHAM STARK and LARRY MARTYN as Private Walker
ARNOLD RIDLEY as Private Godfrey
IAN LAVENDER as Private Pike
JOHN SNAGGE as BBC Announcer for all episodes:

SERIES ONE (BBC RADIO 4, 1974)

1. THE MAN AND THE HOUR
Monday 28/1/74, 6.15–6.45pm
Studio Recording: Sunday 3/6/73
The Man – Mr Mainwaring. The Hour – 11.30am, 14 May 1940, when the Manager of Swallows Bank, Walmington-on-Sea, answers his country's call and forms a platoon of Local Defence Volunteers to defend our island home.
TV: 'The Man and the Hour', Series 1 (1968)
With: Timothy Bateson (Elliott/Gen. Wilkinson/Driver).

2. MUSEUM PIECE
Monday 4/2/74, 6.15–6.45pm
Studio Recording: Thursday 7/6/73
The determination of Captain Mainwaring and his platoon to fight to the last man in defence of our island shores is marred only by one small detail – a total lack of weapons.
TV: 'Museum Piece', Series 1 (1968)
With: Eric Woodburn (George Jones).
Arnold Ridley does not appear.

3. COMMAND DECISION
Monday 11/2/74, 6.15–6.45pm
Studio Recording: Thursday 21/6/73

Above: A light-hearted script conference in Arthur Lowe's dressing room. L–R: John Le Mesurier, Bill Pertwee, Arnold Ridley, Clive Dunn and Arthur Lowe.

*Mr Mainwaring, self-appointed commander of his
platoon of LDV, puts the defence of the realm before
his own personal pride – and nearly comes a cropper.*
TV: 'Command Decision', Series 1 (1968)
With: Geoffrey Lumsden (Colonel Square) and David
Sinclair (the GHQ Driver).
Arnold Ridley and Ian Lavender do not appear.

4. THE ENEMY WITHIN THE GATES
Monday 18/2/74, 6.15–6.45pm
Studio Recording: Thursday 21/6/73
*Captain Mainwaring and his men triumph over the
problems of security, Fifth Columnists and German
parachutists – and make a profit.*
TV: 'The Enemy Within the Gates', Series 1 (1968)
With: Carl Jaffe (Captain Winogrodzki) and David
Sinclair (the German Airman).
John Laurie does not appear.

5. THE BATTLE OF GODFREY'S COTTAGE
Monday 25/2/74, 6.15–6.45pm
Studio Recording: Friday 6/7/73
*When the bells ring out signalling the German invasion,
Captain Mainwaring calls on his trusty lads of the
Home Guard for their supreme effort – only to find that
half of them have gone off to the pictures.*
TV: 'The Battle of Godfrey's Cottage', Series 2 (1968)
With: Bill Pertwee (the ARP Warden), Nan Braunton
(Cissy Godfrey) and Percy Edwards (Percy the Parrot).
James Beck does not appear.

6. THE ARMOURED MIGHT OF LANCE CORPORAL JONES
Monday 4/3/74, 6.15–6.45pm
Studio Recording: Friday 6/7/73
*The members of the Walmington-on-Sea Home Guard
use their initiative and turn Corporal Jones's butcher's
van into a war machine.*
TV: 'The Armoured Might of Lance Corporal Jones',
Series 3 (1969)
With: Bill Pertwee (the ARP Warden), Pearl Hackney
(Mrs Pike), Richard Davies (the Volunteer), Elizabeth
Morgan (Mrs Leonard) and Diana Bishop (Miss
Meadows).
Arnold Ridley and Ian Lavender do not appear.

7. SGT WILSON'S LITTLE SECRET
Monday 11/3/74, 6.15–6.45pm
Studio Recording: Friday 13/7/73
*The freedom of the world pales into insignificance for
Sergeant Wilson when his own freedom is threatened.*
TV: 'Sgt Wilson's Little Secret', Series 2 (1969)
With: Bill Pertwee (the ARP Warden) and Pearl
Hackney (Mrs Pike). John Laurie does not appear.

8. A STRIPE FOR FRAZER
Monday 18/3/74, 6.15–6.45pm
Studio Recording: Friday 13/7/73
*Captain Mainwaring's promotion of Private Frazer also
promotes a state of none-too-friendly rivalry with
Corporal Jones.*
TV: 'A Stripe for Frazer', Series 2 (1969)
With: Geoffrey Lumsden (Captain-Colonel Square) and
Michael Knowles (Captain Bailey).
Arnold Ridley does not appear.
*This is the last episode that James Beck recorded, and is
his last work on* Dad's Army. *The character of Walker
does reappear but not until 'The Showing Up of
Corporal Jones' in which the part is taken over by
Graham Stark.*

9. OPERATION KILT
Monday 25/3/74, 6.15–6.45pm
Studio Recording: Monday 23/7/73
*In their efforts to turn themselves into an efficient
fighting force, Mainwaring and his men pit their wits
against a detachment of Highland Infantry.*
TV: 'Operation Kilt', Series 2 (1969)
With: Pearl Hackney (Mrs Pike) and Jack Watson
(Captain Ogilvy).

10. BATTLE SCHOOL
Monday 1/4/74, 6.15–6.45pm
Studio Recording: Thursday 28/6/73
*Captain Mainwaring and his men undergo training for
guerrilla warfare and get their first experience of live
ammunition – from the wrong end.*
TV: 'Battle School', Series 3 (1969)
With: Jack Watson (Major Smith) and Alan Tilvern
(Captain Rodrigues).
James Beck does not appear.*

This episode was recorded before James Beck's death, but does not feature him.

11. UNDER FIRE
Monday 8/4/74, 6.15–6.45pm
Studio Recording: Friday 27/7/73
When German high explosives rain down on Walmington-on-Sea, Captain Mainwaring and his men demonstrate their great resourcefulness and unearth a spy in their midst.
TV: 'Under Fire', Series 2 (1969)
With: Pearl Hackney (Mrs Pike), Geoffrey Lumsden (Captain-Colonel Square), Avril Angers (Mrs Keane) and David Gooderson (Mr Murphy). Ian Lavender does not appear.

12. SOMETHING NASTY IN THE VAULT
Monday 15/4/74, 6.15–6.45pm
Studio Recording: Monday 23/7/73
Captain Mainwaring and Sergeant Wilson fall upon an explosive situation when the bank is broken into.
TV: 'Something Nasty in the Vault', Series 3 (1969)
With: Bill Pertwee (the ARP Warden), John Barron (Mr West), Frank Thornton (Captain Rogers) and Elizabeth Morgan (Janet King). Arnold Ridley does not appear.

13. THE SHOWING UP OF CORPORAL JONES
Monday 22/4/74, 6.15–6.45pm
Studio Recording: Friday 20/7/73.
Corporal Jones must prove his fitness for the Home Guard by completing an assault course in just 15 minutes.
TV: 'The Showing Up of Corporal Jones', Series 1 (1968)
With: Jack Watson (Major Regan).
This episode features the first appearance of Graham Stark as Private Walker.

14. THE LONELINESS OF THE LONG DISTANCE WALKER
Monday 29/4/74, 6.15–6.45pm
Studio Recording: Friday 20/7/73
When Private Walker's call up threatens the platoon's black market supplies, Captain Mainwaring and his men scheme to avert this disaster.
TV: 'The Loneliness of the Long Distance Walker', Series 2 (1969)
With: Jack Watson (the Sergeant/the Brigadier), Judith Furse (the Chairwoman) and Michael Knowles (the Captain/Mr Rees). Ian Lavender does not appear.

15. SORRY, WRONG NUMBER
Monday 6/5/74, 6.15–6.45pm
Studio Recording: Friday 27/7/73
Captain Mainwaring attempts to instruct the platoon in the use of telephone boxes, hoping to improve communication between men on patrol and his HQ at the Church Hall. But when a German plane crash-lands in the reservoir, Corporal Jones causes nothing but confusion!
TV: 'The Lion Has Phones', Series 3 (1969)
With: Bill Pertwee (the ARP Warden), Pearl Hackney (Mrs Pike), Avril Angers (the Telephone Operator) and John Forest (Lieutenant Hope-Bruce). Arnold Ridley does not appear.

16. THE BULLET IS NOT FOR FIRING
Monday 13/5/74, 6.15–6.45pm
Studio Recording: Thursday 26/7/73
When Corporal Jones and his platoon waste their meagre ration of five rounds of ammunition per man, Captain Mainwaring takes action – a Court Martial.
TV: 'This Bullet is Not for Firing', Series 3 (1969)
With: Frank Williams (the Vicar), Michael Knowles (Captain Pringle), Timothy Bateson (Captain Marsh) and John Whitehall (all the Choir). John Laurie and Ian Lavender do not appear. *In transmission terms, this episode features the last appearance of Graham Stark as Private Walker. The character does not appear in the remaining episodes of Series 1.*

17. ROOM AT THE BOTTOM
Monday 20/5/74, 6.15–6.45pm
Studio Recording: Monday 23/7/73
Exactly one year to the day after Captain Mainwaring assumed command of Walmington-on-Sea Home Guard, Brigade Headquarters discover a slight irregularity – he's never had the authority to do so.
TV: 'Room at the Bottom', Series 3 (1969)
With: Jack Watson (Sergeant Gregory) and John

Ringham (Captain Turner).
Ian Lavender does not appear.

18. THE MENACE FROM THE DEEP
Monday 27/5/74, 6.15–6.45pm
Studio Recording: Tuesday 24/7/73
Marooned on the end of the pier with no food, no communication and no means of getting back to dry land, Captain Mainwaring and his doughty men face the horrors of the sea.
TV: 'Menace from the Deep', Series 3 (1969)
With: Bill Pertwee (the ARP Warden) and David Sinclair (the 2nd ARP Warden). Arnold Ridley does not appear.

19. NO SPRING FOR FRAZER
Monday 3/6/74, 6.15–6.45pm
Studio Recording: Thursday 26/7/73
When Private Frazer loses a vital part, Captain Mainwaring is prepared to waken the dead at this threat to the security of our island fortress.
TV: 'No Spring for Frazer', Series 3 (1969)
With: Edward Sinclair (the Verger), Joan Cooper (Miss Baker) and Timothy Bateson (Mr Blewitt/Captain Turner). Ian Lavender does not appear.

20. SONS OF THE SEA
Monday 10/6/74, 6.15–6.45pm
Studio Recording: Wednesday 25/7/73
When Captain Mainwaring and his men take to the water, their plans go dangerously adrift.
TV: 'Sons of the Sea', Series 3 (1969)
With: Timothy Bateson (Mr Maxwell and everybody else).

CHRISTMAS SPECIAL
(BBC RADIO 4, 1974)

21. PRESENT ARMS
Tuesday 24/12/74, 1.15–2.15pm
Studio Recording: Thursday 18/7/74
Captain Mainwaring and his men pit their wits against Westgate platoon for the honour of guarding a VIP.
TV: 'Shooting Pains', Series 1 (1968) and 'Battle of the Giants', Special Episode for Christmas (1971).
With: Bill Pertwee (Chief Warden), Pearl Hackney (Mrs

Pike), Geoffrey Lumsden (Captain Square), Jack Watson (the Brigadier/Cheerful Charlie Cheeseman) and Norman Bird (Bert Postlethwaite).
This episode features Larry Martyn's first transmitted appearance as Private Walker but was recorded at the end of the recording block for Series 2. The earliest episodes in this series do not feature him – his first performance as Walker can be heard in 'A Brush with the Law', (episode 29).

SERIES TWO (BBC RADIO 4, 1975)

22. DON'T FORGET THE DIVER
Tuesday 11/2/75, 12.27-12.57pm
Studio Recording: Tuesday 16/7/74
Enlisting the additional services of a bird warbler, a scarecrow and a flock of sheep, Captain Mainwaring and his men mount a river attack on Captain Square's HQ.
TV: 'Don't Forget the Diver', Series 4 (1970)
With: Edward Sinclair (the Verger), Geoffrey Lumsden (Captain Square) and Norman Ettlinger (the Sergeant).

23. IF THE CAP FITS …
Tuesday 18/2/75, 12.27–12.57pm
Studio Recording: Wednesday 17/4/74
One way to deal with a persistent grumbler is to give him a taste of responsibility. So Captain Mainwaring hands over command to Private Frazer – with unexpected results.
TV: 'If the Cap Fits …', Series 5 (1972)
With: Edward Sinclair (the Verger), and Frazer Kerr (Major-General Menzies/Sergeant MacKenzie).

24. PUT THAT LIGHT OUT
Tuesday 25/2/75, 12.27–12.57pm
Studio Recording: Tuesday 30/4/74
Put in charge of the observation post in the disused lighthouse, Corporal Jones sets out to prove his qualities of leadership – and ends up endangering the whole town.
TV: 'Put that Light Out', Series 4 (1970)
With: Bill Pertwee (the ARP Warden), Avril Angers (the Telephone Operator) and Stuart Sherwin (the Lighthouse Keeper).

25. BOOTS, BOOTS, BOOTS

Tuesday 4/3/75, 12.27–12.57pm
Studio Recording: Tuesday 16/4/74
The men of Walmington-on-Sea's Home Guard object strongly to Captain Mainwaring's recipe for an efficient fighting force, the three Fs – fast feet, functional feet, and fit feet.
TV: 'Boots, Boots, Boots', Series 4 (1970)
With: Erik Chitty (Mr Sedgewick).

26. SERGEANT – SAVE MY BOY!

Tuesday 11/3/75, 12.27–12.57pm
Studio Recording: Tuesday 16/4/74
When Pike gets the seat of his pants caught on barbed wire in a minefield, Mainwaring springs to his rescue – treading very, very carefully.
TV: 'Sergeant – Save My Boy!', Series 4 (1970)
With: Pearl Hackney (Mrs Pike).

27. BRANDED

Tuesday 18/3/75, 12.27–12.57pm
Studio Recording: Wednesday 17/7/74
Thrown out of the platoon by Captain Mainwaring for being a conscientious objector, spurned by his friends, Godfrey has to prove himself – and does!
TV: 'Branded', Series 3 (1969)
With: Bill Pertwee (Chief Warden Hodges), Nan Braunton (Cissy Godfrey), Michael Segal (the 2nd Warden) and Norman Ettlinger (the Doctor).

28. UNINVITED GUESTS

Tuesday 25/3/75, 12.27–12.57pm
Studio Recording: Thursday 18/4/74
When Chief Warden Hodges and his men try to take over the Church Hall, Captain Mainwaring is determined to make things hot for them…
TV: 'Uninvited Guests', Series 4 (1970)
With: Bill Pertwee (the ARP Warden), Frank Williams (the Vicar) and Edward Sinclair (the Verger).

29. A BRUSH WITH THE LAW

Tuesday 1/4/75, 12.27–12.57pm
Studio Recording: Wednesday 17/7/74
When a light is left switched on in the Church Hall, the Chief Warden achieves his burning ambition – to haul Captain Mainwaring into court.
TV: 'A Brush with the Law', Series 5 (1972)
With: Bill Pertwee (Chief Warden Hodges), Geoffrey Lumsden (Captain Square), Edward Sinclair (the Verger), Michael Segal (the 2nd Warden), Michael Knowles (Mr Wintergreen) and Norman Ettlinger (the Clerk of the Court).
Larry Martyn assumed the role of Private Walker from this episode up to the end of the run.

30. A SOLDIER'S FAREWELL

Tuesday 8/4/75, 12.27–12.57pm
Studio Recording: Wednesday 15/5/74
A cinema visit and an off-the-ration toasted-cheese supper set the scene for Captain Mainwaring at the Battle of Waterloo.
TV: 'A Soldier's Farewell', Series 5 (1972)
With: Bill Pertwee (the ARP Warden) and Pat Coombs (the Clippie/Marie).

31. BRAIN VERSUS BRAWN

Tuesday 15/4/75, 12.27–12.57pm
Studio Recording: Tuesday 30/4/74
During an initiative test, Captain Mainwaring and his men disguise themselves as firemen complete with fire engine, but get diverted to tackle a real blaze.
TV: 'Brawn Versus Brain', Series 5 (1972)
With: Avril Angers (the Waitress/the Policeman), Robert Raglan (Colonel Pritchard) and Stuart Sherwin (Mr Fairbrother/the Corporal).

32. WAR DANCE

Tuesday 22/4/75, 12.27–12.57pm
Studio Recording: Sunday 12/5/74
The enjoyment of a platoon dance – arranged by Captain Mainwaring to boost the morale of his men – is spoiled when Pike announces his engagement.
TV: 'War Dance', Series 3 (1969)
With: Pearl Hackney (Mrs Pike) and Wendy Richard (Violet Gibbons).

33. MUM'S ARMY

Tuesday 29/4/75, 12.27–12.57pm
Studio Recording: Sunday 12/5/74
When Captain Mainwaring opens the ranks of his

Home Guard platoon to the ladies of Walmington, he discovers to his sorrow that the problems caused are not only physical, but also emotional.
TV: 'Mum's Army', Series 4 (1970)
With: Carmen Silvera (Mrs Gray), Mollie Sugden (Mrs Fox/the Waitress) and Wendy Richard (Edith Parrish).

34. GETTING THE BIRD
Tuesday 6/5/75, 12.27–12.57pm
Studio Recording: Monday 15/7/74
Private Walker arranges to supply Corporal Jones with some off-the-ration pigeons. But the question is not where they come from, but where to store them.
TV: 'Getting the Bird', Series 5 (1972)
With: Frank Williams (the Vicar) and Diana Bishop (Sgt Wilson's Daughter).

35. DON'T FENCE ME IN
Tuesday 13/5/75, 12.27–12.57pm
Studio Recording: Thursday 16/5/74
While the Walmington-on-Sea platoon are in charge of a POW Camp, the prisoners escape and a traitor is unearthed in their midst – Private Walker.
TV: 'Don't Fence Me In', Series 4 (1970)
With: Cyril Shaps (General Monteverdi), John Ringham (Captain Turner) and Sion Probert (the POW/the Sentry).

36. THE KING WAS IN HIS COUNTING HOUSE
Tuesday 20/5/75, 12.27–12.57pm
Studio Recording: Wednesday 15/5/74
When a bomb falls on the strong-room of Mainwaring's bank, the platoon is set to guard the money. But first it must be counted in – every penny.
TV: 'The King was in His Counting House', Series 5 (1972)
With: Bill Pertwee (the ARP Warden) and Wendy Richard (Shirley).

37. WHEN DID YOU LAST SEE YOUR MONEY?
Tuesday 27/5/75, 12.27–12.57pm
Studio Recording: Wednesday 15/5/74
Corporal Jones can't remember how he lost £500, so the Platoon try to jog his memory and Private Frazer reveals himself as a hypnotist.

TV: 'When Did You Last See Your Money?', Series 5 (1972)
With: Timothy Bateson (Mr Blewitt/Mr Billings).
Larry Martyn does not appear.

38. FALLEN IDOL
Tuesday 3/6/75, 12.27–12.57pm
Studio Recording: Tuesday 16/7/74
On a weekend exercise, Captain Mainwaring's maxim that he and his men eat together, sleep together and fight together comes badly unstuck – and so does his sobriety.
TV: 'Fallen Idol', Series 4 (1970)
With: Geoffrey Lumsden (Captain Square), Jack Watson (Captain Reed), Michael Brennan (the Sergeant-Major) and Norman Ettlinger (Pritchard).
Larry Martyn does not appear.

39. A. WILSON (MANAGER)?
Tuesday 10/6/75, 12.27–12.57pm
Studio Recording: Wednesday 17/4/74
Captain Mainwaring's complacency is rudely shaken when Wilson, his chief clerk at the bank, is given his own branch – and promoted to second lieutenant.
TV: 'A. Wilson (Manager)?', Series 4 (1970)
With: Edward Sinclair (the Verger), Michael Knowles (Captain Bailey) and Fraser Kerr (Mr West).
Larry Martyn does not appear.

40. ALL IS SAFELY GATHERED IN
Tuesday 17/6/75, 12.27–12.57pm
Studio Recording: Monday 15/7/74
Captain Mainwaring and the men of the Walmington Home Guard try to work alongside the warden to bring in the harvest, but not even the presence of the vicar can ensure peaceful co-existence.
TV: 'All is Safely Gathered In', Series 5 (1972)
With: Bill Pertwee (the ARP Warden), Frank Williams (the Vicar) and Nan Kenway (Mrs Prentice).
Larry Martyn does not appear.

41. THE DAY THE BALLOON WENT UP
Tuesday 24/6/75, 12.27–12.57pm
Studio Recording: Thursday 18/4/75
Captain Mainwaring and Corporal Jones get carried

away in their efforts to secure a runaway barrage balloon.
TV: 'The Day the Balloon Went Up', Series 3 (1969)
With: Bill Pertwee (the ARP Warden), Frank Williams
(the Vicar), Edward Sinclair (the Verger) and Michael
Knowles (Squadron Leader Horsfall).
Larry Martyn does not appear.

SERIES THREE (BBC RADIO 4, 1976)

42. A MAN OF ACTION
Tuesday 16/3/76, 12.27–12.57pm
Studio Recording: Monday 28/4/75
For the benefit of a reporter from the Eastbourne
Gazette, Captain Mainwaring tries to portray himself as
a dynamic, efficient leader in the Churchill mould, only
to come a shade unstuck when Private Pike gets up to
his ears in trouble.
TV: 'A Man of Action', Series 7 (1974)
With: Bill Pertwee (Chief Warden Hodges), Julian
Orchard (Mr Upton – Town Clerk), Jonathan Cecil (Mr
Norris) and Fraser Kerr (Captain Swan/the Inspector).

43. THE HONOURABLE MAN
Tuesday 23/3/76, 12.27–12.57pm
Studio Recording: Monday 28/4/75
On the occasion of the goodwill visit by a distinguished
Russian, the Town Council of Walmington-on-Sea
decides to offer him the Freedom of the Town …
TV: 'The Honourable Man', Series 6 (1973)
With: Bill Pertwee (the ARP Warden), Julian Orchard
(Mr Upton – the Town Clerk) and Fraser Kerr (the
Visiting Russian).

44. THE GODIVA AFFAIR
Tuesday 30/3/76, 12.27–12.57pm
Studio Recording: Monday 5/5/75
The choosing of a local lady to play the part of Lady
Godiva in Walmington's Carnival Procession in aid of
the Spitfire Fund strikes a discordant note for Captain
Mainwaring and his men, who were planning their own
musical surprise.
TV: 'The Godiva Affair', Series 7 (1974)
With: Bill Pertwee (ARP Warden), Frank Williams (the
Vicar), Julian Orchard (Mr Upson) and Mollie Sugden
(Mrs Fox).

45. KEEP YOUNG AND BEAUTIFUL
Tuesday 6/4/76, 12.27–12.57pm
Studio Recording: Monday 12/5/75
When the War Office notifies all Home Guard units
that in future only the younger and healthier members
will be retained, while those older and less fit will be
exchanged with ARP personnel, Captain Mainwaring
and the veteran members of his platoon are driven to
adopt drastic measures.
TV: 'Keep Young and Beautiful', Series 5 (1972)
With: Michael Burlington (the Wig Maker).

46. ABSENT FRIENDS
Tuesday 13/3/76, 12.27–12.57pm
Studio Recording: Tuesday 6/5/75
With mutiny on his hands from within the ranks of his
Home Guard platoon, Captain Mainwaring, battling to
regain his authority, receives unexpected help – from an
escaped convict.
TV: 'Absent Friends', Series 4 (1970)
With: Bill Pertwee (Chief Warden Hodges), Pearl
Hackney (Mrs Pike), Michael Brennan (Tom/George
Pearson) and Stuart Sherwin (the Policeman).

47. ROUND AND ROUND WENT THE GREAT BIG WHEEL
Tuesday 20/4/76, 6.15–6.45pm
Studio Recording: Wednesday 7/5/75
When, during its testing at Walmington-on-Sea, a new
secret weapon runs amok, Mainwaring and his Home
Guard platoon turn the humiliation of spud bashing
into the glory of saving the town.
TV: 'Round and Round Went the Great Big Wheel',
Series 5 (1972)
With: Bill Pertwee (the ARP Warden), John Barron
(Colonel Pierce) and Michael Knowles (Captain
Stewart).

48. THE GREAT WHITE HUNTER
Tuesday 27/4/76, 12.27–12.57pm
Studio Recording: Friday 30/5/75
Private Walker converts a parachute he's found into
several pairs of ladies underwear and, in the process,
causes Captain Mainwaring and his men some
embarrassment.

TV: 'Man Hunt', Series 3 (1969)
With: Pearl Hackney (Mrs Pike), Elizabeth Morgan (Housewife), and Fraser Kerr (the Policeman).

49. THE DEADLY ATTACHMENT

Tuesday 4/5/76, 12.27–12.57pm
Studio Recording: Wednesday 30/4/75
Corporal Jones's life is put in jeopardy when the crew of a German U-Boat and their cunning commander turn the tables on Captain Mainwaring and his platoon, whose task is to guard them.
TV: 'The Deadly Attachment', Series 6 (1973)
With: Frank Williams (the Vicar), Philip Madoc (Captain Muller) and Fraser Kerr (Colonel Winters).

50. THINGS THAT GO BUMP IN THE NIGHT

Tuesday 11/5/76, 12.27–12.57pm
Studio Recording: Wednesday 7/5/75
A storm forces Captain Mainwaring and his men to take shelter for the night in a deserted country mansion, but when they begin to hear weird noises, everyone is convinced that the hounds of Hell are after them.
TV: 'Things that Go Bump in the Night', Series 6 (1973)
With: John Barron (Captain Cadbury).

51. MY BRITISH BUDDY

Tuesday 18/5/76, 12.27–12.57pm
Studio Recording: Tuesday 6/5/75
Captain Mainwaring arranges a 'Welcome to England' party for the first contingent of American troops to arrive in Walmington but his hopes to cement Anglo-US relations come somewhat unstuck when a brawl develops between the visitors and his platoon.
TV: 'My British Buddy', Series 6 (1973)
With: Bill Pertwee (Chief Warden Hodges), Jack Watson (Colonel Schulz), Pearl Hackney (Mrs Pike), Mollie Sugden (Mrs Fox), Wendy Richard (Shirley) and Michael Middleton (the American Sergeant).

52. BIG GUNS

Tuesday 25/5/76, 12.27–12.57pm
Studio Recording: Monday 5/5/75
Captain Mainwaring and his men set their sights on total dominance of Walmington-on-Sea.
TV: 'Big Guns', Series 3 (1969)

With: Julian Orchard (Mr Upton – the Town Clerk) and Michael Middleton (the Pickford's Man).

53. THE BIG PARADE

Tuesday 1/6/76, 12.27–12.57pm
Studio Recording: Friday 2/5/75
When Private Walker offers to provide the Walmington-on-Sea Home Guard platoon with a suitable mascot to lead them on parade, Captain Mainwaring, to his dismay, discovers that the cheapest is not necessarily the best.
TV: 'The Big Parade', Series 4 (1970)
With: Bill Pertwee (Chief Warden Hodges), Edward Sinclair (the Verger) and Pearl Hackney (Mrs Pike).

54. ASLEEP IN THE DEEP

Tuesday 8/6/76, 12.27–12.57pm
Studio Recording: Friday 9/5/75
While attempting to rescue Privates Walker and Godfrey from the bombed water works, Captain Mainwaring and the rest of his men themselves become trapped – with water rapidly rising about them.
TV: 'Asleep in the Deep', Series 5 (1972)
With: Bill Pertwee (the ARP Warden).

55. WE KNOW OUR ONIONS

Tuesday 15/6/76, 12.27–12.57pm
Studio Recording: Thursday 8/5/75
With Captain Mainwaring and his men facing the humiliation of failure in the Home Guard Efficiency Tests and Private Pike on the verge of tears, it takes a shady deal by cunning Joe Walker to save the day.
TV: 'We Know Our Onions', Series 6 (1973)
With: Bill Pertwee (the ARP Warden), Alan Tilvern (Captain Ramsay) and Michael Middleton (Sergeant Baxter).

56. THE ROYAL TRAIN

Tuesday 22/6/76, 12.27–12.57pm
Studio Recording: Tuesday 29/4/75
With the main line at Walmington Station blocked and HM King George VI due to arrive soon, Mainwaring and his men take charge, only to find they are on a runaway train.
TV: 'The Royal Train', Series 6 (1973)

With: Bill Pertwee (the ARP Warden), Frank Williams (the Vicar), Stuart Sherwin (the Station Master), Fraser Kerr (the Train Driver) and Michael Middleton (the Driver's Mate).

57. A QUESTION OF REFERENCE
Tuesday 29/6/76, 12.27–12.57pm
Studio Recording: Monday 12/5/75
Having sent Mainwaring and his Home Guard platoon into the target area by mistake, it's up to Corporal Jones and Private Godfrey to save them being blown to pieces by the 25-pounders.
TV: 'The Desperate Drive of Corporal Jones', Series 5, (1972)
With: Peter Williams (the Colonel) and Michael Burlington (the Signalman).

58. HIGH FINANCE
Tuesday 6/7/76, 12.27–12.57pm
Studio Recording: Friday 27/6/75
When Mainwaring refuses any longer to extend Jones's credit at the bank, the rest of the platoon try to find £50 to save him from bankruptcy.
TV: 'High Finance', Series 8 (1975)
With: Bill Pertwee (Chief Warden Hodges), Pearl Hackney (Mrs Pike) and Frank Williams (the Vicar).

59. THE RECRUIT
Tuesday 13/7/76, 12.27–12.57pm
Studio Recording: Thursday 1/5/75
Sergeant Wilson takes over command of Walmington-on-Sea's Home Guard platoon during Captain Mainwaring's enforced absence and makes the most unusual addition to their strength.
TV: 'The Recruit', Series 6 (1973)
With: Bill Pertwee (Chief Warden Hodges), Frank Williams (the Vicar), Edward Sinclair (the Verger) and Elizabeth Morgan (the Nurse and the Small Boy).

60. A JUMBO-SIZED PROBLEM
Tuesday 20/7/76, 12.27–12.57pm
Studio Recording: Wednesday 18/6/75
Travelling in Jones's butcher's van to a vitally important assignment, Captain Mainwaring and his men get completely bogged down, and it takes two pairs of feet
and a truck to get them out.
TV: 'Everybody's Trucking', Series 7 (1974)
With: Bill Pertwee (Chief Warden Hodges).

61. THE CRICKET MATCH
Tuesday 27/7/76, 12.27–12.57pm
Studio Recording: Thursday 1/5/75
As a relief from their accustomed role as defenders of these island shores against the common foe – Adolf Hitler – Captain Mainwaring and his men propose to do battle with their local adversary, Chief Warden Hodges, on the playing field in whites rather than khaki.
TV: 'The Test', Series 4 (1970)
With: Bill Pertwee (Chief Warden Hodges), Frank Williams (the Vicar), Edward Sinclair (the Verger), and Anthony Smee (G.C.Egan).

62. TIME ON MY HANDS
Tuesday 3/8/76, 12.27–12.57pm
Studio Recording: Tuesday 29/4/75
When a German pilot bales out over Walmington, his parachute gets entangled with the Town Hall clock and so does Captain Mainwaring's platoon when they attempt to rescue him.
TV: 'Time On My Hands', Series 5 (1972)
With: Bill Pertwee (Chief Warden Hodges), Frank Williams (the Vicar), Erik Chitty (Mr Parsons) and Fraser Kerr (the German Pilot).

63. TURKEY DINNER
Tuesday 10/8/76, 12.27–12.57pm
Studio Recording: Friday 2/5/75
When Captain Mainwaring is due to be guest speaker at the local Rotary Club, he and his dress suit have to run the gauntlet of some sloppy work by the men of his own platoon.
TV: 'Turkey Dinner', Series 7 (1974)
With: Bill Pertwee (Chief Warden Hodges), Frank Williams (the Vicar), Pearl Hackney (Mrs Pike) and Harold Bennett (Mr Blewitt).

64. THE CAPTAIN'S CAR
Tuesday 17/8/76, 12.27–12.57pm
Studio Recording: Friday 9/5/75

The running feud between the wardens and the Home Guard of Walmington-on-Sea is sorely aggravated, when Captain Mainwaring is offered the use of a Rolls-Royce for the duration.
TV: 'The Captain's Car', Series 7 (1974)
With: Bill Pertwee (Chief Warden Hodges), Betty Marsden (Lady Maltby) and Gerard Green (Colonel Marsden).

65. THE TWO AND A HALF FEATHERS
Tuesday 24/8/76, 12.27–12.57pm
Studio Recording: Thursday 8/5/75
The bemedalled military career of Lance-Corporal Jones comes under grave suspicion when an old comrade-in-arms dredges up their past service in the Sudan.
TV: 'The Two and a Half Feathers', Series 4 (1970)
With: Bill Pertwee (Chief Warden Hodges), Michael Bates (Private Clarke) and Avril Angers (Edith).

66. IS THERE HONEY STILL FOR TEA?
Tuesday 31/8/76, 12.27–12.57pm
Studio Recording: Friday 11/7/75
When plans for a new airfield are announced, Captain Mainwaring and his men engage bureaucracy in a rearguard action to save Godfrey's cottage from demolition.
TV: 'Is There Honey Still For Tea?', Series 8 (1975)
With: Joan Cooper (Cissy Godfrey) and Fraser Kerr (Sir Charles Renfrew-McAllister/the Colonel).
Larry Martyn does not appear.

67. TEN SECONDS FROM NOW
Tuesday 7/9/76, 12.27–12.57pm
Studio Recording: Wednesday 18/6/75
The climax to Captain Mainwaring's position comes when his platoon is chosen to take part in a world-wide radio broadcast that culminates in a speech from HM King George VI.
TV: 'Christmas Night with the Stars: Broadcast to the Empire', (1972).
With: Frank Thornton (the BBC Producer) and Roger Gartland (Bert – the BBC Engineer).

RADIO PRODUCTION CREDITS
Adapted by: Michael Knowles and Harold Snoad from

TV Scripts written by Jimmy Perry and David Croft.
Produced by: John Dyas.
Recorded at: The Playhouse Theatre, Northumberland Avenue, London and at Paris Studios, Lower Regent Street, London. Recorded in Mono.

TV EPISODES NOT ADAPTED FOR RADIO
'Gorilla Warfare', 'Ring Dem Bells', 'When You've Got To Go', 'Come In, Your Time Is Up', 'The Face On The Poster', 'My Brother And I', 'The Love of Three Oranges', 'Wake Up Walmington', 'The Making of Private Pike', 'Knights of Madness', 'The Miser's Hoard', 'Number Engaged' and 'Never Too Old'.

COLONEL OR CAPTAIN SQUARE?
This is indeed a very interesting subject. I have had to listen to all the radio shows which included this character, paying particular attention to the dialogue to clarify the situation.

'Command Decision'
This is before Colonel Square joins the Home Guard and therefore he has retained his military rank; perhaps it should say (Retired). In the show he is referred to as 'Colonel' and the credits confirm this.

'A Stripe For Frazer'
This is where the character first joins the Home Guard as a corporal in the Walmington platoon. In the show he is referred to as 'Corporal Colonel Square', however in the credits he is announced as Colonel Square.

'Under Fire'
Again in the show he is referred to as 'Corporal Colonel' and again the credits announce it as Colonel.

'A Brush With The Law'
The character has now taken up his duties with the Eastgate platoon as their captain. However in the show he is a civilian and a magistrate, so should it be 'Colonel' or 'Captain'? During the show he is referred to as 'Captain' and in the credits this is confirmed.

'Fallen Idol' and 'Present Arms'
In both shows and credits he is referred to as Captain.

FILM STARS

The Columbia Pictures feature film of *Dad's Army* was made early in the show's career in 1970 and was premiered in March 1971.

One of the locations for the film was Chalfont St Peter in Buckinghamshire. This pretty little town was transformed into Walmington-on-Sea, complete with some small boats, fishing nets, the Swallow Bank, Hodges' greengrocer's shop, Jones' butcher's shop, etc, all of which had only been seen in interior studio mock-ups in the television series.

Another location was Chobham in Surrey, where two hair-raising scenes occurred, one causing John Laurie to finish up with very badly bruised ribs. There was a long scene in which a white horse had to cross the river on a raft with our heroes on board. The raft was being towed downstream by way of ropes that were handled from the river bank. The rather jerky movements of the tow lines unbalanced the horse and it slipped and fell, hitting John Laurie. It was not a pleasant thing to happen to anyone, let alone to someone in their seventies who suffered from asthma. However, John recovered and luckily everyone else was unharmed.

Other locations that were used for filming were Seaford in Sussex, various streets around Shepperton in Middlesex, and the interior filming at Shepperton Studios.

The film was produced by John Sloan and directed by Norman Cohen. It was not an easy assignment for the director or actors. Columbia Pictures were determined to make the film on time – eight weeks was their target – although it did take a little longer. Jimmy Perry and David Croft, the writers and advisers for the production, spent a great deal of time and energy in trying to make sure that the film was kept in the 1940s style. It was, of course, not so easy for an American film company to think of the era in the same way as we did. David and Jimmy and all the television crew knew the actors well, and they always ensured that they were comfortable and happy and not being hurried into their work.

The feature film was a slightly different matter. The producer constantly pressurised the director to get so many minutes in the can per day, and this in turn pressurised the production. We did have some very helpful assistants among the film crew, which was a great advantage. John Le Mesurier, who was the most experienced film actor among us, knew a few of the crew from previous films in which he had acted, so that also helped.

Actors tend to find amusement in off-screen incidents, and one such occasion was when Arthur Lowe was given a rather heavy and cumbersome revolver to use, without ammunition, because it didn't actually have to be fired. Arthur commented that as this was the case could not the prop department find a plastic replica which would be easier to handle and quicker to get out of the holster he was wearing. The prop department said they didn't think they could, so Arthur decided to look for one himself. He ordered a unit car and, accompanied by one or two other actors, including Paul Dawkins who was playing the German general, drove from the studios to the nearest Woolworth's store. The sight of a large limousine pulling up outside Woolworth's and Arthur, plus the German general in full military uniform, caused a few raised eyebrows among the passers-by. The Woolworth's staff were even more surprised at being confronted by Captain Mainwaring and a German general asking for a plastic revolver.

Above: 'Right men, get that furniture across the road. It will stop the Hun in his track'; a scene from the feature film.
Overleaf: Another scene from the feature film.

The store couldn't help, however, and Arthur, left the shop muttering, 'You could always buy a sixpenny pistol in Woolworth's when I was a lad'. There were some very funny sequences in the feature film, although it didn't have the overall atmosphere of the television production. It was not an expensive film to produce and many cinema managers have been delighted financially with the business they have done with it, particularly at holiday times. All of the actors and production team associated with it have agreed that

it has improved with age. The public certainly enjoys it because some of them have gone out of their way to say so each time it has an airing on television, which it has had on more than one occasion.

The official London premiere of the movie took place at the Columbia Cinema in London, and we all did some publicity appearances for it at various cinemas around the Home Counties when it was on general release.

In 1970 it was just another sequence of events during the reign of *Dad's Army*, but we all had to get back to work quickly in the television studios to make more episodes for the small screen.

THE FEATURE FILM

ARTHUR LOWE as Captain Mainwaring
JOHN LE MESURIER as Seargent Wilson
CLIVE DUNN as Lance Corporal Jones
JOHN LAURIE as Private Frazer
JAMES BECK as Private Walker
ARNOLD RIDLEY as Private Godfrey
IAN LAVENDER as Private Pike

Britain 1939, Walmington-on-Sea on the south coast of England ... George Mainwaring, Manager of Martin's Bank, has to refuse credit to a customer who wants to cash a cheque. The man, a Major-General Fullard, is angered by this and storms off.

Later that morning, Mainwaring and his two subordinates hear the Rt Hon Anthony Edens call for a national network of Local Defence Volunteers. They go to the Police Station to sign on, only to find chaos. Mainwaring decides to take charge and reconvenes the meeting at the Church Hall, where he forms the Walmington-on-Sea platoon of the LDV, appointing himself as captain, Wilson as his sergeant and Jack Jones, the town butcher, as lance corporal – but only after Jones bribes him with a pound of sausages! The men meet again that evening and as Mainwaring gives a lecture on their aims – despite virtually no means of defence – the Germans across the English Channel are drawing up plans to invade our island shores. They feel that their Operation 'Sealion' cannot fail to succeed ...

After a week, the first pieces of LD equipment arrive – armbands and ammunition, but no guns! One evening, as Mainwaring demonstrates the construction of petrol bombs, two workmen arrive at the church to remove all but one of the church bells, so that they can be melted down for the war effort. The vicar, an enthusiastic campanologist, cannot resist one last ringing of his beloved bells before they are

taken away. Unfortunately, Mainwaring and his LDVs misinterpret this as a warning of imminent invasion by the Germans and proceed to blockade the High Street with all manner of household items – including beds, wardrobes, and a large pot-plant courtesy of Private Godfrey! – and shortly hear the sounds of gunshots coming from the town. Expecting Germans, they instead discover that the shots are caused by the faulty exhaust of the bell workers' van, and feel rather foolish.

Time passes and the Dunkirk evacuation takes place. Frank Pike notices that Wilson is spending more and more time with Frank's widowed mother, Mavis. Meanwhile, Lance Corporal Jones comes up with various ingenious weapons for the now renamed Home Guard. These include a dive-bomber rocket gun (which blows up a barn housing the platoon), a one-man bullet-proof tank, constructed from an old bath (which nearly ends up causing the drowning of the operator, Private Walker) and finally Frazer presents his anti-vehicle device, which, in the event of invasion, could flood roads with oil, making them unpassable. However, due to gross negligence on the part of Jones, the machine is activated prematurely, floods the road and causes the Staff Car of Major-General Fullard to skid wildly and is almost written off. Fullard is furious – in fact, even more so when he recognises Mainwaring as the bloody bank clerk who wouldn't cash his cheque. A bad omen! Finally, the platoon are issued with proper uniforms and

guns and go on their first weekend manoeuvres in Jones' armoured butcher's van – which has recently been converted to run on gas. Jones manages to burst the gas bag during a false alarm, which results in Mainwaring's men arriving five hours late at camp. They use a traction engine to get them to the site but lose control of it and destroy the tents they were to have been using that night …

After sleeping in the open, they all miss breakfast (except Wilson). They are especially upset about this as they had already missed dinner the previous evening. However, they get on with their exercise, which is to guard a pontoon bridge on the river. Unbeknown to the platoon, part of the pontoon has been sabotaged by another group. Private Walker notices the cut rope and Jones and the others try to hold thee structure together. Just at this point, Major-General Fullard rides his horse, unawares, onto the loose section of the bridge and insists on a salute from Jones and his men. Jones tries to explain to his superior that it really isn't available, but fullard is adamant and they reluctantly let go of the rope to oblige his order. The Major-

General receives the salute as he and his horse drift off slowly downstream. Mainwaring and the platoon manage to lift Fullard off the horse onto an overhanging bridge, but in the process Jones falls onto the horse and pontoon section himself. He, in turn, is rescued by Mainwaring, Wilson and Frazer, who unwittingly become stranded themselves until later that evening when they run aground in the shallows. It is therefore unsurprising when, the next morning, Fullard informs Mainwaring that his position as leader of the platoon is in serious doubt after the weekend's mishaps.

A dejected platoon travel home to Walmington whilst, at the same time, a German aircraft crew have to bail out over the town. They land near the Church Hall, where the mayor is holding a meeting and quickly take the townspeople present hostage. Chief ARP Warden Hodges manages to escape and warn Major–General Fullard of the situation. The Home Guard arrives back in the church grounds

at this time, and Hodges informs them of the events. Fullard tells Mainwaring and his men to go home as this is a job for the Regular Army. However, Jones has the idea that the platoon could enter the church via the crypt and surprise the Germans. They do so and, once in the church, disguise themselves as choir members, enter the room and force the Germans to surrender. By the time Fullard and the others enter, the situation is under control. Mainwaring later reveals to Wilson that his gun was unloaded when he threatened one of the German airmen (as was the airman's own weapon). However, all the platoon are now heroes in the town and Mainwaring's position as captain of the Walmington-on-Sea Home Guard is secure.

FEATURE FILM SUPPORTING CAST

Liz Fraser (Mrs Pike), Bernard Archard (Major–General Fullard), Derek Newark (RSM), Bill Pertwee (Hodges), Frank Williams (the Vicar), Edward Sinclair (the Verger), Anthony Sagar (Police Sergeant), Pat Coombs (Mrs Hall), Roger Maxwell (Peppery Old Gent), Paul Dawkins (Nazi General), Sam Kydd (Nazi Orderly), Michael Knowles (Staff Captain), Fred Griffiths (Bert King), John Baskcomb (Mayor), Alvar Liddell (Newsreader) George Roubicek (German Radio Operator), Scott Fredericks (Nazi Photographer), Ingo Mogen-dorf (Nazi Pilot), Franz van Norde (Nazi Co-Pilot), John Henderson (Radio Shop Assistant), Harriet Rhys (Girl in Bank), Dervis Ward (AA patrolman), Robert Raglan (Inspector Hardcastle), John D. Collins (Naval Officer) and Alan Haines (Marine Officer).

The Platoon: Desmond Callum-Jones, Colin Bean, Frank Godfrey, Freddie Wiles, Freddie White, Leslie Noyes, David Fennell, Hugh Hastings, George Hancock, Bernard Severn.

FEATURE FILM PRODUCTION CREDITS

Screenplay by: Jimmy Perry and David Croft, using, in part, many sequences from 'The Man and the Hour' (TV Series One, 1968) and sections of other episodes.

Music Composed and conducted by: Wilfred Burns.

Produced by: John R. Sloan

Directed by: Norman Cohen

Studio sequences filmed at: Shepperton Studios, Shepperton, Middlesex.

Location sequences filmed at: Chalfont St Giles, Buckinghamshire (Walmington-on-Sea); Chobham, Surrey; Seaford, Sussex; and various streets around Shepperton, Middlesex.

Film Running Time: 94 minutes (Cinema); 90 minutes (TV/Video)

Copyright: 1971 Columbia (British) Productions Ltd.

Above: It's a good job we all use Persil ... The newly formed platoon keeping fit for the fight – even though the rest of the uniform hasn't arrived!

Opposite: L–R Bill Pertwee, Clive Dunn and John Le Mesurier during filming.

Below: 'War or no war, you can't leave that van here' – an AA patrolman antagonises Captain Mainwaring by failing to grasp the military importance of the Walmington-on-Sea Home Guard.

TREADING THE BOARDS

The stage musical of *Dad's Army* was a major event in our lives in 1975 and 1976. We had heard about it some time before, but in no great detail. We were all asked whether we would be available and if we wanted to do it. Bernard, now Lord Delfont, who had already produced many large-scale musicals and pantomimes, not only in London but all over the country, was to combine with Louis Michaels and Duncan Weldon of Triumph Theatre Productions in presenting the stage show. The television series was popular with the public and they all thought it would be a good box office attraction. Contracts were arranged, but as yet no London theatre had been decided upon. All the principal actors would be in the show, with the exception of John Laurie, who felt that working in the theatre every night and travelling between Buckinghamshire and London every day would be too tiring for him. The show was also to include Frank Williams, Teddy Sinclair, Pam Cundell, Janet Davies and myself, all of us regular members of the television series. Replacements had to be found for John Laurie and Jimmy Beck, who had died some time before. There was no question that John or Jimmy could be replaced, but the characters had to be reproduced. It was not an easy task, particularly for the actors who would be playing the well-known characters of Privates Frazer and Walker, but still creating a personality of their own, which is very important on stage. The two actors who were eventually cast in these difficult roles were John Bardon as Walker and Hamish Roughead as Frazer.

The ideas for the script and content of the show had been discussed but not in detail, and it was while we were filming, before we had received out scripts, that Jimmy Perry informed us what the show would be about. Jimmy is a very enthusiastic person at the best of times, but when he is in a dynamic mood, perhaps charged with a glass or two of red wine, he is unstoppable. The particular evening at the Bell Hotel in Thetford when he decided to explain to a few of us what he and David had in mind was both exhilarating and funny. He asked Frank Williams, Ted Sinclair and myself to come up to his room where he could explain the details. Once Jimmy had begun, he gave us a solo performance of the proposed show. He dashed about his bedroom, leapt on the bed, rushed to the door, and went in and out of the bathroom, depicting various scenes. He explained how the show would open up with some film of the 1940s on a back projection screen; he demonstrated this by mimicking Winston Churchill in front of the large mirror. He explained how Warden Hodges would make his first entrance from the audience, interrupting the verger and vicar who were singing a chanting-type song about the blackout. Private Pike would have to sing a big production number entitled, 'When can I have a banana again?', which we were to hear a lot more of once rehearsals began. Ian (Pike) was to be zipped up in a huge plastic banana (not seen in this country during World War II). Jimmy looked so funny leaping about the bedroom as a banana that Frank Williams laughed uncontrollably until he had to plead for Jimmy to stop. Jimmy, however, continued unabated. He then started to sing, 'Follow the

White Line', a song that advised people what to do when they were walking home in the black-out. This he demonstrated, taking us in tow in conga fashion around the room, and so he continued, demonstrating various acts, playing all the characters and singing all the songs until he finally sat down on his bed and said, 'Well, how does that sound?' Ted Sinclair, who had sat motionless through it all, said, 'I'm tired out and the show hasn't even started yet!'

The first day of rehearsal for the show was at the Richmond Theatre, the lovely Victorian playhouse in Surrey. The director was a young man called Roger Redfarn who had, among other things, been artistic director at the successful Belgrade Theatre in Coventry. David Croft and Jimmy Perry were obviously going to be very much in evidence, advising, suggesting and keeping a close eye on the production. The musical director who was in charge of a large orchestra was an American, Ed Coleman. Ed proved to be a tremendous help to us as rehearsals got underway and afterwards during the actual production. For Ed cajoled, shouted, encouraged and complimented the cast, all in the space of a few minutes. On the first day of rehearsal he got the whole company together and made us sing collectively and solo the first two bars of 'Somewhere over the Rainbow'.

Above: The main cast members outside the Theatre Royal, Newcastle. L–R: Jack Haig, Frank Williams, Edward Sinclair, Arthur Lowe, John Le Mesurier, Ian Lavender and Bill Pertwee.

His experience was such that he could judge our singing range with that short burst of song. The choreographer was Sheila O'Neill, who had the task of teaching people of all shapes and sizes, some with two left feet like me, and several of them new to a full stage musical, but each and every one very enthusiastic. Also in the cast was Joan Cooper, Arthur Lowe's wife, who was to play Private Godfrey's sister Dolly, as she had done on numerous occasions in the television series; Eric Longworth who had played the town clerk in several episodes; and Michael Bevis who was to feature in one of the production numbers. Also taking part were Norman MacLeod, Bernice Adams, Debbie Blackett, Ronnie Grange, Graham Hamilton, Vivian Pearman, Peggy Ann James, Barrie Stevens, Jan Todd, David Wheldon Williams, Alan Woodhouse, Michelle Summers, June Shand, Kevin Hubbard and Jeffrey Holland, who would be playing a mad German inventor as well as being part of the general production team.

Jeffrey did his audition for the show while he was playing a season at the Chichester Festival

 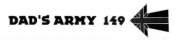

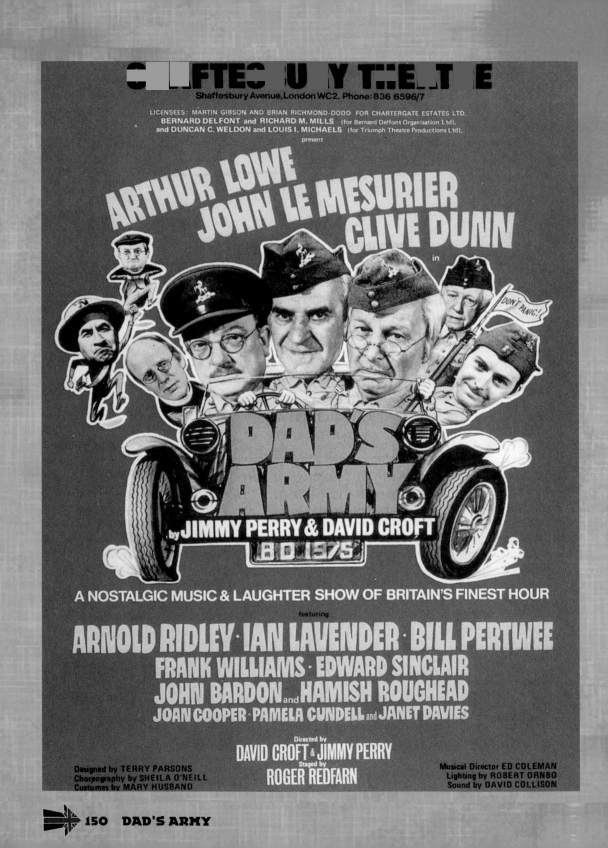

Theatre and on the recommendation of Roger Redfarn. Jeffrey was very depressed that he had been booked for only one of the plays at Chichester and not for all four plays in the repertoire as was usual. He had grown fond of that lovely city in the heart of the Sussex countryside so he was not in the best of spirits when he travelled up to London for the audition for the *Dad's Army* stage musical. Being a true professional, Jeffrey determined to do well in the audition and then to return for his last weeks at Chichester. He had learned the song 'When can I have a banana again?' as he knew this was going to be part of the show. He did the audition and was engaged immediately by David and Jimmy so he returned to Chichester in delight.

Jeffrey had considerable experience as an actor after he gave up an office job when he was young and decided to follow a career in the theatre. Four and a half years at the Belgrade Theatre in Coventry near his home town of Walsall and small parts in television had smoothed the rough edges, but *Dad's Army* was a turning point in his career. He later joined us for an episode in the television series as a driver of a heavy-duty service vehicle. In 1980 Jeffrey was cast by Jimmy and David as the comedian Spike in their new series *Hi-de-Hi* and from there he has never looked back. He recalls the time in his life when he went to audition for the stage musical of *Dad's Army*. 'I had a marvellous year with that show. Six months in London and six months on tour. From an audition I really wasn't too bothered about I got a job that was an absolute joy and afforded me the privilege of working with a cast and a show that were then and are now a legend. Just think, if I had done the four plays at Chichester instead of just one it would never have happened and my life and career in the theatre would almost certainly have been quite different.'

After three weeks rehearsal at Richmond we made out way north to Billingham, in Cleveland, for the out-of-town opening of the show.

We were due to run it in at the Forum Theatre there before moving into the Shaftesbury Theatre, London, in the autumn.

The Forum is a modern, well-equipped theatre, part of an entertainments complex with swimming-pool, squash courts, snooker, etc. Les Jobson, and ex-schoolmaster, the artistic director and his staff all combined to make us very welcome. However, the stage doorkeeper was obviously confused about our names for when John le Mesurier arrived, he greeted him with the words, 'Good morning, Sir, are you Arnold Lowe?'

The extensive workshops of the Forum had made all the sets, most of which were quite complicated and extra staff had to be drafted in to handle them. They were designed to represent the two sides of the English Channel and consisted of two electrically controlled trucks that moved on to the stage from the wings. Corporal Jones was on top of one truck guarding the British coast, while the German general (played by me) and the mad inventor sat on top of the opposite truck looking out from France.

Opposite and Below: Advertising material for the stage play of *Dad's Army*.

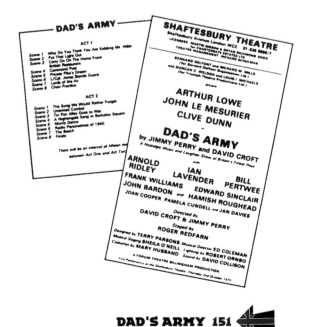

Above: Jeffrey Holland.
Opposite: A scene from the production: German General (the author) and mad inventor (Jeffrey Holland).

On another occasion Private Godfrey would glide on stage on a truck that represented his cottage garden, talking to his sister Dolly (who was so adept at making upside-down cakes) about the current cricket scores, which to him were more important than anything else. On another truck Field Marshall Goering would be extolling the virtues of the Luftwaffe and how they were going to blast the British out of the skies. The scene finished with Godfrey reciting 'Lords of the Air' and the boys and girls forming a choir in the background. This was a very moving moment in the show and it was played superbly by Arnold Ridley and Joan Cooper. We were very lucky to have such a good company of boys and girls as a back-up to the established principals. They had been picked for their singing and dancing abilities, but were also to prove accomplished actors.

During the technical rehearsal there were moments of anxiety concerning whether certain equipment was going to work or whether a scene that had been envisaged on paper would prove successful in practice. One such scene was the banana production that some of us had been privy to in Jimmy's bedroom at Thetford. It was rehearsed and re-rehearsed many times. We would get to the theatre in the morning only to be told that for the next couple of hours, only the banana people were required. So some of us would simply walk around the Billingham shopping precinct. We all agreed that we would never eat another banana! The problems with the song were finally sorted out and it proved to be a big success in the show, much to Ian Lavender's relief because he had been in and out of that plastic banana skin many times over.

On other occasions some members of the company would be given the whole day off because scenes were being rehearsed that did not include them, so we would pile into a car and take a trip out on the moors for a pub lunch, or go down to the North Yorkshire coastal harbours of Staithes and Robin Hood's Bay. The beautiful scenery and friendliness of the Yorkshire people act as a tonic, and to walk into the little resort of Staithes from the car park on the hill and wander among the fisherman's cottages is a joy. Whitby is a much larger place, but is certainly worth a visit and, apart from a particular little establishment near Yorkshire's Headingly cricket ground, has the best fish and chip shops in the country, and even one or two pubs make sure their fish luncheons taste like gourmet dishes.

Opening night at the Forum was now getting very close. We were working long hours on some days and Roger Redfarn was becoming oblivious of the time of day as we went through songs, dance routines, dialogue and costume rehearsals. At two o'clock one morning I realised that the uncomplaining boys and girls had had no supper, not even a sandwich, and our strength was beginning to sag. I therefore walked on to the stage and, quite out of turn, announced that everyone has obviously had enough for that night. There was a silence in which you could have heard a pin drop. Suddenly Arthur Lowe said, 'I quite agree', and that was the end of rehearsals for that night.

Above: Mainwaring: 'Now if a Nazi stormtrooper comes cycling into view, pick up the nearest chair, push the chair legs through his spokes, grab his gun and there's another Jerry in the bag, simple!'

L–R: Hamish Roughhead (back to camera), Arnold Ridley, Clive Dunn, Arthur Lowe, Graham Hamilton, Norman Macleod, John Le Mesurier, Ian Lavender, Eric Longworth, John Bardon. A scene from the production at the Shaftesbury Theatre, London.

Below: Rehearsal of the 'Floral Dance' for the Royal Variety Performance at the London Palladium.

Apart from all the production numbers they were involved in, some of the boys and girls were understudying the principals and had to learn their lines as well, which was a considerable task. Eric Longworth was covering for Arthur Lowe, Michael Bevis for John Le Mesurier and Norman Macleod for Clive Dunn. Norman was one of the principal singers and had at one time been lead singer with a famous Canadian group, The Maple Leaf Four. There was a very complicated production number called 'Too Late' about the killing of General Gordon at Khartoum which featured Clive Dunn recalling Corporal Jones' experiences as a young soldier. John Le Mesurier had a scene with Private Pike and his mother, which led into 'A Nightingale Sang in Berkeley Square', sung by John. This was given all the experience of John's theatrical technique and proved to be one of those quiet but delightful moments that you occasionally experience in the theatre.

Several of us were involved in a scene that concerned radio personalities of the 1940s. Arthur Lowe did a very passable impersonation of Robb Wilton, with all the comic mannerisms of that great humourist. In fact, as I have mentioned earlier, Arthur's timing and general approach to comedy was reminiscent of Wilton.

Pam Cundell and Joan Cooper appeared as Elsie and Doris Waters (Gert and Daisy), sisters of Jack Warner (the *Dixon of Dock Green* policeman); three of the girls combined in a very good presentation of the American favourites, the Andrews sisters; and Arthur also played Mr Lovejoy with Michael Bevis as Ramsbottom and Ian Lavender as Enoch as 'We Three in Happidrome' fame who were a huge radio success during the war. I was given the opportunity to portray the cheeky chappy, Max Miller. I was slightly worried about performing this at Billingham, because although Miller had been a great bill topper in his heyday in variety at the London Palladium and else-where, he had never performed in the most northern areas of the country. I had actually worked with Max Miller when I was playing in variety in the 1950s, so I had some idea of his style and this helped considerably.

To complete the entertainment scene of the 1940s, Arthur Lowe and John Le Mesurier appeared as Flanagan and Allen, those great stars of the Crazy Gang. The song 'Hometown' began with Arthur and John walking across the stage and when they got to the other side they picked up two more members of the cast who were dressed the same way, they then walked back again and picked up two more members from the other side, and so it went on, with the whole cast eventually arriving on stage with those in the back rows carrying life-size cut-outs of Flanagan and Allen and all singing 'Hometown'. It was a tremendously effective scene. The only two members of the cast who were not involved in 'Hometown' were myself and Jeffrey Holland; we followed high up on our truck, commenting on the uncertainties of our future now that it looked as if the Allies were going to win the war.

One of the most enjoyable pieces to perform was the Morris Dance, which involved a disciplined routine that went haywire when it was performed by Mainwaring's boys, together with the Warden who started arguing with Jones and brandishing his club, causing chaos until Mainwaring restored order. The sight of people dressed in white costumes, panama hats, bells and colourful tassels looked most attractive.

Another enjoyable piece was the Floral Dance, a comedy routine that also involved the whole cast and which was a rehearsal for the Home Guard and citizens of Walmington of a choir concert they were going to give in aid of wounded soldiers. It not only included some wonderful visual comedy but also very funny dialogue. Both 'The Morris Dance' and 'The Choir Practice' had been adapted for the stage from the television episodes, so there was a

certain amount of confidence in them.

The opening night suddenly arrived and we just hoped that the packed theatre would receive the show well. We need not have worried, however, for apart from one or two minor technical hitches and over-running a little, most people enjoyed it. It hadn't been easy for Roger Redfarn or Jimmy and David, but no matter what the directors do, everything depends on the actors and actresses once the curtain goes up.

The rest of our short stay at Billingham went well, with crowds coming in from all over the North East to see us. We had a very friendly array of dressers and stage staff, which certainly helped the overall atmosphere.

Once back in London we were to open our West End run at the Shaftesbury Theatre. Some cuts had to be made during the two or three days' rehearsal at the Shaftesbury as we were still over-running. At this time I was asked to record a song for EMI that had been written around a phrase that I often used in the television series describing Mainwaring's mob as 'hooligans'; the reverse side was to be an oldie, 'Get Out and Get Under the Moon'. This was recorded in company with Norman Macleod from the stage show.

We had a few days of previews at the Shaftesbury and then came the official opening night. The atmosphere was electric, with a packed house that included friends and relations, and it seems we would stay at the London venue for a while yet. One night at the theatre Norman Macleod recognised the former prime minister Sir Alec Douglas Home in the audience. On his way home to Brighton Norman found himself standing next to Sir Alec on the platform of the Underground station and asked him if he had enjoyed the show. Sir Alec replied, 'Very much, I'm a fan of *Dad's Army*'. Some of us had met Sir Alec previously when he was our host at a Saints and Sinners charity lunch in London. He was kind and thoughtful on that occasion and proved to be a charming person.

Very early into the run we were all asked to stay on stage after the show. We were then informed that we had been invited to take part in the annual Royal Variety Performance at the London Palladium in the presence of Her Majesty the Queen and the Duke of Edinburgh. This was exciting news and it was decided that we should perform the Floral Dance choir item, as this was not only a good comedy piece which was going well at the Shaftesbury, but it also included the whole cast. We had had one or two bomb scares in London during the autumn of 1975 and on a couple of occasions it had affected our theatre. The audience was asked to leave halfway through a performance and we also had to go. It was amusing to see Arthur Lowe in Mainwaring style saying, 'Right, follow me men', and off we would march up the road to the pub where we would have a drink before we were told that it was a false alarm and then we would return to the theatre to continue the show. As a result of these bomb scares there was a tremendous amount of security around the Palladium for the royal show.

When the weekend arrived for the royal performance we used the Shaftesbury Theatre as our base and were shuttled backwards and forwards to the Palladium by coach for rehearsal. On Sunday and Monday (the day of the show) we were driven back and forth along Oxford Street with packs of sandwiches and flasks of coffee. We were continually being searched and given identity papers. After we had finished the final rehearsal on Monday we were all dispersed to different buildings around the Palladium because there is only limited dressing-room accommodation there and with over 350 people taking part in the show we could not all be accommodated. The Kwa Zulu dancers were housed with the Rhos Male Voice Choir in a pub somewhere near – I wonder what they made of one another.

The finale of the Royal Variety performance must be as well rehearsed as any other item to ensure that the entire cast can fit on to the stage.

Above: The line-up for the final curtain rehearsal of the 1975 Royal Variety Performance: L–R: Harry Secombe, Vera Lynn, Michael Crawford, Telly Savalas, Count Basie, Charles Aznavour, Bruce Forsyth, the cast of *Dad's Army*, Dukes and Lee, Kris Kremo and (behind) all the artistes taking part.

Below: An early Royal Performance at the BBC Television Centre in 1971. R–L: Vera Lynn, Eric Morecambe, Ernie Wise, Eddie Braben, Dave Allen, Huw Weldon (back to the camera), Dudley Moore, Her Majesty The Queen and the cast of *Dad's Army* – Ian Lavender is just out of shot.

There was Count Basie and his Band, the Rhos Male Voice Choir, Kwa Zulu dancers, the *Billy Liar* company from Drury Lane Theatre, Telly Savalas (Kojak) and his cabaret company, the cast of *Dad's Army*, plus all the other principals, Bruce Forsyth, Vera Lynn, Charles Aznavour, Dukes and Lee, Harry Secombe and the huge orchestra.

We were called over to the Palladium from our hiding place nearby just before the Royal Family arrived. We were on stage early, so had a long wait until the final curtain. We certainly saw the Duke of Edinburgh laughing at our performance and it was an exciting moment to stand on the stage in front of a huge audience and in the presence of the royal couple. The entire cast were lined up after the show and introduced to Her Majesty and His Royal Highness, and although it is a long evening for the performers it is equally long for them.

A moment in the evening that made me laugh was when we were waiting for the final line-up. I was standing next to Arthur Lowe and next to him were members of the Kwa Zulu African dancers. With so many people involved, each performer is only concerned with taking his right position on the stage. On this particular occasion Arthur and I were suddenly conscious that something was happening next to him. We looked around and saw one of the dancers next to Arthur breast-feeding her baby. The baby and his mother's breast were

Above: Some of the cast are presented to the Queen and the Duke of Edinburgh at the Royal Variety Performance, 1975.

level with Arthur's eye line. Arthur did one of his double takes and then said to the lady, 'He enjoys a drink does he? I could do with one right now!'

Other notable happy occasions when we were at the Shaftesbury theatre included celebrating Arnold Ridley's 80th birthday. This was performed on stage with a huge cake and the national press in attendance. It was remarkable to think that this dear man of 80 was still playing nightly, plus two matinees a week, in the theatre.

Several of the cast were invited to a tea party at 10 Downing Street where Prime Minister Harold Wilson was hosting a party for underprivileged children. We were greeted by Harold, his wife Mary and Marcia Williams. Several of our friends were there including Eric Morecambe and Ernie Wise. It was a marvellous experience to be in that historic residence and to be in the same rooms where so many great statesmen and women had been in the past. Harold Wilson made everybody feel welcome. He said to me at one stage, 'Come and sit here, this is Henry Kissinger's favourite chair'. It was wonderful to see how the Prime Minister together with Morecambe and Wise gave all the children their presents. Although Eric cracked plenty of jokes, Harold Wilson

kept up with him and sometimes even outwitted him. Before we let Mary Wilson asked us to come and see the kitchen. It was huge, with large scrubbed tables. Mary had just made a Christmas cake and she asked us if we had children and would we like to take a slice of cake home for them. As we left Number 10 I took note of all the wonderful pictures that were hanging on the staircase.

By February 1976 we were told that we would be finishing at the Shaftesbury and making a long tour around the country. A few items would have to be changed and the scenery altered because at times we would be playing to much smaller theatres. The orchestra was also to be reduced, but we were still going to have our wonderful musical director, Ed Coleman, with us. Clive Dunn was only doing half the tour as he had prior commitments, so Jack Haig was to play Corporal Jones when Clive left. We opened the tour at the Opera House, Manchester. The pre-publicity at the theatre left something to be desired, and for the first few days we were dashing about doing radio, news-paper and television interviews, and even dropping hand-bills into shops, which should have been handed out well before we arrived in the city. Audiences increased after the first week and by the end of the third they were quite large. After Manchester we moved on to Blackpool which, out of season, had only a few senior citizens on holiday. We had some good social evenings in Blackpool after the performances, but that resort out of season is not exactly Las Vegas!

After Blackpool we moved to Newcastle and not only did we enjoy full houses at nearly every performance but the weather improved and it became one of the hottest summers for years. The Geordies are great people, very friendly and they like their theatre.

We played Bournemouth and some of the cast's families joined us there. We then moved to Birmingham and on to Nottingham, where we were able to get in some cricket practice. A match had been arranged for us to play when

Below: Arnold Ridley celebrates his 80th birthday in style.

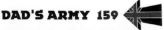

we arrived in Bradford so we thought we should loosen up a bit. At Nottingham we practised at the famous Trent Bridge ground, the headquarters of Nottinghamshire CC. A few of us, including 80 year old Arnold Ridley, had a gentle practice in the outdoor nets and then went in to the indoor cricket school. At one point Ian Lavender was bowling to me and hit me fair and square on my big toe. Brian Clough, the Nottingham Forest football manager, was also having some net practice and he drove me straight over to the football ground across the road and called the doctor to drill my toe which had already turned black. The drill did the trick and I had no after-effects.

While we were in Nottingham we were invited to a very peculiar film party after the show one night. All those invited went, with the exception of Arthur Lowe, and I reckon he must have known something. The party was in a fairly small semi-detached house and a couple of cars had been laid on to take us there. We were shown into a lounge which had a bar and a huge Hammond organ which went right up into the ceiling above. Cheese and ham rolls were handed around by the host and his wife and then their two small daughters came in and proceeded to play the enormous Hammond organ. The whole house, and probably the adjoining house next door too, shook like crazy with the vibrations, and when it finished the little girls took a bow and went to bed. The host then asked us if we would like to see some funny films. Arnold Ridley, who had been having a doze in spite of the noise of the organ, said, 'How nice, we like comedy films', thinking of vintage Lloyd or Laurel and Hardy. It took us a few seconds to understand that the films were not to be 'funny ha ha!', but 'funny very peculiar', so we beat a hasty retreat out of the house and back to our hotels.

During our stay in Brighton on the Sussex coast, the theatre was completely sold out. We also had the chance to see relations and renew old acquaintances; it was pleasant for me as my wife and I with our baby son had lived in that busy resort some years earlier.

It is always enjoyable to spend a week or two in Yorkshire and this we did when we played Bradford Alhambra. Within fifteen minutes' drive outside any big town in that part of the country you will find yourself in the most beautiful countryside. It was from Bradford that we travelled to play our cricket match for which we had practised in Nottingham. Arthur Lowe was the President of the Hayfield Cricket Club in Derbyshire, as his father had been before him. The club wanted to build a new pavilion and the cast of *Dad's Army* were going to play Hayfield to raise the money to make this possible. Luckily, it was a lovely sunny Sunday when we set off by coach from Bradford. The idea was to make a weekend of it, staying in various pubs in Hayfield overnight. When we arrived the little village was seething with people who had literally turned out in their thousands 'to see their television idols', as one gentleman put it.

We all had a good lunch accompanied by plenty of the local brew. As Arthur said, 'By gum, we've stopped a few barrels going sour today.' He inspected his side before the match in good military fashion and the game got under way. Every stroke played by the *Dad's Army* team drew applause from the huge crowd and a catch made by them was more than the onlookers could bear. I was batting and had two or three when Arnold Ridley came in and it was decided that he should have a runner. Arnold played one or two fine strokes and then became rather excited. He hit a full toss into the outfield and started to run, together with his runner and myself. We all finished up in a heap at one end and it was deemed that I was out.

At the end of the match enough money had been collected from the sale of programmes and raffles to make it possible for work to begin immediately on the new pavilion and Arthur officially opened it a year or two later. We stopped a few more barrels going sour in the evening and started off next morning for the

Below: Arthur Lowe inspecting his 'troops' before the cricket match at Hayfield.

Right: Arthur Lowe and General Roosevelt admiring Chamberlain's famous umbrella.

Bottom: Lunch party with Mrs Chamberlain.

Overleaf: The cast of the stage show.

return journey to Bradford. Arthur was in one of his skittish moods and when the coach was stopped to allow the gentlemen in the party to relieve themselves on the side of the road, hidden by the coach, Arthur quietly told the coach driver to move on. The sight of a dozen males standing in a straight line hastily adjusting their dress was like something out of a French farce.

We played the Richmond Theatre, where it had started with those early rehearsals, and this allowed most of us to live at home that week. It also coincided with my 50th birthday, and as a special surprise the company had a huge cake made in the shape of my white warden's helmet. It was here at Richmond that just before the finale of the mid-week matinee Jeffrey Holland received the news that his wife had gone into labour in hospital in Coventry. Jeffrey asked his understudy to take over for the evening show and by a miracle of good rail connections was in Coventry in two hours. As was expected it was a difficult birth, but the result was a lovely boy. Although Arthur Lowe quite naturally, and with reason, scolded Jeff on his return to the show next day for unprofessional conduct in the theatre, the first bouquet of flowers to arrive at the hospital for Jeff's wife Ellie was 'From Arthur and Joan Lowe, with love'.

The last date of the tour was at Bath and it was a most memorable finale to the six months we had been on the road. During the first week in Bath the Duke of Beaufort, whose famous home Badminton is not far away, brought in a party to see the show one night and asked us to have drinks with him afterwards. Among his party was Neville Chamberlain's daughter-in-law who invited us to have lunch with her and her two teenage children while we were in the city. This we did and it turned out to be a fascinating day. Among her guests was General Roosevelt, the late American president's son. Mrs Chamberlain's husband (Neville Chamberlain's son) had been an MP himself, but had died fairly young. Mrs Chamberlain and her

children were the complete hosts that day in Bath. We were shown all the mementoes concerning her father-in-law, his gifts from King George VI who was a close friend, and the letters he sent to his son during the Munich Crisis in 1938. These letters were smuggled out of Germany by various means at the time and were not even trusted to the diplomatic bag. They state quite clearly that Chamberlain was

buying as much time as possible because he knew that Hitler was not to be trusted. To see those actual handwritten letters concerning a period I remember so vividly as a youngster was an extraordinary experience. Suddenly it felt as if one was back in 1938 reliving those nerve-racking days, and it made us all realise what agonising moments our parents had gone through just waiting to see what Chamberlain could do to save the country from going to war. When he arrived back in England with that piece of paper, and on the steps of the aeroplane announced that it was 'peace in our time', a huge sigh of relief went through the country.

So a year with the stage show came to an end. We however still had another television series to make before we finally said farewell to *Dad's Army*.

THE STAGE SHOW
(1975-76)

ARTHUR LOWE as Captain Mainwaring
JOHN LE MESURIER as Sergeant Wilson
CLIVE DUNN and JACK HAIG as Lance Corporal Jones
ARNOLD RIDLEY as Private Godfrey
IAN LAVENDER as Private Pike
JOHN BARDON as Private Walker
HAMISH ROUGHEAD as Private Frazer

ACT 1

Scene 1 WHO DO YOU THINK YOU ARE KIDDING, MR HITLER?
Orchestra and company
The show opens with black-and-white back-projected World War II news footage. The cast slowly descend a flight of stairs to the strains of 'Who Do You Think You Are Kidding Mr Hitler?' (This is an orchestral version with accompanying vocals from all the company).

Scene 2 PUT THAT LIGHT OUT
Bill Pertwee, Frank Williams, Edward Sinclair and ensemble
Hodges, making his entrance from the audience, warns the vicar and the verger that they are showing a light. He then leads them in a song, performed in a chanting fashion, explaining blackout regulations. The vicar's and the verger's input highlights how awkward it is to blackout a church!

Scene 3 CARRY ON ON THE HOME FRONT
Bill Pertwee, Frank Williams, Edward Sinclair, Pamela Cundell, Janet Davies, Joan Cooper and ensemble
A musical number which leads into a scene in Walmington-on-Sea's British Restaurant, where Mainwaring and the platoon have gone to eat.

Scene 4 COMMAND POST
Arthur Lowe and John Le Mesurier
Mainwaring and Wilson keep watch on the
waters of the English Channel from the cliff-top.

Scene 5 PRIVATE PIKE'S DREAM
Ian Lavender, John Bardon, Bernice Adams and ensemble
Aided by John Bardon as Walker, Ian Lavender as Private Pike sings a big production number entitled, 'When Can I Have a Banana Again?', whilst zipped into a huge plastic banana. (Because of a government import ban, bananas were not available in Britain during the war.)

Scene 6 LANCE CORPORAL JONES STANDS GUARD
Clive Dunn, Bill Pertwee and ensemble
Jones stands guard on the English Coast, while the German general (a dual role for Bill Pertwee) and the Mad Inventor look across the English Channel from occupied France.

Scene 7 LORDS OF THE AIR
Arnold Ridley and ensemble
Private Godfrey and his sister Dolly sit outside their cottage, drinking tea, while across the Channel Field Marshall Goering is extolling the virtues of the Luftwaffe he commands, pronouncing that they will blast the British Squadrons from the skies. The scene culminates in a moving reading, by Arnold Ridley, of the poem 'Lords of the Air', backed by a choir of girls and boys.

Scene 8 CHOIR PRACTICE
Arthur Lowe and company
Rounding off the first act, this scene depicts a re-

hearsal for the platoon and the people of Walmington-on-Sea of a planned choir concert they are to give in aid of wounded soldiers. The scene closes with the cast performing the Floral Dance.

ACT 2

Scene 1 THE SONG WE WOULD RATHER FORGET

Bill Pertwee, Frank Williams, Edward Sinclair, Pamela Cundell, Janet Davies, Joan Cooper and ensemble
A rendition of 'We're Going to Hang Out the Washing on the Siegfried Line', which leads into 'We'll Meet Again'.

Scene 2 UNARMED COMBAT

Scene 3 TIN PAN ALLEY GOES TO WAR

Scene 4 A NIGHTINGALE SANG IN BERKELEY SQUARE

John Le Mesurier and Ian Lavender
After discussing women with Private Pike, Sergeant Wilson, nostalgically recalling a past acquaintance – who was completely different from his current love – performs 'A Nightingale Sang in Berkeley Square'.

Scene 5 MORRIS DANCE

Scene 6 RADIO PERSONALITIES OF 1940

Arthur Lowe, John Le Mesurier, Ian Lavender, Bill Pertwee, Pamela Cundell, Joan Cooper, Michael Bevis and company.
This scene is composed of several set pieces and involves the cast impersonating the radio stars of the day. Arthur Lowe portrays Robb Wilton, while Pamela Cundell and Joan Cooper showcase their talents as the Elsie and Doris Waters' creations Gert and Daisy. Three young female members of the company join in the fun as the Andrew Sisters, and Bill Pertwee becomes the cheeky chappie – Max Miller. The tribute concludes with a rendition of 'Hometown', featuring Arthur Lowe and John Le Mesurier as Flanagan and Allen.

Scene 7 THE BEACH

Arthur Lowe, John Le Mesurier, Clive Dunn and Graham Hamilton
We end up on the beach, saying goodbye, rolling up the barbed wire: the war's over and we're going back to our business. And at the end, the beach is deserted, Mainwaring goes down to the

floats and delivers the epilogue and we get through to the truth of the man – all the fooling's over, all the pomposity's pricked – and find out what he really believes. He says: 'The Home Guard never went into battle, but the two million men – shop assistants, factory workers, doctors, lawyers, men from every walk of life – gave of their spare time and, in some cases, their lives, to defend their homeland. And if ever this island were in danger again, men like those would be there once more – standing ready.'

Scene 8 FINALE

Orchestra
Leading on from Mainwaring's speech, a strident, upbeat orchestral version of the Dad's Army *theme brings the show to its conclusion.*

STAGE SHOW SUPPORTING CAST

Joan Cooper as Miss Godfrey, **Pamela Cundell** as Mrs Fox, **Janet Davies** as Mrs Pike, **Jack Haig** (Lance Corporal Jones, for half of the tour) with: Eric Longworth, Michael Bevis, Norman MacLeod, Bernice Adams, Debbie Blackett, Ronnie Grange, Graham Hamilton, Vivien Pearman, Peggy Ann James, Barrie Stevens, Jan Todd, David Wheldon Williams, Alan Woodhouse, Michelle Summers, June Shand, Kevin Hubbard and Jeffrey Holland.

STAGE SHOW PRODUCTION CREDITS

Written by: Jimmy Perry and David Croft
Directed by: David Croft and Jimmy Perry
Staged by: Roger Redfarn

An LP was released by Warner Bros that featured many musical numbers and sections of dialogue. The recording was made at the Forum Theatre, Billingham, and produced by Alan A. Freeman.

Performed at:

The Forum theatre, Billingham Cleveland, (late Summer 1975): Shaftesbury Theatre, Shaftesbury Avenue, London, (October 1975–February 1976). First Performance: Thursday 2 October 1975.

On tour:

February-August 1976 (theatres unknown unless specified): Manchester (the Opera House), Blackpool, Newcastle (Theatre Royal: Tuesday 22 June for two weeks), Bournemouth (the Winter Gardens), Birmingham, Nottingham, Brighton (the Theatre Royal), Bradford (the Alahambra), Richmond (The Richmond Theatre), the run finishing in Bath.

DEMOB

Although rumours were flying around in the summer of 1977 that we might be recording the last series of *Dad's Army*, I don't think it made any great impression on the actors as we had heard the possibility before. However, when we had the final scripts in our possession, which were all very funny with some intriguing situations, the last episode did give a certain suggestion that the end might be in sight. We thought that if it was the end of the series, at least we would go out on a high note and not outstay our welcome with the public who had shown so much affection for us, even including the show's 'baddie', Air Raid Warden Bert Hodges.

In the entertainment business actors are always moving to pastures new and are used to change, and it has to be remembered that *Dad's Army* had lasted for nine years. The writers, Jimmy and David, had done a marathon job in creating 80 episodes altogether, as well as the feature film and stage show.

We had enjoyed the pre-filming of the last series at Thetford, the last episode of which, 'Never Too Old', showed our gallant lads drinking a toast to the Home Guard and Mainwaring declaring that 'Men will always stand together whenever Britain needs them.' The episode also included the marriage of Corporal Jones to Mrs Fox, who, incidentally, was given away by Captain Mainwaring. So Jones had finally beaten his rivals for his sweetheart's hand.

A nice touch by David and Jimmy was to include the wives and girlfriends (those with Equity membership) of the cast to play the wedding guests. It was, in fact, the last ever episode of *Dad's Army* and it had finished without fuss and with no dramatic ending as

Above: Inspecting the troops: the 'Magnificent Seven' with (at left) Bernard Archard.

Opposite: Cheers! A smiling platoon raise a glass to the show that made them household names.

generally happens in television series' nowadays. The series ended quietly, just as it had begun in 1968.

We had become a working family and as all families we enjoyed the social life connected with the series. Apart from the social occasions already mentioned, we had several parties in our various homes and on Arthur Lowe's boat during the rehearsal and recording weeks in London. Arthur also arranged a marvellous day for us on the Regent's Canal by way of a promotion, which started off with drinks at his nearby flat. The craft we were using was quite new and a regular floating restaurant on the canal. It was a gloriously sunny day with plenty of good food and wine, and our wives were included too, which was not always possible on other occasions.

Another unusual trip was when we went to Blackpool to switch on the illuminations. We assembled with our wives at Euston Station, and we were greeted by a gold-braided station master who showed us to our own dining car. An agreeable lunch on the train, accompanied by much conversation, eventually brought us

to Blackpool in what seemed no time at all. We were given a civic welcome by the mayor, and after various media interviews, we changed into our uniforms ready to throw the switch that would illuminate the famous Golden Mile. It was now pouring with rain, but the job was done very cheerily with a little assistance from a wee dram or two. We then boarded an open-top tram to make our journey, as is customary on these occasions, along the 'mile'. In spite of the rain the public turned out in great numbers to cheer us on our way. The evening finished with a dinner in the company of the civic dignitaries. It had all been quite an experience.

We were asked to open a charity fete on the Isle of Wight on one occasion and some dear friends of ours, Tony and Sybil Snelling, were part of the organising committee. We had a rehearsal in London on the day in question, but David Croft allowed us to finish at midday. We were picked up at the BBC by a minibus and driven to Fairoaks Aerodrome, near Woking, where an Islander aircraft was waiting to fly us to the island. The Britten Islander was an aircraft that had been developed at Bembridge Airport for sale around the world as an executive jet. We crowded into the aircraft on yet another wonderfully sunny day and made our way over the Surrey hills and the Hampshire coastline with glorious views of the Solent below and on to Bembridge Airport. Before landing, the pilot circled around over the area of the fete a few times, dipping his wings, and the huge crowd below responded by waving anything they could lay their hands on. Some of our families had gone on earlier by ferry from Portsmouth. We were met at Bembridge Airport by cars waiting to whisk us off to the venue. The crowds seemed even bigger when we got there and as well as walking round the stalls and joining in the general fun, we went into a tent in shifts to sign autographs. Again with a little assistance from a tot or two accompanied by a

Above: Mrs Fox with her intended, Corporal Jones.
Opposite: Hodges: 'Well, it's all over Mainwaring.'
Mainwaring: 'Yes, indeed.'
Hodges: 'I know what you're thinking.'
Mainwaring: 'Yes, you'll have to go back to being just an ordinary greengrocer now.'
Hodges: 'And you'll have to go back to being just an ordinary bank manager.'
(Dialogue by Jimmy Perry and David Croft.)

lot of ice, because it was extremely hot. We finished the day at the Snelling residence with all sorts of edible goodies (and another tot or two!) before we were driven back to Bembridge airport for the return flight to Fairoaks after a wonderful day.

Receiving the BAFTA award for the best situation comedy programme was a night to remember. Not only did we receive the prize from Princess Anne, but we wined and dined at London's Albert Hall in the company of some of the great entertainers of our business. Sitting on the next table to us, and there to present one of the awards, was the American

 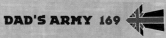

film star Ray Milland, someone we had all admired and seen many times on our cinema screens. We had to wait in a tunnel, one of the many that led up to the stage, and when we were called it was a memorable experience to walk on stage to the programme's signature tune, 'Who do you think you are kidding, Mr Hitler?', and to face the hundreds of people from our   profession, and then to be introduced by Richard Attenborough to the Princess. The thunderous applause which greeted our presentation was still ringing in our ears as we walked off. It was raining when we finally left the Albert Hall at the end of the evening, but even having to wait for a taxi outside did not dampen our spirits. I was just about to step in to one with my wife when I noticed astronomer Patrick Moore also waiting with his mother. We ushered them into our cab, and years later Patrick reminded me of this when were were playing cricket together for the Lord's Taverners.

When the series did finally finish I think it slipped the minds of the BBC hierarchy to give us the sort of send off that would have been appreciated at the time, but the *Daily Mirror* stepped in after their television critic announced their news in their columns. The *Mirror* invited us and our wives, plus a few friends, to a sumptuous dinner at London's Cafe Royal, and they presented us with medals which were inscribed 'for services to television entertainment'. Speeches were made, some slightly ribald in content, and a good time was had by all. There was however more to come. We did get an invitation from the Board of Governors, no less, of the BBC at a later date to have lunch with them and compliments about the series were gratefully received. At the end of nine years, we had been blessed with two writers and a host of backroom boys and girls who we will always remember with great affection.

Centre: Switching on the Blackpool Illuminations.
Clockwise, from left: A scene from : 'Menace from the Deep'; John Le Mesurier during shooting; a signed frontispiece of the very last script; and a scene from 'Come in, Your Time is Up".

LIFE AFTER DAD'S

Forty years on, people ask me whether any of us from *Dad's Army* still get together, and I'm always pleased to tell them that we do, although, because Clive lives in Portugal we don't see him as often as we would like. He did however come over for the large celebration held at the Imperial War Museum to mark the 40th anniversary of the show. That event got a lot of television and other media coverage, as did the whole phenomenon that is *Dad's Army*. During 2008, as well as the repeats of episodes, there were many programmes and interviews about the series, including a special chat show, hosted by Jonathan Ross, which was luckily made before he got into trouble!

Apart from Ian Lavender of course, who's always in some show or other, and the indefatigable Pam Cundell, the rest of us still work, but only when it suits us. I enjoy doing the odd show or after-dinner speech and I'm also involved in raising money for various charities, including a children's hospice in Cornwall.

The continuing popularity of *Dad's Army* can be measured by the size of its fan club: the Dad's Army Appreciation Society started with about 300 members in 1993 and now has over 1700, and thanks largely to this very well-run club we are able to meet up, not only with our fellow performers but also with our loyal audience, some of whom are very young indeed! There was an attempt to start a club in 1990, by a fan who lived near Exeter, but he had to give it up due to work commitments, and it was then taken over by a young Yorkshire lad, Tadge Muldoon. Tadge really got it going and wasted no time in producing a newsletter entitled *Permission to Speak, Sir!* The year 1995 was a turning point for the society as there was enough interest to arrange the first 'convention'. This was held in March in London and the following month, a New Zealand branch was set up and launched by a student, Dave Homewood.

Sadly in May 1995 came the news that Tadge had been involved in a serious accident and he later died as a result of his injuries, leaving his wife and two sons. We all felt it was important not to let all Tadge's hard work go to waste, so, in my role as President of the Society, I appointed a charming retired draughtsman, Jack Wheeler, as 'Commander-in-Chief'. Jack subsequently enlisted the help of two fans who were happy to assist: Paul Carpenter, and, a little later, Tony Pritchard, both of whom had full-time jobs, but put all their spare hours into helping with the huge amount of administration involved in supporting such a thriving organisation. They're still at it today!

In the period after Tadge's death, a newsletter was issued, imparting the sad news and change of leadership. While the finances were being sorted out, it was decided to inject some stability into the society by promising to issue newsletters on a regular basis and asking members to contribute articles for future inclusion.

Another 'convention' was arranged for October 1996, held in York, attended by myself, Frank Williams and Eric Longworth, and at this event Frank was made Vice President. Since that date the DAAS has kept its promise and produced regular quarterly full colour newsletters, as well as arranging many members' events, including guided tours of filming locations, meals attended by cast members and local events. A website was created in September 1997, keeping members

Above: The last recording of *Dad's Army*.

up to date with events and giving anyone new to *Dad's Army* facts and information about the series. See Appendix 5 for more information.

In April 1998 the DAAS arranged a 30th Anniversary Convention at the Oval Cricket Ground in central London. This was a major event, attended by most of the surviving cast members and the following year, in July, a Dad's Army Day was held at Bressingham Steam Museum in Norfolk. The museum collection included some of the vehicles used in the series, so the DAAS approached them with a view to displaying some of the society's collection of memorabilia, taking up no more than a cabinet or two. Later in the year, the Bressingham management asked myself, Jack Wheeler, Paul and Tony to come to a meeting. Imagine our surprise when they produced elaborate plans to convert a large hall into a reproduction of Walmington-on-Sea, including the Church Hall, Vicar's Office, Jones'

Butchers, Frazers Funeral Parlour, Swallows Bank, complete with a street, lamp posts – the lot. Space would be set aside for the DAAS collection within the project and it was scheduled for completion by May 2000, when the next convention was due to be held there.

Knowing that the opening of the Dad's Army Collection (as it was to be called) would be a major event, the society contacted Thetford Town Council to arrange another event for the day before the opening, as it was hoped to invite as many involved in *Dad's Army* as possible. The Town Council backed this idea and arranged a Civic Reception for their special guests.

13th May 2000 started off as a cool grey miserable day. There were dozens of period vehicles, including Jones' van, to carry the celebrities on a procession through the town and many people were in 1940s clothes.

 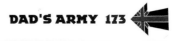

Above: Official opening of the *Dad's Army* Museum at Bressingham, Norfolk, 2000.

The Civic Reception was held in the Council Office grounds and after a time all the guests boarded different vehicles for a parade around the town, ending up at the Guildhall, (used in the series as the Town Hall). By this time the sun had come out and the temperature was rising. The parade made its way through the town and by the time it reached the Guildhall there were in excess of 5,000 people waiting for them!

The following day all the cast gathered at Bressingham, where they and DAAS members had a private preview of the museum before Jimmy Perry and David Croft officially opened the collection to the general public.

Since then a *Dad's Army* Day has been a yearly event at the Museum each May, still drawing huge crowds, including visitors from all over the world. It's a terrific day out for all the family, because Bressingham is on the site of Blooms Nurseries, so, as well as the *Dad's Army* and steam museums, there are also two

small-gauge railways and a lovely old-fashioned carousel to ride on, lovely gardens to explore – and plants to buy.

Sadly dear Jack Wheeler died in 2005, so Paul and Tony have been left to carry on Jack's good work, and they're doing this very well indeed. In 2004 they produced a handbook called the *Dad's Army Companion*, which pinpoints all the locations used in the series and, such is the depth of their knowledge, that when the BBC have been producing retrospectives on the show, they've come to them for advice. I'm sure it's thanks to the society that the BBC has re-shown so many episodes, as its members are always writing in, suggesting yet another of their favourites that they'd like to see back on their screens.

The 40th anniversary also prompted a group of people in Thetford to put their town on the map by marking its association with *Dad's Army*. Quite a few thought this should have been done before, considering the impor-

tance of its connection with the series, as the *Dad's Army* company stayed at the Bell Hotel for the whole nine years when they did the exterior filming in and around that area.

The movement for its recognition was initially headed up by two ladies, Corinne Fulford and Sarah Wilson, and they were very soon joined by some members of the town council. The result has been amazing. They marked the anniversary in July 2008 with a huge parade around the town and the opening of a small museum. This has now expanded, with help from the town council, and has been completely refurbished and looks marvellous. Many volunteers, 'Friends of the Museum', have helped with this refurbishment, and with the original museum.

That July weekend, Thetford welcomed back David Croft, Ian Lavender, Colin Bean, Harold Snoad and myself. The Saturday night finished with a dance and cabaret at the Guildhall. Sunday was an open day in the town which was roped off so that hundreds of people could line the pavements, collecting autographs. Coach tours now pay visits all year round and the council, as well as providing leaflets about the museum and the town's association with the series, have arranged guided walks around the town, covering areas that were used as locations in 'Walmington-on-Sea'. Nearby of course is the Stamford Battle Area which was regularly used for many filmed episodes.

As if all this wasn't enough, Corinne and co are raising money in all sorts of ways to have a statue of Arthur Lowe, in the guise of Captain Mainwaring, built for Thetford. A terrific idea, which everyone knows will be a great draw for visitors to the town.

I'm proud and delighted to say I've been invited to become a patron of the museum. Does this mean that 'Hodges' will have to contribute to the fund for 'Mainwaring'? He'll have to put up the price of his veg to pay for it. You see, once again Napoleon has put one over on the warden! It's all a dream come true for Corinne Fulford and her team.

Another interesting development over the last fifteen years or so has been the finding of missing episodes. Back in the late 1960s, in spite of David Croft's wishes, video tapes were usually re-used or discarded. In fact, 19 film cans were pulled out of a skip at Elstree film studios in the 1970s by someone who was working there. One of the missing *Dad's Army* cans contained a card which read: 'Return to David Croft.' Apparently the man who found them kept them for many years

Below: Thetford's proposed statue of Arthur Lowe as the inimitable Captain Mainwaring.

before his daughter insisted he must throw them out. He passed them on to a friend for safekeeping, who responded to a BBC appeal for lost archive material and came forward. The episodes, from 1969 are 'The Battle of Godfrey's Cottage' and 'Operation Kilt'. Two other episodes came to light in Australia in 2001. It is thought they were recorded to show to executives at Columbia Pictures during discussions on the structure of the *Dad's Army* feature film.

Thanks to digital technology, all these finds can now be safely preserved for future generations. Talking of 'digital technology' and, as you can imagine it's a phrase that doesn't pass my lips very often, near the end of 2008, thanks to a 'colour recovery' process which I can't begin to explain, a terrific episode first shown in 1969, 'Room at the Bottom' was screened in very natural-looking colour when it had only been seen in black and white for years. Ralph Montagu, co-ordinator of the *Dad's Army* DVD releases, explains: 'Of the 80 *Dad's Army* episodes, only three are now missing, and these are all from the second series made in black and white. 'Room at the Bottom' almost suffered the same fate as the tape for this episode was also wiped, but not before a black and white film recording was made. It was from this film that we were able to recover the colour information using this new technology. Wiping video tapes was common practice in the BBC at that time as it was considered too expensive for every programme to be kept.' The episode was screened in December 2008, as a part of a whole evening on *Dad's Army*, and it was preceded by an introduction by Ian Lavender and James Insell, one of the people responsible for developing the new colour process. I must say it looked great, and is yet more proof that *Dad's Army* doesn't have to be relegated to a pre-digital age, but can be enhanced by it.

Another proof of the continuing popularity of the series is the fact that, in the last ten years there have been very successful theatre shows, based on various episodes. In 2002, an amateur company based at The Court Theatre in Tring, Hertfordshire, performed the first stage version of two *Dad's Army* episodes, 'The Deadly Attachment' and 'The Godiva Affair', and this version is now in print, published by French's. In 2003 there was another production at Tring, where the Dad's Army Appreciation Society celebrated its 10th anniversary, along with original cast members, watching the Tring Festival Company's production of *Dad's Army, The Lost Episodes*.

About that time I myself directed an amateur production, mounted by the WHIPS, (West Horsley Independent Players), in my local village hall. It went really well and did great business. How can you fail with a poster that says '*Dad's Army* on stage at the hall?' Again, several of the original cast were able to come down to a performance, which I'm sure must have made their 'doubles' pretty nervous, though one of the younger members, Joe Sanders, so enjoyed the experience that he was inspired to go on to train as an actor. Joe's story is quite extraordinary. With just four days to go before the dress rehearsal, the chap who was going to play Private Pike dropped out as he was involved in other things. The following day I was having a drink in my local and a fellow behind the bar looked a bit like Pike so I asked him if he'd done any acting. He said 'No,' but I said, 'Why not have a go?' He came along to rehearsals that evening and I gave him a script to learn. In four days he was pretty much word-perfect. Some time after that, he went to drama college and is now doing very well, having already worked at the National Theatre. Not bad, eh, from village hall to the National? Horsley is very proud of him.

The so-called 'lost episodes' are clearly 'lost' no longer but very much with us, as, starting in September 2007, theatre producer

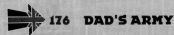

Ed O'Driscoll mounted a long tour, based around three episodes, the first two having been 'lost', 'The Loneliness of the Long-Distance Walker' and 'A Stripe for Frazer', and ending with that all-time favourite, 'The Deadly Attachment'. David Croft and Jimmy Perry were responsible for the adaptation for the stage and the star of the show was Leslie Grantham, playing Walker. The tour was so successful that there are plans to send out a new version in 2010.

Any final thoughts I have about *Dad's Army* undoubtedly bring me back to David Croft and Jimmy Perry, a couple of extraordinarily gifted people. Through all their classic comedy series' over the years, they've had a sure instinct for what families want to watch, and their audiences are made up not just of mums and dads but all age groups, from young children upwards. The hallmarks of their writing are strong characters in real situations, slightly exaggerated but played for real. The casting of those characters has been wonderful and the research into every aspect of their productions has been meticulous in whatever period their programmes have been set. I believe their last co-operation together, *You Rang, M'Lord?* set in the 1920s, was their crowning glory. After that, quite naturally after so many years together, Jimmy and David felt it was time for a rest and to reassess their futures.

After this respite, starting with a pilot in 1995, David once more assembled a team, many of whom he had enjoyed working with in the past, for a new sitcom, *Oh Dr Beeching!* This was set in the 1960s, during the period of closure of so much of our national rail network, and ran for two series. Not one to retire, in the recent past David has written his autobiography and formed his own production company, along with his daughter Penny, to produce a new sitcom, *Here Comes the Queen*, which he wrote with Jeremy Lloyd; it will be available on DVD soon.

Jimmy has always had a few ideas up his sleeve, one of which was a four-part radio series based on the very early days of the BBC under its authoritarian boss, Sir John Reith. The research for this series took Jimmy a long time but it was well worth the preparation when it appeared in 1994. I had the pleasure of being included in this light-hearted look at the beginnings of broadcasting. Jimmy also wrote a musical play based on the world of the bygone twice-nightly variety theatre in this country which was produced in the autumn of 1997. Jimmy and David value their friendship and regularly discuss their various activities. As the phenomenon that is *Dad's Army* marches on into the 21st century, no doubt the fruits of their great collaboration will continue to be heard on the radio and seen on television and DVD. Who knows, Mainwaring and Co may even be coming to a theatre near you!

Below: Ian, Clive and the Author 'being silly' at a *Dad's Army* event at the Imperial War Museum.

APPENDICES

1. IT STICKS OUT HALF A MILE

When *Dad's Army* finally finished in 1977, the possibility of transferring the show to one of the ITV companies was discussed but the idea didn't go any further. Both the writers and the actors felt that there was not much more they could get out of the characters and the situation. It was generally agreed that it should finish while it was popular – but there were also thoughts about whether it could be continued in another form.

It was suggested that the characters could perhaps become involved in the peacetime activities of Walmington-on-Sea as members of the Town Council – not a bad thought.

However, Harold Snoad and Michael Knowles, who had been responsible for adapting the original TV episodes for radio, came up with an alternative idea. The suggestion they put forward to BBC Radio was for a series called 'It Sticks Out Half a Mile', which would involve Arthur Lowe (still in his *Dad's Army* character of Mainwaring) purchasing a disused pier further along the coast from Walmington at 'Frambourne'.

Harold Snoad explains the plot of the first pilot episode: 'George Mainwaring returns from living abroad for a couple of years (because of Elizabeth's health) and learns that Frambourne pier is up for sale. It has been closed since the war and he is excited at the prospect of putting it back on its feet. Needing a loan, he calls into the local bank at Framborne and is taken aback to discover that the manager is Arthur Wilson, his old chief clerk at Walmington. Swallowing his pride, with difficulty, he takes Wilson to see the pier and gets his loan. They then attend a meeting with members of the Town Council and the deal is done. Flushed with success he toasts himself as the new owner of Frambourne pier, only to have Wilson point out that the real owner is the Swallow Bank!'

Arthur Lowe died on 15 April 1982, soon after the making of the pilot programme, which was never broadcast. It doesn't even exist in the BBC archives. However, following a remark by Arthur's widow Joan that such a good idea should not be abandoned for ever ('Arthur thought it had so much potential'), Snoad and Knowles suggested to the BBC that, with a rewrite, it could still work. Consequently a second pilot was commissioned, with a cast that was to feature John Le Mesurier, Ian Lavender, Bill Pertwee and Vivienne Martin. This pilot programme was recorded on 11 September 1982 and became the first in a series of 13 episodes.

CAST

ARTHUR LOWE as George Mainwaring (1st Pilot)
JOHN LE MESURIER as Arthur Wilson
IAN LAVENDER as Frank Pike (2nd Pilot onwards)
BILL PERTWEE as Bert Hodges (2nd Pilot onwards)

1st PILOT EPISODE (BBC RADIO 2, 1982): IT STICKS OUT HALF A MILE

Not broadcast.
Studio Recording Date: early 1982.
With: Josephine Tewson (Miss Perkins).

2nd PILOT EPISODE (BBC RADIO 2, 1983): 1. THE BUSINESS PROPOSITION

Sunday 13/11/83, 1.30–2.00pm
Studio Recording: Saturday 11/9/82
(Broadcast as Episode One of the series).
The war has been over three years. Arthur Wilson is now Manager of the Swallow's Bank in Frambourne-on-Sea. Frank Pike has moved there too, but their peacetime lives are shattered when Bert Hodges suddenly appears with a business proposition for Frank.
With: Vivienne Martin (Miss Perkins), Robin Parkinson (Mr Hunter), Edward Burnham (Mr Short), Gordon Peters (Mr. Rawlings) and Spencer Banks (Council Employee).

SERIES ONE (BBC RADIO 2, 1983-4):

2. THE BANK LOAN

Sunday 20/11/83, 1.30–2.00 pm

Studio Recording: Saturday 19/2/83

Bert Hodges and Frank Pike have persuaded Arthur Wilson reluctantly to loan them £5,000 from Swallows Bank, to renovate the pier at Frambourne, but on the pier they meet resistance from its Caretaker, Guthrie, and Hodges almost goes to a watery grave.

With: Vivienne Martin (Miss Perkins), Glynn Edwards (Fred Guthrie) and Michael Bilton (Mr Johnson).

3. WHO OWNED THE PIER?

Sunday 27/11/83, 1.30–2.00pm

Studio Recording: Wednesday 23/2/83

Hodges, Pike and Wilson continue their renovations of the pier at Frambourne and visit the local library to do some research on the previous pre-war owners.

With: Vivienne Martin (Miss Perkins), Glynn Edwards (Fred Guthrie), Barry Gosney (Mr Watkins/the Electrician), James Bryce (the Bank Cashier/the Librarian) and Stuart Sherwin (Electricity Showroom Assistant).

4. INSPECTING THE PILES

Sunday 4/11/83, 1.30–2.00pm

Studio Recording: Wednesday 23/2/83

In an effort to save money, Hodges, Pike and Wilson decide to inspect the foundations of Frambourne Pier themselves and put to sea at night in an inflatable rubber dinghy.

With: Vivienne Martin (Miss Perkins).

5. PIKE IN LOVE

Sunday 11/12/83, 1.30–2.00pm

Studio Recording: Saturday 19/2/83

Pike is unable to concentrate on the pier renovations, because he is in love. Mrs Pike is worried and calls in Mr Wilson to lecture her son on the birds and the bees.

With: Vivienne Martin (Miss Perkins), Carol Hawkins (Avril), Janet Davies (Mavis Pike), and Gordon Salkild (the Telephone Engineer).

This is the only episode of *It Sticks Out Half A Mile* that exists at the BBC Sound Archive.

6. THE FRIENDS OF FRAMBOURNE PIER

Sunday 18/12/83, 1.30–2.00pm

Studio Recording: Saturday 26/2/83

Pike and Hodges decide to launch a campaign asking for volunteers to save the pier. And so the Friends of Frambourne Pier Association is born.

With: Vivienne Martin (Miss Perkins), Glynn Edwards (Fred Guthrie), Michael Knowles (Ernest Woolcot) and Hilda Braid (Olive Briggs).

7. THE FIRST MEETING

Sunday 1/1/84, 1.30–2.00pm

Studio Recording: Saturday 5/3/83

The first meeting of the Friends of Frambourne Pier Association is convened. Arthur Wilson attends but has to explain his evening out to a suspicious Mrs Pike.

With: Glynn Edwards (Fred Guthrie), Michael Knowles (Ernest Woolcot), Hilda Braid (Olive Briggs), Michael Bilton (the Elderly Man), Madi Hedd (the Woman) and Jill Lidstone (the Young Lady).

8. MAROONED

Sunday 8/1/84, 1.30–2.00pm

Studio Recording: Tuesday 8/3/83

A Visit to the Pier Theatre, which can only be reached by Bosun's Chair, ends in disaster when Arthur Wilson and romantically inclined Miss Perkins are marooned together.

With: Vivienne Martin (Miss Perkins) and Paul Russell (Derek).

9. THE FANCY DRESS NIGHT

Sunday 15/1/84, 1.30–2.00pm

Studio Recording: Saturday 5/3/83

The Friends of Frambourne Pier Association arrange a Fancy Dress Night on the Pier to raise money, but problems arise for Arthur Wilson when Miss Perkins and Mrs Pike choose the same costumes.

With: Janet Davies (Mavis Pike), Michael Knowles (Ernest Woolcot), Hilda Braid (Olive Briggs), Gordon Clyde (Willoughby Smallpiece) and Miranda Forbes (the Waitress).

10. EPISODE TEN
THE BUILDER
Tuesday 21/8/84, 10.30–11.00pm
Studio Recording: Saturday 26/2/83
Pike and Hodges find a builder to repair the Pier, but old hostilities are renewed when they discover his nationality.
With: Vivienne Martin (Miss Perkins), Glynn Edwards (Fred Guthrie), Stella Tanner (Myrtle Spivy), Gordon Clyde (Mr Fisher), Carole Harrison (the Builder's Receptionist) and Katherine Parr (the Irish Nun).

11. EPISODE ELEVEN
WAR DAMAGE
Tuesday 4/9/84, 10.30–1100pm
Studio Recording: Tuesday 8/3/83
Wilson, Pike and Hodges go to London to claim War Damage Compensation for the pier.
With: Vivienne Martin (Miss Perkins), Reginald Marsh (Sir Wensley Smithers), Gordon Clyde (Civil Servants 1 and 5), Jon Glover (Civil Servants 2 and 4) and Michael Bilton (Mr Thorndyke/ Civil Servant 3).

12. EPISODE TWELVE
THE PIN UP GIRL
Tuesday 18/9/84, 10.30–11.00pm
Studio Recording: Tuesday 15/3/83
Pike and Hodges decide to update the photographs in the Pier's 'What the Butler Saw' machine and persuade Miss Perkins to pose as their pin-up girl.
With: Vivienne Martin (Miss Perkins), Christopher Biggins (Dudley Watkins) and Robin Parkinson (Mr Hunter)

13. EPISODE THIRTEEN
HIDDEN TREASURE
Tuesday 9/10/84, 10.30–11.00pm.
Studio Recording: Tuesday 15/3/83
Pike and Hodges discover that there may be hidden treasure on the Pier and clairvoyant Madame Zara is called in to help them.
With: Vivienne Martin (Miss Perkins), Glynn Edwards (Fred Guthrie) and Betty Marsden (Madame Zara).

BACKGROUND INFORMATION
Radio Times preview article by Robert Ottaway, for the week of 12–18 November 1983:
'There are TV characters who cling to our memories long after their series have been laid to rest. I'm sure many have speculated about those indomitable triers of *Dad's Army*. Whatever would happen to them when their pikes were taken away?

'And that's the inspiration behind *It Sticks Out Half a Mile*, which transports John Le Mesurier, Ian Lavender and Bill Pertwee into 1948 – into a situation where John is now a bank manager, timid Ian is now a trainee manager at Woolworths and Bill is a wheeler-dealer.

'Missing from the contingent are Arthur Lowe and John Laurie, now sadly dead. Ian Lavender says, "I played with that team for 10 years. The atmosphere …was so great between us – and I think that carries on, now we are supposed to be three years older." The advantage of radio, he says, "is that I don't need so much Brylcreem and eyeshadow to disguise myself, my voice is more or less the same."

'NOSTALGIA AT THE END OF THE PIER'
Radio Times preview article by David Gillard, for the week of 14–20 July 1984:
"Yes, I think we all felt this was the last – the end of the road for *Dad's Army*," says Bill Pertwee of *It Sticks Out Half a Mile*, the radio sequel to TV's enduring Home Guard comedy success. The series – which begins a repeat run on Tuesday and includes a bonus of four previously unheard episodes – was recorded early last year (1983) and was to be the last ever completed by the late John Le Mesurier.

'Bill – who, of course, plays that dirty-fingered greengrocer and one-time Air Raid Warden Bert Hodges – believes the whole cast knew that it probably was the last time they would all work together, though such feelings went unspoken. "The series had originally been mainly written around Arthur Lowe and John, and when Arthur died it had to be re-jigged. John had not been well, though he was feeling better when we recorded the series, but I think we all realised that we'd had a great run – the programmes started on TV in 1968 – and we were coming to the end of it. We'd lost

so many of the original cast – Arthur, John, Laurie, Arnold Ridley, Edward Sinclair, James Beck and a few months later, John was dead too."

'I asked Bill to assess the show's enduring appeal. "When it started there was a lot of kitchen sink drama around and people were pleased to sit back and laugh at this rather gentle company of people," he says. "The younger viewers enjoyed the Mack Sennett routines – the chases and so on – while the older viewers found it extremely nostalgic."

'Bill himself had come from a variety background, including playing at the Windmill, and has recently returned to farce with two big hits for the Theatre of Comedy Company in London. "The rest of the *Dad's Army* cast were all actors, really, so I'd never worked with any of them before. We were all terribly different but there was a tremendous camaraderie between us. It was very hard work, but we had wonderfully happy times. You can't help but be sad when you look back now, can you?"

BILL PERTWEE'S COMMENT

Harold Snoad has always felt it somewhat sad that after the original pilot episode the project was abandoned because of the death of Arthur Lowe and then, having re-jigged the idea and completed 13 episodes (possibly an unfortunate number!), John Le Mesurier also died and put paid to there being any more.

Later Harold Snoad and Michael Knowles wrote a pilot episode for TV called *Walking the Planks*, which starred Michael Elphick with Richard Wilson as the bank manager and, like the radio series, featured Vivienne Martin as his secretary. This was transmitted on BBC1 but in spite of it being well received there was no immediate interest shown by the BBC in continuing with the idea. Harold Snoad, therefore , took the idea to Yorkshire Television who were very enthusiastic and produced an initial series of seven. Although the series went down reasonably well it was certainly not helped by the fact that, for a number of reasons, Yorkshire TV wasn't able to do any location filming and the obvious absence of the sea, the horizon, gulls, the effect of wind, etc, for a series which is set on a pier didn't exactly help!

PRODUCTION CREDITS

Written by: Harold Snoad and Michael Knowles
The characters of Wilson, Pike and Hodges were originally created by Jimmy Perry and David Croft.
Recorded in stereo.

PRODUCERS:

Jonathon James Moore (1st Pilot)
Martin Fisher (2nd Pilot and series)
Episodes were not preserved by the BBC Transcription Service as the series was thought to be of little interest to an international audience.

2. RELATED APPEARANCES BY *DAD'S ARMY* REGULARS

CHRISTMAS NIGHT WITH THE STARS

Wednesday 25 December 1968, BBC1 B/W
A *Dad's Army* sketch formed a part of this programme, which was presented by Eric Morecambe and Ernie Wise. Edward Sinclair guested in the sketch which featured multiple Father Christmases including one looking suspiciously like Mr Jones, Walmington-on-Sea's butcher. This item does not exist in the BBC Archive.

CHRISTMAS NIGHT WITH THE STARS

Thursday 25 December 1969, BBC1 Colour
'Resisting the Aggressor Down the Ages'
Extract included in BBC2's *Fry & Laurie Host a Christmas Night with the Stars* special (27/12/94).
The *Dad's Army* team contributed a 20-minute item for this programme, which was compered by Val Doonican. The item concerned the platoon's rehearsal for a Christmas town pageant – their item depicting Britain's dogged defiance of the many aggressors who had tried to overthrow her people in the past. Bill Pertwee (the ARP Warden) and Robert Aldous (the German Pilot) also appeared in the *Dad's Army* sketch, which exists in its entirety in the BBC Archive, although sadly the remainder of the 1969 *Christmas Night with the Stars* does not.

THE COWARD REVIEW
26 December 1969 produced by James Gilbert.
Featured Arthur Lowe, John Le Mesurier and Clive Dunn. This item exists in the BBC Archive.

ROYAL TELEVISION GALA PERFORMANCE
Sunday 24 May 1970, BBC1 Colour
'Guarding Buckingham Palace'
In the presence of HM the Queen and the Duke of Edinburgh, the *Dad's Army* team performed an item at the BBC TV Theatre, Shepherd's Bush as part of the Gala Performance. The sketch, performed live on stage, concerned the platoon being asked to stand guard at Buckingham Palace. This item exists in the BBC Archive.

CHRISTMAS NIGHT WITH THE STARS
Friday 25 December 1970, BBC1 Colour
The *Dad's Army* team, featuring Bill Pertwee as the ARP Warden, contributed a 15-minute item for this programme, which was introduced by Cilla Black. The item concerned a rehearsal for a performance of the Cornish Floral Dance by Mainwaring's men, the wardens and some of the ladies of Walmington-on-Sea. This item was subsequently revived for the stage show in 1975, with few alterations. (It was also the item chosen for inclusion in the 1975 Royal Variety Performance.) It does not exist in the BBC Archive. However, an incomplete audio recording exists in a private collection.

THIS IS YOUR LIFE
Wednesday 24 March 1971, ITV Colour
Clive Dunn was the featured guest in this edition, which was hosted by Eamonn Andrews.
This programme no longer exists in the Thames TV archive, though two short clips are known to exist on audio tape in a private collection.

THE MORECAMBE AND WISE SHOW
Thursday 22 April 1971, BBC2 Colour
Arthur Lowe was the featured guest and appeared in several sequences featuring Janet Webb. Later, in one of Ernie's plays based upon *Mutiny on the Bounty*, he portrayed Captain Bligh, while members of the platoon

(John Le Mesurier, John Laurie, James Beck, Arnold Ridley and Ian Lavender) made cameo appearances as the few members of the ship's crew still loyal to Bligh. This item exists in the BBC Archive. (Sketch called 'Monty On The Bonty').

SOUNDS FAMILIAR
Thursday 19 October 1972, BBC Radio 1 & 2
Arthur Lowe, John Le Mesurier, John Laurie and Bill Pertwee were special guests on the gameshow.

ASK ASPEL
Sunday 22 December 1972, BBC1 Colour
Arthur Lowe was interviewed as Michael Aspel's special guest.

CHRISTMAS NIGHT WITH THE STARS
Broadcast to the Empire:
Monday 25 December 1972, BBC1 Colour
The *Dad's Army* team, featuring Bill Pertwee as the ARP Warden, contributed a 15-minute item for this programme which was presented by the 'Two Ronnies' – Ronnie Barker and Ronnie Corbett.
The item concerned a special broadcast being made from the Church Hall, in which the platoon are to perform a short play. The broadcast is to follow a speech by the King – and Mainwaring is particularly pleased that after the King finishes, his will be the next voice to be heard … if all goes well. This item exists in the BBC Archive.

THE ROYAL VARIETY PERFORMANCE
Sunday 16 November 1975, ITV Colour
The *Dad's Army* regulars performed the Floral Dance item from the Stage Show. The programme was recorded on Monday 10/11/75 at the London Palladium. It exists in the London Weekend Television Archive, running for 8.5 minutes.

THIS IS YOUR LIFE
Wednesday 10 March 1976, ITV Colour
Arnold Ridley was the featured guest in this edition, which was hosted by Eamonn Andrews. The programme exists in the Thames TV archive.

THE MORECAMBE AND WISE CHRISTMAS SHOW

Sunday 25 December 1977, BBC1

Produced several months after the completion of work on the final series of *Dad's Army*, stars Arthur Lowe, John Le Mesurier and John Laurie reprised the Home Guard roles in a brief sequence with singer Elton John, who asked them to direct him to the TV studio where *The Morecambe and Wise Show* was being recorded. This item exists in the BBC Archive.

DEFINITELY DUNN

1. 'Pubs and Parents'
2. 'Flat Feet and Concert Parties'
3. 'Relieving General Gordon'
4. 'Glamorous Nights in a Prison Camp'
5. 'Grandad and the Elephant'
6. 'The Men from Walmington'

Wednesday 6/7 to Wednesday 10/8/88, BBC Radio 2, 10.00–10.15pm.

A series of six 15-minute programmes. Clive Dunn recalled highlights from his years in showbiz. In front of a studio audience, Clive told stories and sang songs, accompanied by Ronnie Bridges.

NOEL'S HOUSE PARTY

Saturday 27 November 1993

Featured Clive Dunn as Corporal Jones.

WOGAN

Monday 1 August 1988, BBC1

Clive Dunn, Ian Lavender, Bill Pertwee, David Croft and Jimmy Perry were interviewed by Terry Wogan to mark the 20th anniversary of the first *Dad's Army* episode. Clips taken from 'The Man and the Hour' and 'Battle of the Giants'.

DAYTIME LIVE

Tuesday 24 November 1989, BBC1

Bill Pertwee, Clive Dunn, Ian Lavender and Frank Williams were interviewed by Judy Spiers to celebrate 21 years of the programme and to promote Bill Pertwee's new book. David Croft and Jimmy Perry were also interviewed via a video link from the North Acton Rehearsal Rooms, where they were supervising

rehearsals for their then-upcoming series *You Rang, M'Lord?* A clip from 'The Face on the Poster' was featured. This item exists in the BBC Archive.

JIM DAVIDSON SPECIAL

Featured Bill Pertwee, Clive Dunn, Windsor Davies, Melvyn Hayes.

OPEN AIR

Ian Lavender, Bill Pertwee and Jimmy Perry were interviewed on 6 December 1989.

THE ARTHUR LOWE STORY

Tuesday 28 December 1993, BBC Radio 2

I had the privilege to write and present this tribute on the life of Arthur – a life that was not just Captain Mainwaring of *Dad's Army*, wonderful as his portrayal of the platoon commander was. Many of his colleagues and friends who had worked with him from the start of his amazing career in repertory in Manchester through to his appearances and beyond, talked to me about Arthur's life and times. Listeners who knew only part of Arthur Lowe's career were very surprised at his very varied career. It was a programme with which I was delighted to be associated.

OMNIBUS; PERRY & CROFT – THE SIT-COMS

Tuesday 18 April 1995, BBC1

This long-overdue 50-minute documentary celebrated the collaborative works of Jimmy Perry and David Croft. Concentrating on their three main successes – *Dad's Army, It Ain't Half Hot Mum* and *Hi-De-Hi!* – the programme boasted interviews with Perry and Croft, contributions from many of the regular artistes who appeared in each series, plus comments from celebrity admirers and from representatives of academia and the media. *Dad's Army* received much praise from those interviewed, many citing it as a masterpiece of television comedy. Of the surviving personnel from *Dad's Army*, only Clive Dunn, Bill Pertwee and Ian Lavender were interviewed for this tribute, with Frank Williams, Colin Bean and Pamela Cundell sadly not appearing. The main *Dad's Army* section of the documentary lasted some 15 minutes in total, and featured clips from many episodes. The closing credit sequence

 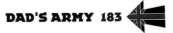

featured the wonderful scene from 'A Soldier's Farewell' where Mainwaring is trampled under the feet of the platoon as they leave the cinema. It is interesting to note that the documentary ignored completely their most recent collaboration – *You Rang M'Lord* – which featured several of the actors interviewed.

Programmes repeated on consecutive Tuesdays (BBC1) to accompany this documentary were: *It Ain't Half Hot Mum* 'The Road to Bannu' (18/4/95), *Dad's Army* 'The Deadly Attachment' (25/4/95) and *Hi-Di-Hi!* 'A Night Not to Remember' (2/5/95). This item exists in the BBC Archive.

GOODNIGHT SWEETHEART
'Don't Get Around Much Any More'
Monday 20 February 1995, BBC1

Although not featuring any original *Dad's Army* cast members, this episode featured an affectionate tribute to its comic precursor. The series, written by Laurence Marks and Maurice Gran, concerns a TV repairman named Gary Sparrow (Nicholas Lyndhurst), who, having discovered a way to travel back in time to wartime Britain, finds himself romantically entangled with two women 50 years apart. 'Don't Get Around Much Any More' opened the second series of this light-hearted comedy and saw Gary depositing money at the Stepney branch of the Provincial bank in 1940, planning to pick it up with interest in the present. However, when the bank manager and his chief clerk reveal themselves to be Mainwaring and Wilson, Gary is quite dumbstruck. He soon recovers enough to sing a particularly tuneless rendition of 'Who Do You Think You Are Kidding, Mr Hitler' and discovers that they are, indeed, Home Guard members, too. When a gangly youth brings in the tea in a most clumsy fashion, Lyndhurst's character is sure it must be Frank Pike, but some sanity is restored to the proceedings, when it transpires that he is called Major. The sequence ends with Gary Sparrow delighting in referring to him as 'a stupid boy'!

Mainwaring was played by Alec Linstead, who, despite a reasonable likeness to Arthur Lowe, turns in a lacklustre performance. Fortunately, Terrence Hardiman is far better as Wilson, getting John Le Mesurier's wonderful affectations off to a tee. Max Digby played Major. The episode was directed by Robin Nash.

LAST NIGHT AT THE PARIS
BBC Radio 2

Compèred by Bob Hoskins, this was the very last programme recorded at the BBC Paris Studios on Lower Regent Street, London on 26/2/95 and transmitted on 11/3/95. The *Dad's Army* sketch called 'The Boy Who Saved England', featuring Ian Lavender, Frank Williams, Bill Pertwee and Jimmy Perry the writer, was part of a programme called *Full Steam A-Hudd*, compèred by Roy Hudd. This was recorded on 30/4/95, as a gala opening event from the Concert Hall in Broadcasting House, now a regular venue for many BBC Radio shows. The programme was transmitted on 3/6/95 on BBC Radio 2.

THIS IS YOUR LIFE: DAVID CROFT
Wednesday 20 December 1995, BBC1

David Croft's contribution to British television and to the lives of his friends, colleagues and family was recognised in this edition of the programme. Actors from his many television shows, including *Dad's Army*, appeared on the programme, paying tribute to a man who had helped shape their careers.

THE STORY OF *DAD'S ARMY* (A TELEVISION LEGEND)

A cassette I recorded for Polygram, produced by Barry Johnston and Chris Seymour in 1995, was based on the first edition of this book. It took 25 hours to record, quite a strain on the old voice. I did have to smile one day when stopped at traffic lights: the driver alongside me was listening to it. I almost called out, 'Enjoying it are you?', but I thought better of it. He might have said, 'No'!

THE JAMESONS
Tuesday 14 January 1997, BBC Radio 2
Interview with Bill Pertwee and Ian Lavender.

CROFT ORIGINALS
Tuesday 29 April 1997, BBC Radio 2
Presented by Ian Lavender and featuring David Croft.

Above: The most famous air raid warden in the world!

THE *DAD'S ARMY* STORY
Saturday 27 May 2000
Victoria Wood presented a programme dedicated to *Dad's Army*. Included interviews with Clive Dunn, Jimmy Perry, David Croft, Ian Lavender, Frank Williams, Pamela Cundell, Wendy Richard.

THE UNFORGETTABLE ARTHUR LOWE
Monday 18 September 2000
A tribute to Arthur Lowe, featuring many rare clips and interviews with co-stars and production staff.

REPUTATIONS
Saturday 21 September 2002, BBC2
The life and career of Arthur Lowe, one of Britain's favourite comic actors. As Captain Mainwaring he appeared in 81 episodes of *Dad's Army*, and will remain forever etched on the nation's memories. Considered one of the greatest actors of his generation by his peers, Lowe had the chance of playing theatre's great classical roles and a shot at Hollywood. But in many ways such potential remained unfulfilled. The programme also examined Lowe's relationship with his wife, Joan Cooper.

BRITAIN'S BEST SITCOM
Saturday 20 March 2004, BBC2
Presented by Jonathan Ross. The celebrity advocate for the show was Phill Jupitus. *Dad's Army* placed fourth overall. With 'talking heads' appearances from David Croft, Graham McCann, Jimmy Perry, Bill Pertwee and Frank Williams.

COMEDY CONNECTIONS
Friday 29 August 2008, BBC1
Dad's Army was the featured programme in Episode 7 of Season 6 of this series, which looked at the stories behind the making of Britain's best comedies and examined comedic and theatrical links with other shows. Narrated by Doon Mackichan, there were contributions and reminiscences from Frank Williams, Wendy Richard, Harold Snoad, Jimmy Perry, Ann Croft, David Croft, Ian Lavender, Bill Pertwee, Clive Dunn and Pamela Cundell.

JONATHAN ROSS SALUTES *DAD'S ARMY*
Wednesday 3 December 2008
A one-off special to commemorate the 40th anniversary of the classic show. Self-confessed *Dad's Army* fan Jonathan Ross was joined by the show's stars, including Ian Lavender, Clive Dunn, Bill Pertwee and Frank Williams, plus celebrity fans Ronnie Corbett, Jon Culshaw and John Thomson.

DAD'S ARMY NIGHT
Saturday 13 December 2008, BBC2
Evening schedule as follows:
'Life On The Box – Arthur Lowe', 7.10pm
'Missing Presumed Wiped', 7.55pm
'Dad's Army in Colour' – 'Room At The Bottom', 8.25pm
'Comedy Connections (rpt) – *Dad's Army*', 9pm
This entire evening of *Dad's Army*-related programming included a very special episode of the show, 'Room At The Bottom', in colour for the first time in nearly 40 years, which was the centrepiece of the evening's viewing. The vintage episode was preceded by a short introduction in which Ian Lavender, one of the original cast members of the show, interviewed James Insell, BBC archivist, about the colour recovery process and the technology used to restore such programmes from black and white to full colour.

3 TV SHOW AND FILM ARTISTS

ARTIST	ROLE	EPISODE
Bernice Adams	*ATS Girl*	Number Engaged
Robert Aldous	*German Pilot*	Man Hunt, Gala Sketch 1970
Joy Allen	*Clippie*	Soldier's Farewell
	Lady with Pram	Gorilla Warfare
Avril Angers	*Tel Operator*	Lion Has Phones, Put That Light Out
Bernard Archard	*Maj-Gen Fullard*	Film
John Ash	*Raymond*	Two and a Half Feathers
Roger Avon	*The Doctor*	Branded
Ralph Ball	*Man at Station*	Sons of the Sea
John Bardon	*Harold Forster*	Ring Dem Bells
Tim Barrett	*Capt Pringle*	Bullet is Not for Firing
	Doctor	When You've Got To Go
John Baskcomb	*Mayor*	Film
Colin Bean	*Pte Sponge*	Regular Extra (28 shows, as listed below):

The Battle of Godfrey's Cottage, Battle School, Room at the Bottom, The Big Parade, Don't Forget the Diver, A. Wilson (Manager)?, Battle of the Giants, Asleep in the Deep, A Soldier's Farewell, The King Was In His Counting House, All Is Safely Gathered In, Time On My Hands, Deadly Attachment, Things That Go Bump In the Night, Everybody's Trucking, Man Of Action, The Godiva Affair, When You've Got To Go, Come In Your Time Is Up, High Finance, The Face On the Poster, My Brother and I, The Love of Three Oranges, Wake Up Walmington, Knights Of Madness, Miser's Hoard, Number Engaged, Never Too Old

ARTIST	ROLE	EPISODE
James Beck	*Pte Joe Walker*	Appeared in 59 TV Shows, Film (Last TV: Things That Go Bump In the Night)
Harold Bennett	*Old Man*	Armoured Might of Cpl Jones
	Mr Blewitt	Bullet is Not For Firing, Day the Balloon Went Up, No Spring for Frazer, The Test, When Did You Last See Your Money?, Time On My Hands, Everybody's Trucking, Man of Action, Turkey Dinner, Come In Your Time Is Up, Face On the Poster, Wake Up Walmington
Michael Bevis	*Police Sgt*	Face on the Poster
Michael Bilton	*Mr Maxwell*	Sons of the Sea
Sue Bishop	*Ticket Collector*	Royal Train
Dennis Blanch	*2nd Lt*	If the Cap Fits
Derek Bond	*Minister*	Keep Young and Beautiful
Roger Bourne	*Regular Extra*	
Felix Bowness	*Driver*	Everybody's Trucking, Number Engaged
	Special Constable	Ring Dem Bells
Ronnie Brandon	*Mr Drury*	No Spring for Frazer
Nan Braunton	*Miss Godfrey*	Battle of Godfrey's Cottage, Day the Balloon Went Up, War Dance, Branded
Ronnie Brody	*Bob*	Royal Train
	Mr Swan	High Finance

ARTIST	ROLE	EPISODE
Ronnie Brody (cont.)	*GPO Man*	Number Engaged
Arthur Brough	*Mr Boyle*	A. Wilson (Manager)?
Jennifer Browne	*WAAF Sgt.*	Day the Balloon Went Up
Julia Burbery	*Miss Ironside*	Mum's Army
Blake Butler	*Mr West*	A. Wilson (Manager)?
David Butler	*Farmhand*	Turkey Dinner
Peter Butterworth	*Mr Bugden*	Face On the Poster
Desmond C-Jones	*Regular Extra*	
Timothy Carlton	*Lt Hope Bruce*	Lion Has Phones
Andrew Carr	*Ops Officer*	Day the Balloon Went Up
John Cater	*Pte Clarke*	Two and A Half Feathers
Hugh Cecil	*Regular Extra*	
Jonathan Cecil	*Capt Cadbury*	Things That Go Bump In The Night
Geoffrey Chater	*Col Pierce*	Round and Round Went the Big Wheel
Erik Chitty	*Mr Sedgewick*	Boots, Boots, Boots
	Mr Clerk	Gorilla Warfare
John Clegg	*Radio Operator*	Round and Round Went the Big Wheel
John D Collins	*Naval Officer*	Film
Pat Coombs	*Mrs Hall*	Film
Patrick Connor	*Shamus*	Absent Friends
Joan Cooper	*Miss Baker*	No Spring For Frazer
	Miss Fortescue	Time On My Hands
	Dolly	Is There Honey Still For Tea?, Love of Three Oranges, Never Too Old
James Copeland	*Capt Ogilvy*	Operation Kilt
Tina Cornioli	*Olive*	All Is Safely Gathered In
Leon Cortez	*Milkman*	Museum Piece
	Small Man	Man Hunt
Deirdre Costello	*Buffet Attendant*	Mum's Army
Brenda Cowling	*Mrs Prentice*	All Is Safely Gathered In
Pamela Cundell	*Mrs Fox*	Armoured Might of Cpl Jones, Big Parade, Mum's Army, Getting the bird, My British Buddy, Honourable Man, Everybody's Trucking, Godiva Affair, Turkey Dinner, Love of Three Oranges, Making of Private Pike, Never Too Old
	Lady in Queue	Lion Has Phones
Amy Dalby	*Unknown*	Battle of Godfrey's Cottage
Colin Daniels	*Boy*	Lion Has Phones
David Davenport	*MP Sgt.*	Enemy Within the Gates
Janet Davies	*Mrs Pike (Mavis)*	(30 shows, as listed below):

The Man and the Hour, Museum Piece, The Showing Up of Corporal Jones, Shooting Pains, Operation Kilt, The Battle of Godfrey's Cottage, Sergeant Wilson's Little Secret, Under Fire, The Armoured Might of Corporal Jones, The Lion Has Phones, This Bullet Is Not for Firing, Something Nasty in the Vault, War Dance, Man Hunt, Big Parade, Boots Boots Boots, Sergeant Save My Boy!, Absent Friends, Mum's Army...

 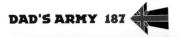

ARTIST	ROLE	EPISODE
Janet Davies (cont.)	*Mrs Pike (Mavis)*	

A. Wilson (Manager)?, My British Buddy, Honourable Man, The Godiva Affair, Turkey Dinner, When You've Got To Go, High Finance, The Love of Three Oranges, The Making of Private Pike, Knights of Madness, Never Too Old

ARTIST	ROLE	EPISODE
Paul Dawkins	*Nazi General*	Film
Gladys Dawson		Under Fire
Andrew Daye	*Choir*	Bullet is Not For Firing
Roy Denton	*Mr Bennett*	Big Guns
Jay Denyer	*Inspector Blake*	Man of Action
J.G. Devlin	*Regan*	Absent Friends
Arnold Diamond	*Major General*	My Brother and I
Maggie Don	*Waitress*	Brain v Brawn
Robert Dorning	*Bank Inspector*	Something Nasty in the Vault
Sally Douglas	*Blodwen*	War Dance
Caroline Dowdeswell	*Janet King*	Man and the Hour, Museum Piece, Command Decision, Enemy Within the Gates, Shooting Pains
Vernon Drake	*Regular Extra*	
Clive Dunn	*L/Cpl Jack Jones*	All 80 TV Shows, Film
Lindsey Dunn	*Small Boy*	The Recruit
Freddie Earlle	*Henry*	Royal Train
	Italian Sgt	When You've Got To Go
Arthur English	*Policeman*	Absent Friends
Don Estelle	*Pickford's Man*	Big Guns
	2nd ARP	Don't Forget the Diver
	Gerald	The Test, Uninvited Guests
Edward Evans	*Unknown*	Loneliness of the Long-Distance Walker
	Mr Rees	Big Guns
	Gen Monteverdi	Don't Fence Me In
Ewan Evans	*Regular Extra*	
Blain Fairman	*US Sgt*	My British Buddy
Rosemary Faith	*Ivy Samways*	Mum's Army
	Barmaid	Battle of the Giants
	Waitress	Godiva Affair
Hilda Fenemore	*Queenie Beal*	Ring Dem Bells
Kate Forge	*Choir*	Bullet is Not For Firing
Liz Fraser	*Mrs Pike*	Film
Scott Fredericks	*Nazi Photographer*	Film
Chris Gannon	*Clerk of Court*	Brush With the Law
Jeffrey Gardiner	*Mr Wintergreen*	Brush With the Law
Rex Garner	*Capt Ashley-Jones*	Fallen Idol
David Gilchrist	*Serviceman*	Mum's Army
Robert Gillespie	*Charles Boyer*	Soldier's Farewell
Jean Gilpin	*Sylvia*	Making of Private Pike
Frank Godfrey	*Regular Extra*	

ARTIST	ROLE	EPISODE
Graham Twins	*Doris and Dora*	War Dance
Carson Green	*Boy*	Lion Has Phones
Fred Griffiths	*Bert King*	Film
Jack Haig	*Gardener*	Day the Balloon Went Up
	Landlord	Ring Dem Bells
Alan Haines	*Maj Smith*	Battle School
	Marine Officer	Film
Miranda Hampton	*Sexy Lady*	Man Hunt
George Hancock	*Pte Hancock*	Godiva Affair
	Regular Extra	
Graham Harboard	*Young Arthur*	Sgt Wilson's Little Secret
John Hart-Dyke	*French General*	Captain's Car
Hugh Hastings	*Pianist*	War Dance
	Pte Hastings	A. Wilson (Manager)?
	Regular Extra	
Nigel Hawthorne	*Angry Man*	Armoured Might of Cpl Jones
Dick Haydon	*Raymond*	Armoured Might of Cpl Jones
John Henderson	*Radio Shop Asst*	Film
Charles Hill	*The Butler*	Command Decision, Wake-up Walmington
	Sergeant	Battle of the Giants
Rose Hill	*Mrs Cole*	Uninvited Guests
Jeffrey Holland	*Soldier*	Wake-Up Walmington
Frankie Holmes	*Fish Fryer*	When You've Got to Go
Jonathan Holt	*2nd Soldier*	Sons of the Sea
Peter Honri	*Pte Day*	Godiva Affair
Bob Hornery	*City Gent*	Royal Train
Geoffrey Hughes	*Bridge Corporal*	Brain v Brawn
Neville Hughes	*The Soldier*	Man and the Hour
Tony Hughes	*Mr Billings*	When Did You Last See Your Money?
Penny Irving	*Chambermaid*	My Brother and I
Richard Jacques	*Mr Cheesewright*	Lion Has Phones
	Regular Extra	
Carl Jaffes	*Capt Winogrodzki*	Enemy Within the Gates
Linda James	*Betty*	Lion Has Phones, Two and a Half Feathers
Natalie Kent	*Miss Twelvetrees*	High Finance
Suzanne Kerchiss	*Ivy*	My British Buddy
Diana King	*Chairwoman*	Loneliness of the Long-Distance Walker
Michael Knowles	*Capt Cutts*	Loneliness of the Long-Distance Walker, Bullet is Not for Firing
	Engineering Officer	Sgt Save My Boy!
	Capt Reed	Fallen Idol
	Capt Stewart	Round and Round Went the Big Wheel
	Staff Capt.	Film
Sam Kydd	*Yokel*	Wake-Up Walmington

ARTIST	ROLE	EPISODE
Sam Kydd (cont.)	*Nazi Orderly*	Film
Vicki Lane	*Girl on Tandem*	Day The Balloon Went Up
Robert Lankesheeer	*Unknown*	Loneliness of the Long-Distance Walker
John Laurie	*Pte James Frazer*	All 80 TV Shows, Film
Ian Lavender	*Pte Frank Pike*	All 80 TV Shows, Film
John Leeson	*1st Soldier*	Sons of the Sea
John Le Mesurier	*Sgt Arthur Wilson*	All 80 TV Shows, Film
Jack Le White	*Porter*	Mum's Army
Arthur Lewis	*Choir*	Bullet is Not For Firing
Alvar Liddell	*Newsreader*	Getting the Bird, Film
Barry Linehan	*Van Driver*	Wake-Up Walmington
Michael Lomax	*2nd ARP*	Absent Friends
Eric Longworth	*Mr Gordon*	Time On My Hands, Honourable Man, Man Of Action, Godiva Affair, Captain's Car, When You've Got To Go, Love of Three Oranges, Knights of Madness
Arthur Lowe	*Capt George Mainwaring*	All 80 TV Shows, Film
Geoffrey Lumsden	*Col Square*	A Stripe for Frazer, Under Fire, Command Decision, Don't Forget the Diver, Fallen Idol, Battle of the Giants, Brush with the Law, Wake-Up Walmington
Jimmy Mac	*Regular Extra*	
Fulton Mackay	*Capt Ramsey*	We Know Our Onions
	Dr McCeavedy	Miser's Hoard
Kenneth MacDonald	*Army Sgt*	Number Engaged
Philip Madoc	*U-Boat Capt*	Deadly Attachment
Janet Mahoney	*Barmaid*	Ring Dem Bells
Susan Majolier	*Nurse*	The Recruit
Melita Manger	*Waitress*	Mum's Army
	Nora	The Making of Private Pike
Pamela Manson	*NAAFI Girl*	We Know Our Onions
Larry Martyn		Loneliness of the Long Distance Walker
	2nd Soldier	Menace From the Deep
	Italian POW	Don't Fence Me In
	Signals Pte	Desperate Drive of Cpl Jones
Roger Maxwell	*Peppery Old Gent*	Film
Alex McAvoy	*Sergeant*	If The Cap Fits, We Know Our Onions
Parmell McGarry	*Elizabeth*	Two and a Half Feathers
Stanley McGeagh	*Sgt Waller*	Lion has Phones
Stuart McGugan	*Scottish Sgt*	Number Engaged
Therese McMurray	*Girl in Window*	Showing Up of Cpl Jones, Shooting Pains
	Girl in Haystack	The Day the Balloon Went Up
Eilidh McNab	*Choir*	Bullet Is Not for Firing
Fred McNaughton	*Mayor*	Royal Train, Honourable Man, Captain's Car,

ARTIST	ROLE	EPISODE
Fred McNaughton (cont.)	Mayor	Knights of Madness
Tom Mennard	Mess Orderly	Fallen Idol
Olive Mercer	Mrs Casson	Armoured Might of Cpl Jones
	Lady in queue	Lion Has Phones
	Mrs Yeatman	War Dance, Getting the Bird, Everybody's Trucking, Turkey Dinner, Love of Three Oranges, Knights of Madness
	Fierce Lady	Man Hunt
Robert Mill	Capt Swan	Man of Action
	Army Capt	Number Engaged
Bernadette Milnes	Lady in Queue	Lion Has Phones
Norman Mitchell	Capt Rogers	Something Nasty in the Vault
Ingo Mogendorf	Nazi Pilot	Film
Michael Moore	Regular Extra	
Robert Moore	Large Man	Man Hunt
William Moore	Station Master	Royal Train
Charles Morgan	2nd MP	Keep Young and Beautiful
Verne Morgan	Landlord	Don't Forget the Diver, Absent Friends, My British Buddy
	Farmer	Gorilla Warfare
Donald Morley	Glossip	Captain's Car
Derek Newark	RSM	Film
Franz Van Norde	Nazi Co-Pilot	Film
Leslie Noyes	Regular Extra	
Michael Osborne	Boy Scout	Museum Piece
James Ottaway	1st MP	Keep Young and Beautiful
Robin Parkinson	Lt Wood	Gorilla Warfare
Denys Peek	German Pilot	Enemy Within the Gates
Toby Perkins	The Usher	Brush with the Law
Gilda Perry	Don't Know	Loneliness of the Long-Distance Walker
	Doreen	Lion Has Phones, Two and a Half Feathers
Jimmy Perry	Charlie Cheeseman	Shooting Pains
Bill Pertwee	ARP Warden	(60 shows, as listed below):
	(Mr Bert Hodges)	Man and the Hour, Enemy Within the Gates, Battle of Godfrey's Cottage, Under Fire, Amoured Might of Cpl Jones, Lion Has Phones, Something Nasty in the Vault, Day the Balloon went Up, Menace from the Deep
	Chief Warden	

Branded, Man Hunt, Big Parade, Don't Forget the Diver, Boots Boots Boots, Sgt Save My Boy, Absent Friends, Put That Light Out, Two and A Half Feathers, The Test, Uninvited Guests, Battle of the Giants, Asleep In the Deep, Keep Young and Beautiful, Soldier's Farewell, Getting the Bird, Desperate Drive of Cpl Jones, If the Cap Fits, King Was in His Counting House, All Is Safely Gathered In, When Did You Last See Your Money?, Brain v Brawn, Brush With the Law, Round and Round Went the Big Wheel, Time On My Hands, ...

ARTIST	ROLE	EPISODE
Bill Pertwee (cont.)	*Chief Warden*	

The Deadly Attachment, My British Buddy, The Royal Train, We Know Our Onions, Honourable Man, The Recruit, Everybody's Trucking, A Man of Action, Gorilla Warfare, Godiva Affair, Captain's Car, Turkey Dinner, Ring Dem Bells, When You've Got To Go, Is There Honey Still For Tea, Come In Your Time Is Up, High Finance, Face On the Poster, My Brother and I, The Love of Three Oranges, Wake-Up Walmington, Making Of Private Pike, Knights of Madness, Miser's Hoard, Number Engaged, Never Too Old, film

ARTIST	ROLE	EPISODE
Arnold Peters	*Fire Officer*	Man of Action
Gordon Peters	*The Soldier*	Command Decision
	Caretaker	A Stripe for Frazer
	Man with Door	Is There Honey Still For Tea?
	Lighthouse Keeper	Put That Light Out
June Petersen	*Unknown*	Under Fire
Hana-Maria Pravda	*Interpreter*	Honourable Man
Mavis Pugh	*Lady Maltby*	Captain's Car
Robert Raglan	*HQ Sgt*	Don't Forget the Diver
	Capt Pritchard	A. Wilson (Manager)?, Fallen Idol
	The Colonel	Battle of the Giants, Keep Young and Beautiful, Desperate Drive of Cpl Jones, If the Cap Fits, Brain v Brawn, Deadly Attachment, My British Buddy, Honourable Man, Gorilla Warfare, Captain's Car, Ring Dem Bells, Is There Honey Still For Tea?, Wake-Up Walmington, Never Too Old
	Insp Hardcastle	Film
Harriet Rhys	*Girl in Bank*	Film
Wendy Richard	*Edith Parish*	Two and a Half Feathers, Mum's Army
	Shirley	King Was In His Counting House, My British Buddy
Nigel Rideout	*German Pilot*	Enemy Within the Gates
Arnold Ridley	*Pte Charles Godfrey*	All 80 TV Shows, Film
John Ringham	*Bracewell*	Man and the Hour
	Capt Bailey	A Stripe for Frazer, Under Fire, Room at the Bottom, Don't Fence Me In
David Rose	*Dump Cpl*	Brain v Brawn
George Roubicek	*Radio Operator*	Film
Anthony Roye	*Mr Fairbrother*	Brain v Brawn
Anthony Sagar	*Sgt Gregory*	Room at the Bottom
	Sgt-Maj	Fallen Idol
	Police Sgt	Film
Kathleen Saintsbury	*Cissy*	Is There Honey Still For Tea?
Chris Sandford	*German Pilot*	Time On My Hands
Joan Savage	*Greta Garbo*	Soldier's Farewell
Jeffrey Segal	*The Minister*	Round and Round Went the Big Wheel
	Brigadier	Making of Private Pike

ARTIST	ROLE	EPISODE
Anthony Sharp	*Unknown*	Loneliness of the Long-Distance Walker
	Colonel	Making of Private Pike
Stuart Sherwin	*2nd ARP*	Menace from the Deep, Branded, Put that Light Out
	Junior Warden	Brush with the Law
Michael S. Martin	*Lieutenant*	Gorilla Warfare
Carmen Silvera	*Mrs Gray*	Mum's Army
Edward Sinclair	*The Caretaker*	Showing Up of Cpl Jones, A Stripe for Frazer

The Verger (Maurice Yeatman) (47 shows, as listed below):

This Bullet is Not For Firing, Room at the Bottom, Big Guns, The Day the Balloon Went Up, War Dance, No Spring for Frazer, Big Parade, Don't Forget the Diver, Absent Friends, The Test, A. Wilson (Manager)?, Uninvited Guests, Battle of the Giants, Getting the Bird, Desperate Drive of Cpl Jones, If the Cap Fits, King Was In His Counting House, All is Safely Gathered In, When Did You Last See Your Money?, Brain V Brawn, Brush with the Law, Time On My Hands, Deadly Attachment, My British Buddy, Royal Train, We Know Our Onions, Honourable Man, The Recruit, Everybody's Trucking, A Man of Action, Gorilla Warfare, Godiva Affair, Captain's Car, Turkey Dinner, Ring Dem Bells, When You've Got To Go, Come In Your Time Is Up, High Finance, Face On the Poster, My Brother and I, Love of Three Oranges, Wake-Up Walmington, Making Of Pte Pike, Knights Of Madness, Miser's Hoard, Number Engaged, Never Too Old, Film

Campbell Singer	*Maj-Gen Menzies*	If The Cap Fits
	Sir Charles McAllister	Is There Honey Still For Tea?
Eleanor Smale	*Mrs Prosser*	War Dance, Mum's Army
Jean St Clair	*Miss Meadows*	Armoured Might of Cpl Jones
Michael Stainton	*Frenchy*	Wake-Up Walmington
Adele Strong	*Lady with Umbrella*	Ring Dem Bells
Bill Tasker	*Fred*	Face On the Poster
James Taylor	*Artillery Officer*	Desperate Drive of Cpl Jones
Vic Taylor	*Regular Extra*	
Rachel Thomas	*Mother Superior*	Gorilla Warfare
Talfryn Thomas	*Mr Cheeseman*	My British Buddy, Man of Action
	Pte Cheeseman	Gorilla Warfare, Godiva Affair, Captain's Car, Turkey Dinner
Alan Tilvern	*Cpt Rodrigues*	Battle School
	US Colonel	My British Buddy
Fred Tomlinson	*Choir*	Bullet is Not for Firing
Cy Town	*Mess Steward*	We Know Our Onions
Bill Treacher	*1st Sailor*	Menace from the Deep
Freddie Trueman	*E.C. Egan*	The Test
Patrick Tull	*The Suspect*	Man Hunt
Ernst Ulman	*Sigmund Murphy*	Under Fire
Edward Underdown	*Maj-Gen Holland*	Round and Round Went the Big Wheel
Gabor Vernon	*The Russian*	Honourable Man
	Polish Officer	Face On the Poster
Patrick Waddington	*The Brigadier*	Showing Up of Cpl Jones, Loneliness of The Long-Distance Walker

ARTIST	ROLE	EPISODE
April Walker	*Judy*	All Is Safely Gathered In
Dervis Ward	*AA Man*	Film
May Warden	*Mrs Dowding*	Bullet is Not for Firing
Kenneth Watson	*RAF Officer*	The Day the Balloon Went Up
Queenie Watts	*Mrs Keane*	Under Fire
	Mrs Peters	Armoured Might of Cpl Jones
	Edna	Two and a Half Feathers
Freddie White	*Regular Extra*	
Freddie Wiles	*Regular Extra*	
Marjorie Wilde	*Lady Magistrate*	Brush with the Law
Frank Williams	*The Vicar*	(39 shows, as listed below):
	(Rev Timothy Farthing)	

Armoured Might of Cpl Jones, Bullet is Not for Firing, Day the Balloon Went Up, War Dance, No Spring for Frazer, Don't Forget the Diver, The Test, A. Wilson(Manager)?, Uninvited Guests, Battle of the Giants, Soldier's Farewell, Getting the Bird, Desperate Drive of Cpl Jones, King Was In His Counting House, All Is Safely Gathered In, When Did You Last See Your Money?, Brush with the Law, Time On My Hands, My British Buddy, Royal Train, Honourable Man, The Recruit, Everybody's Trucking, Man of Action, Godiva Affair, Captain's Car, Turkey Dinner, Ring Dem Bells, When You've Got To Go, Come In Your Time Is Up, High Finance, Face On the Poster, My Brother and I, Love of Three Oranges, Making of Private Pike, Knights of Madness, Miser's Hoard, Number Engaged, Never Too Old, Film

Alister Williamson	*Bert*	Wake-Up Walmington
Seretta Wilson	*Wren*	Getting the Bird
Barbara Windsor	*Laura La Plaz*	Shooting Pains
Eric Woodburn	*Museum Caretaker*	Museum Piece
Martyn Wyldeck	*Maj Reagan*	Showing Up of Cpl Jones, Shooting Pains

NB: Some show names and character names have been truncated to save space.

4 RADIO SHOW ARTISTS

Avril Angers	*Mrs Keane*	Under Fire
	Operator	Sorry Wrong Number, Put that Light Out
	The Waitress	Brain v Brawn
	Edna	The Two and a Half Feathers
John Barron	*Mr West*	Something Nasty in the Vault
	Col Pierce	Round and Round Went the Great Big Wheel
	Capt Cadbury	Things That Go Bump in the Night
Michael Bates	*Pte Clarke*	The Two and a Half Feathers
Timothy Bateson	*Elliott*	The Man and the Hour
	Capt Marsh	The Bullet is not for Firing
	Mr Blewitt	No Spring for Frazer...
		When Did You Last See Your Money?
	Capt Turner	No Spring for Frazer
	Mr Maxwell	Sons of the Sea
James Beck	*Pte Joe Walker*	(7 Shows) The Man and the Hour, Museum Piece,

ARTIST	ROLE	EPISODE
James Beck (cont.)	*Pte Joe Walker*	Command Decision, Enemy Within the Gates, Armoured Might of L/Cpl Jones, Sgt Wilson's Little Secret, A Stripe for Frazer
Harold Bennett	*Mr Blewitt*	Turkey Dinner
Norman Bird	*Bert Postlethwaite*	Present Arms
Diana Bishop	*Miss Meadows*	Armoured Might of L/Cpl Jones
	Sgt Wilson's Daughter	Getting the Bird
Nan Braunton	*Cissie Godfrey*	The Battle of Godrey's Cottage, Branded
Michael Brennan	*Sgt-Maj*	Fallen Idol
	Tom & George Pearson	Absent Friends
Michael Burlington	*Wig Maker*	Keep Young and Beautiful
	Signaller	A Question of Reference
Jonathan Cecil	*Mr Norris*	A Man of Action
Erik Chitty	*Mr Sedgewick*	Boots, Boots, Boots
	Mr Parsons	Time on My Hands
Pat Coombs	*The Clippie & Marie*	A Soldier's Farewell
Joan Cooper	*Miss Baker*	No Spring For Frazer
	Cissie Godfrey	Is There Honey Still For Tea?
Richard Davies	*The Volunteer*	Armoured Might of L/Cpl Jones
Clive Dunn	*L/Cpl Jack Jones*	All 67 shows
Percy Edwards	*Percy the Parrot*	The Battle of Godfrey's Cottage
Norman Ettlinger	*Sergeant*	Don't Forget the Diver
	The Doctor	Branded
	Clerk of Court	A Brush with the Law
	Pritchard	Fallen Idol
John Forest	*Lt Hope-Bruce*	Sorry Wrong Number
Judith Furse	*Chairwoman*	The Loneliness of the Long Distance Walker
Roger Gartland	*Bert*	Ten Seconds From Now
David Gooderson	*Mr Murphy*	Under Fire
Gerald Green	*Col Masters*	The Captain's Car
Pearl Hackney	*Mrs Mavis Pike*	Armoured Might of L/Cpl Jones, Sgt Wilson's Little Secret, Operation Kilt, Under Fire, Sorry Wrong Number, Present Arms, Sgt Save My Boy!, War Dance, Absent Friends, The Great White Hunter, My British Buddy, The Big Parade, High Finance, Turkey Dinner
Carl Jaffe	*Capt Winogrodzki*	The Enemy Within the Gates
Nan Kenway	*Mrs Prentice*	All Is Safely Gathered In
Fraser Kerr	*Maj-Gen Menzies**	If the Cap Fits (*and Sgt MacKenzie)
	Capt Swan and Inspector	A Man of Action
	Mr West	A. Wilson (Manager)?
	Russian Visitor	The Honourable Man
	Policeman	The Great White Hunter
	Col Winters	The Deadly Attachment
	Train Driver	The Royal Train
	German Pilot	Time On My Hands

ARTIST	ROLE	EPISODE
Fraser Kerr (cont.)	*Sir Charles McAllister*	Is There Honey Still For Tea?
Michael Knowles	*Captain Bailey*	A Stripe for Frazer, A. Wilson (Manager)?
	Capt and Mr Rees	The Loneliness of the Long Distance Walker
	Capt Pringle	The Bullet is not for Firing
	Mr Wintergreen	A Brush with the Law
	Squadron Leader	The Day the Balloon Went Up
	Capt Stewart	Round and Round Went the Great Big Wheel
John Laurie	*Pte James Frazer*	(64 shows, as listed below):

The Man and The Hour, Museum Piece, Command Decision, The Battle of Geoffrey's Cottage, Armoured Might of L/Cpl Jones, A Stripe for Frazer, Operation Kilt, Battle School, Under Fire, Something Nasty in the Vault, The Showing Up of Cpl Jones, The Loneliness of the Long Distance Walker, Sorry Wrong Number, Room at the Bottom, The Menace from the Deep, No Spring for Frazer, Sons of the Sea, Present Arms, Don't Forget the Diver, If the Cap Fits, Put that Light Out, Boots Boots Boots, Sgt Save My Boy!, Branded, Uninvited Guests, A Brush with the Law, A Soldier's Farewell, Brain v Brawn, War Dance, Mum's Army, Getting the Bird, Don't Fence Me In, The King Was in His Counting House, When Did You Last See Your Money?, Fallen Idol, A. Wilson (Manager)?, All Is Safely Gathered In, The Day the Balloon Went Up, A Man of Action, The Honourable Man, The Godiva Affair, Keep Young and Beautiful, Absent Friends, Round and Round Went the Great Big Wheel, The Great White Hunter, The Deadly Attachment, Things that Go Bump in the Night, My British Buddy, Big Guns, The Big Parade, Asleep in the Deep, We Know Our Onions, The Royal Train, A Question of Reference, High Finance, The Recruit, A Jumbo-Sized Problem, The Cricket Match, Time On My Hands, Turkey Dinner, The Captain's Car, The Two and a Half Feathers, Is There Honey Still For Tea?, Ten Seconds From Now

Ian Lavender	*Pte Frank Pike*	(59 shows, as listed below):

The Man and The Hour, Museum Piece, The Enemy Within the Gates, The Battle of Godfrey's Cottage, Sgt Wilson's Little Secret, A Stripe For Frazer, Operation Kilt, Battle School, Something Nasty in the Vault, Sorry Wrong Number, The Menace from the Deep, Sons of the Sea, Present Arms, Don't Forget the Diver, If the Cap Fits, Put that Light Out, Boots, Boots, Boots, Sgt Save My Boy!, Branded, Uninvited Guests, A Brush with the Law, A Soldier's Farewell, Brain v Brawn, War Dance, Mum's Army, Getting the Bird, Don't Fence Me In, The King Was in His Counting House, When Did You Last See Your Money?, Fallen Idol. A. Wilson (Manager)?, All Is Safely Gathered In, The Day the Balloon Went Up, A Man of Action, The Honourable Man, The Godiva Affair, Keep Young and Beautiful, Absent Friends, Round and Round Went the Great Big Wheel, The Great White Hunter, The Deadly Attachment, Things That Go Bump In The Night, My British Buddy, Big Guns, The Big Parade, Asleep in the Deep, We Know Our Onions, The Royal Train, Question of Reference, High Finance, The Recruit, A Jumbo-Sized Problem, The Cricket Match, Time On My Hands, Turkey Dinner, The Captain's Car, The Two and a Half Feathers, Is There Honey Still For Tea?, Ten Seconds From Now

John Le Mesurier	*Sgt Wilson*	All 67 Shows
Arthur Lowe	*Capt George Mainwaring*	All 67 Shows
Geoffrey Lumsden	*Col Square*	Command Decision
	Col Square	A Stripe For Frazer, Under Fire (In the show Referred to as Corporal-Colonel)
	Capt Square	Present Arms, Don't Forget the Diver, A Brush With the Law, Fallen Idol
Philip Madoc	*Cpt Muller*	The Deadly Attachment

ARTIST	ROLE	EPISODE
Larry Martyn	*Pte Joe Walker*	(32 shows, as listed below):

Present Arms, A Brush with the Law, A Soldier's Farewell, Brain V Brawn, War Dance, Mum's Army, Getting the Bird, Don't Fence Me In, The King Was in His Counting House, A Man of Action, The Honourable Man, The Godiva Affair, Keep Young and Beautiful, Absent Friends, Round and Round Went The Great Big Wheel, the Great White Hunter, The Deadly Attachment, Things that Go Bump in the Night, My British Buddy, Big Guns, The Big Parade, Asleep in the Deep, We Know Our Onions, A Question of Reference, High Finance, The Recruit, A Jumbo-Sized Problem, The Cricket Match, Time On My Hands, Turkey Dinner, The Captain's Car, The Two and a Half Feathers, Ten Seconds From Now

Betty Marsden	*Lady Maltby*	The Captain's Car
Michael Middleton	*American Sergeant*	My British Buddy
	The Pickford Man	Big Guns
	Sgt Baxter	We Know our Onions
	Driver's Mate	The Royal Train
Elizabeth Morgan	*Mrs Lennon*	Armoured Might of L/Cpl Jones
	Janet King	Something Nasty in the Vault
	The Nurse	The Recruit
	Housewife	The Great White Hunter
Julian Orchard	*Town Clerk (Mr Upton)*	A Man of Action, The Honourable Man, The Godiva Affair, Big Guns
Bill Pertwee	*ARP Warden Hodges*	(33 shows, as listed below):

The Battle of Godfrey's Cottage, Armoured Might of L/Cpl Jones, Sgt Wilson's Little Secret, Something Nasty in the Vault, Sorry Wrong Number, The Menace from the Deep, Present Arms, Put that Light Out, Branded, Uninvited Guests, A Brush with the Law, A Soldier's Farewell, The King Was in His Counting House, All Is Safely Gathered In, The Day the Balloon Went Up, A Man of Action, The Honourable Man, The Godiva Affair, Absent Friends, Round and Round Went the Great Big Wheel, My British Buddy, The Big Parade, Asleep in the Deep, We Know Our Onions, The Royal Train, High Finance, The Recruit, A Jumbo Sized Problem, The Cricket Match, Time On My Hands, Turkey Dinner, The Captain's Car, The Two and a Half Feathers

Sion Probert	*POW & Sentry*	Don't Fence Me In
Robert Raglan	*Col Pritchard*	Brain v Brawn
Wendy Richard	*Violet Gibbons*	War Dance
	Edith Parrish	Mum's Army
	Shirley	The King was in his Counting House
		My British Buddy
Arnold Ridley	*Pte Charles Godfrey*	(60 shows, as listed below):

The Man and The Hour, The Enemy Within the Gates, The Battle of Godfrey's Cottage, Sgt Wilson's Little Secret, Operation Kilt, Battle School, Under Fire, Showing Up of Cpl Jones, The Loneliness of the Long Distance Walker, The Bullet is not for Firing, Room at the Bottom, No Spring for Frazer, Sons of the Sea, Present Arms, Don't Forget the Diver, If the Cap Fits, Put that Light Out, Boots, Boots, Boots, Sgt. Save My Boy!, Branded, Uninvited Guests, A Brush with the Law, A Soldier's Farewell, Brain v Brawn, War Dance, Mum's Army, Getting the Bird, Don't Fence Me In, The King Was in His Counting House, When Did You Last See Your Money?, Fallen Idol, A. Wilson (Manager)?, All Is Safely Gathered In, The Day the Balloon Went Up, A Man of Action, The Honourable Man, The Godiva Affair, Keep Young and Beautiful, Absent Friends, Round and Round Went the Great Big Wheel, Great White...

 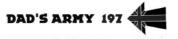

ARTIST	ROLE	EPISODE
Arnold Ridley (cont.)	*Pte Charles Godfrey*	

Hunter, The Deadly Attachment, Things That Go Bump in the Night, My British Buddy, Big Guns, The Big Parade, Asleep in the Deep, We Know our Onions, The Royal Train, A Question of Reference, High Finance, The Recruit, A Jumbo-Sized Problem, The Cricket Match, Time On My Hands, Turkey Dinner, The Captain's Car, The Two and a Half Feathers, Is There Honey Still For Tea?, Ten Seconds From Now

ARTIST	ROLE	EPISODE
John Ringham	*Capt Turner*	Room at the Bottom, Don't Fence Me In
Michael Segal	*2nd Warden*	Branded, A Brush with the Law
Cyril Shaps	*General Monteverdi*	Don't Fence Me In
Stuart Sherwin	*Lighthouse Keeper*	Put That Light Out
	Mr Fairbrother	Brain v Brawn
	Policeman	Absent Friends
	Station Master	The Royal Train
Carmen Silvera	*Mrs Gray*	Mum's Army
David Sinclair	*GHQ Driver*	Command Decision
	German Airman	The Enemy Within The Gates
	2nd ARP Warden	The Menace From the Deep
Edward Sinclair	*The Verger*	No Spring For Frazer, Don't Forget the Diver, If the Cap Fits, Branded, Uninvited Guests, A Brush with the Law, A. Wilson (Manager)?, The Day the Balloon Went Up, The Big Parade, The Recruit, The Cricket Match
Anthony Smee	*G.C.Egan*	The Cricket Match
Graham Stark	*Pte. Walker*	The Showing Up of Cpl Jones, The Loneliness of Long Distance Walker, Sorry Wrong Number, The Bullet Is Not For Firing
Mollie Sugden	*Mrs Fox*	Mum's Army, The Godiva Affair, My British Buddy,
Frank Thornton	*Capt Rogers*	Something Nasty in the Vault
	BBC Producer	Ten Seconds From Now
Alan Tilvern	*Capt Rodrigues*	Battle School
	Capt Ramsay	We Know Our Onions
Jack Watson	*Capt Ogilvy*	Operation Kilt
	Maj Smith	Battle School
	Maj Regan	The Showing Up of Cpl Jones
	Sgt and Brig	The Loneliness of the Long Distance Walker
	Sgt Gregory	Room at the Bottom
	Brigadier	Present Arms
	Capt Reed	Fallen Idol
	Col Schulz	My British Buddy
John Whitehall	*Choir*	The Bullet is not for Firing
Frank Williams	*The Vicar*	(14 shows, as listed below):

The Bullet is Not for Firing, Absent Friends, Uninvited Guests, Getting the Bird, All is Safely Gathered In, The Day the Balloon Went Up, The Godiva Affair, The Deadly Attachment, The Royal Train, High Finance, The Recruit, The Cricket Match, Time On My Hands, Turkey Dinner

ARTIST	ROLE	EPISODE
Peter Williams	*The Colonel*	A Question of Reference
Eric Woodburn	*George Jones*	Museum Piece

Above: 'Captain Mainwaring, I'm drowning!' 'Stop whining, Pike!'
Below: A scene from 'We Know Our Onions.'

5 THE DAD'S ARMY APPRECIATION SOCIETY

The *Dad's Army* Appreciation Society was first formed in 1990. Since then it has overcome many trials and tribulations to become the large organisation of around 1700 members that it is today. Run by Paul Carpenter and Tony Pritchard, the Society publishes a quarterly newsletter-magazine called 'Permission to Speak, Sir', which carries articles about the show and details of events involving the surviving cast, the society and its members. Regular gatherings are held, in addition to annual events at the Bressingham Steam Museum, home of the National *Dad's Army* Collection. Members have joined from far and wide, and their ideas and suggestions are always given attention. Many of them contribute serious, erudite and humorous articles for the magazine. Some of the members do their own voluntary research into the series and the results are also published for the benefit of the worldwide membership. If you would like to find out more about the society, or if you are interested in becoming a member, please visit the website; www.dadsarmy.co.uk.

6 THE BARMY ARMY FILM CLUB

Take a group of *Dad's Army* fans, add a few period vehicles, some old uniforms and a digital video camera and you have the unique Barmy Army Film Club. Since its formation in 1987, the club has produced five of its own comedy dramas set on the British Home Front during World War Two.

'The thought of dressing up and "playing soldiers" at weekends as a relaxation from our weekday jobs seemed as if it could be a bit of fun, so we started our first venture. Our initial aim was to create our own entertainment, but as the project gained momentum, the local press started to show an interest, followed by regional television. At this stage we decided that we could do some good for charity, so in 1990 we adopted the RAF Benevolent Fund and through video sales, and other fund raising ventures, we have regularly raised money for this worthy cause. As more television and press coverage followed we were being approached to perform slapstick events at museums, vehicle rallies and steam railway opening days. The BAFC has striven to research and obtain or replicate the correct uniforms and equipment. This has also seen members collect and restore World War II vehicles. To date we have approximately 10 vehicles in members' hands which are used in productions'.

The club's fictitious platoon, Wellington-in-the-Mire, has an array of characters very similar to those that made up the platoon of Walmington-on-Sea. Colin Bean, who played Private Sponge in the original series, was the club's patron until he died in 2009. I first met the team at Tenterden in Kent where they were 'on parade' helping with charitable events on that day. Long may the 'Barmy Army' continue to enjoy all their activities.

7 THE "REAL" DAD'S ARMY

The 'Real' Dads Army has its origins in the Home Guard section of the Fort Newhaven Military Display Team, a multi-unit World War Two re-enactment group founded in 1983. In 1993 a serious attempt was made to

Above: The 'Real' Dad's Army display team at Newhaven Fort.

compile a 'hands on' tribute to *Dad's Army*; the result being a lookalike platoon. They are much in demand for 1940s events, advertising promotions and corporate entertainments, and do both commercial and charitable work. The section is spearheaded by actor Ralph Harvey (Captain Mainwaring) and historian Richard Hunt. They are supported by a loyal and professional group of veterans of many fine performances. I have met the group on a couple of occasions. One of their finest moments came when they depicted the Home Guard at the VJ-Day parade, marching down the Mall, saluting the Queen and the royal family. Previously, Prince Philip had inspected the unit at Newhaven and had suggested it might be a good idea for them to take part in the Victory parade. The CO explained to HRH that they had already been invited. 'Good,' came the reply, 'I'll look out for you!' On the day, Prince Philip did notice them, pointed them out to the Queen and waved – it was no surprise that they got some of the biggest cheers that day from the crowds lining the Mall.

8 THE DAD'S ARMY COLLECTION

Situated at Bressingham, near Diss, in Norfolk, the *Dad's Army* collection includes memorabilia and artefacts from the series, housed in an authentic reproduction of Walmington-on-Sea, featuring key locations such as the Church Hall, Jones' Butchers and Swallows Bank. The collection opened in 2000 and is now just one of the attractions at Bressingham, which also boasts botanical gardens, the Blooms garden centre, a steam engineering exhibition and four working steam railways.

9 THE DAD'S ARMY MUSEUM

In recent years the Norfolk town of Thetford (where location shots for *Dad's Army* were

Below: 'Walmington' shopfronts at Bressingham, Norfolk.

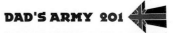

filmed from 1968 to 1977) has celebrated its long association with the show by opening a small but dedicated museum. Exhibits on show include numerous photographs of the cast and crew, both in action and relaxing off set. The museum was opened to the public on Friday 7 December 2007 by David Croft, and since then it has received nearly 4000 visitors. Staffed entirely by volunteers, all costs are met from sales of museum shop items and donations. The museum is open seasonally, every Saturday from 10am–2pm. Private openings, special events and location tours of Thetford can also be booked.

Right: Mick Whitman loves playing the part of Captain Mainwaring for the Thetford Museum. Ever since watching the filming of 'The Captain's Car' Mick was hooked and has been a fan of all things *Dad's Army* ever since. He loves to get out and about, raising the profile of the Museum and sharing stories with other fans. Mick is pictured here with the Author and 'superfan' Katie Bennett, who had a fabulous time at the 2009 DAAS event.

Below: 'Where's the fire?' Bill Pertwee, Pamela Cundell and Frank Williams at Bressingham.

Above: A scene from 'Wake-Up Walmington'.

Below: 'Steady on, I don't even know your name'. An embarrassed Wilson in 'The Captain's Car'.

 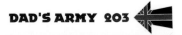

Hugh Cecil

I am sure we all have a certain number of 'lucky' days in our lives, and one of mine was when my agent rang up and gave me two days a week for seven weeks as a walk-on in **Dad's Army**. That was in October 1968 and I little thought I would still be in the show nine years later! Right from the start it was a very happy show and I always said the 'bonhomie' began at the top because David Croft and Jimmy Perry were two of the nicest people I have worked for, and in comparison with many other directors I have had since then it was remarkable how many shots were completed with just one take. Unfortunately I had to miss two series as I was already booked for some summer work in my usual capacity as a children's entertainer, but as soon as I was available I was back again with the platoon, for which I was very grateful. It's a wonderful feeling to be able to claim that one was almost a fixture on such a successful show. The success came largely, I think, because it was just the right time for a change of direction on the box – a healthy comedy programme suitable for all the family.

LEST WE FORGET...
They defended our shores against seemingly insurmountable odds and gave us happy memories that we will never forget...

JAMES BECK (1929–1973)

EDWARD SINCLAIR (1914–1977)

ERIK CHITTY (1907–1977)

PETER BUTTERWORTH (1919–1979)

JOHN LAURIE (1897–1980)

HAROLD BENNETT (1899–1981)

ARTHUR LOWE (1915–1982)

TALFRYN THOMAS (1922–1982)

JOHN LE MESURIER (1912–1983)

GEOFFREY LUMSDEN (1914–1984)

ARNOLD RIDLEY (1896–1984)

ROBERT RAGLAN (1906–1985)

JANET DAVIES (1927–1986)

FULTON MACKAY (1922–1987)

JACK HAIG (1913–1989)

EDWARD UNDERDOWN (1908–1989)

ROBERT DORNING (1913–1989)

LARRY MARTYN (1934–1994)

ARTHUR ENGLISH (1919–1995)

JOHN SNAGGE (1904–1996)

WILLIAM MOORE (1915–2000)

CARMEN SILVERA (1922–2002)

DON ESTELLE (1933–2003)

ERIC LONGWORTH (1918–2008)

WENDY RICHARD (1943–2009)

COLIN BEAN (1927–2009)

EPILOGUE: Long after the last episode of *Dad's Army*, the series is still as popular as ever, its characters have become almost legendary and the stars no longer with us are all sadly missed. *Dad's Army* has a special place in the hearts of the British public and is certain to remain at the pinnacle of our TV comedy heritage for many years to come.

Opposite: Break during filming 'Dont Forget the Diver'.
Below: Jimmy Beck in characteristic Walker mode.

 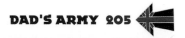

INDEX

This index is restricted to names of people and places connected to the various productions of *Dad's Army*. Page numbers in **bold** indicate a photograph of the subject.